S-04-91   4

S0-AVO-301

THE TRIAL OF FRANK JAMES
FOR MURDER

The Jingle Bob Press was established more than twenty years ago by James D. Horan, novelist and historian, and his wife, Gertrude, with the goal of eventually reprinting many of the rare books on the Wild West from their collection.

The Jingle Bob imprint is derived from the brand used by John Chisum, the cattle king of New Mexico. The brand was known as Jingle Bob because of Chisum's practice of splitting the steer's ear, causing the lower part to hang loosely. Also called "Long Rail" or "Fence Rail," the brand was used by Chisum during the period of the Lincoln County War in the 1870s and was kept up by his heirs until 1894.

Curiously, photographs or sketches of the brand are rare. This one is reproduced by courtesy of V. C. Roybal, Reference Librarian, New Mexico Highlands University, Las Vegas, New Mexico.

To maintain the flavor of the rare Western classics reprinted in this series, the original versions have been reprinted without change, including any original misprints or errors in spelling or grammar.

THE JINGLE BOB BRAND

PRESS OF E. W. STEPHENS,
COLUMBIA, MISSOURI.
1898.

THE TRIAL OF
FRANK JAMES
FOR MURDER.

WITH

CONFESSIONS OF
DICK LIDDIL AND CLARENCE HITE

AND

HISTORY OF THE "JAMES GANG."

PUBLISHED BY
GEORGE MILLER, JR.,
Water Works Building, Kansas City, Mo.

With an Introduction by James D. Horan

JINGLE BOB/CROWN PUBLISHERS, INC.
NEW YORK

Printed in the United States of America
Published simultaneously in Canada by
General Publishing Company Limited

Library of Congress Cataloging in Publication Data

James, Frank, 1844–1915, defendant.
   The trial of Frank James for murder, with confessions of Dick Liddil and Clarence Hite, and history of the "James gang".

   (Jingle Bob series)
   Reprint of the 1898 ed. published by G. Miller, Kansas City, Mo.
   1. James, Frank, 1844–1915. I. Liddil, James Andrew, 1852–
II. Hite, Clarence B. III. Title:
The trial of Frank James for murder . . .
KF223.J34M54 1977   345′.73′02523   77–3708
ISBN 0–517–53117–8

BIBLIOGRAPHY

BOOKS

Buel, James W. *The Border Bandits*. St. Louis: 1881.
———. *The James Boys*. Chicago: n.d.
Connelley, William Elsey. *Quantrill and the Border Wars*. Cedar Rapids, Iowa: 1909.
Crittenden, Henry Huston. *The Crittenden Memoirs*. New York: 1936.
Cummins, Jim. *Jim Cummins' Book*. Denver: 1903.
Donald, Jay. *Outlaws of the Border*. Philadelphia: 1882.
Edwards, Jennie, John N. Edwards. *Biography, Memoirs, Reminiscences, and Recollections*. Kansas City, Missouri: 1889.
Edwards, John N. *Noted Guerrillas; or The Warfare on the Border*. Chicago: 1877.
Harlow, Alvin. *Old Waybills*. New York: 1934.
Horan, James D. *Desperate Men* (revised). New York: 1962.
James, Jesse Edwards. *Jesse James, My Father*. Independence, Missouri: 1899.
———. *Frank James and His Brother, Jesse*. Baltimore: 1915.
Lawson, John D. *American State Trials* (XI), St. Louis: 1914.
Settle, William A., Jr. *Jesse James Was His Name*. Columbia, Missouri: 1966.
Wallace, William H. *Speeches and Writings of William H. Wallace, and Autobiography*. Kansas City, Missouri: 1914.

NEWSPAPERS

St. Louis Missouri Republican, October 6, 1882, Frank O'Neill's interview with Frank James.
For accounts of James's surrender: *St. Louis Globe-Democrat, Kansas City Times, Sedalia Democrat, Kansas City Daily Journal*, October–November, 1882.

All Missouri newspapers had reporters at the trial of Frank James and gave it complete if biased coverage.

PREFACE.

HE editor of this volume has taken great pains to make the account here given of the trial of Frank James, a true and complete narrative of the proceedings had. It gives all the evidence in an abridged and readable form; this being done for the benefit of the reader, as it would have been very tiresome for any one to have attempted to read all the evidence verbatim. We have selected two speeches out of the eight delivered by the attorneys in the case, —one on each side of the case, and these speeches are here printed in full, and are worthy of the attention of any reader. In the confessions of Dick Liddil and Clarence Hite, here published, the reader will observe that there are parts omitted. That which is omitted in Liddil's confession is only a repetition of what is given in his testimony; and that omitted from Hite's confession is a repetition of the details given by Liddil. The history here given is a brief account of the organization of the "James Gang" from the close of the war to its final downfall, giving the principal depredations committed by it and how its final destruction was accomplished. This is not a detailed account of their lives and exploits, as such an account would make a large volume in itself, but is a brief history given for the benefit of the readers of the Trial, and gives only facts.

THE EDITOR.

INTRODUCTION

FRANK JAMES "COMES IN" AND IS
TRIED FOR MURDER
By James D. Horan

On the afternoon of October 5, 1882, two men left the lobby of the McCarty House in Jefferson City, Missouri, and walked to the state capitol. The one who had registered as "B. F. Winfrey, Marshal, Mo." was stocky, balding, and quiet, but during the two days he had sat in the lobby his blue-gray eyes had missed nothing. From the cordial greetings and hearty handshakes of his companion anyone could have told you that he was John Newman Edwards, the well-known, fiery editor of the *Kansas City Times,* who had molded the legend for the James-Younger gang, written a history of Quantrill's guerrillas, was a devoted Democrat and staunch defender of anything connected with the Confederacy.[1]

Only a trusted few knew that "Winfrey" was Frank James, brother of Jesse, who had come to Jefferson City to surrender to Missouri's Governor Thomas H. Crittenden.

For over three years Frank had been living as a respectable farmer in Tennessee with his wife, Annie, and their children.[2]

It had been generally accepted that Frank would seek vengeance against the Ford brothers for the killing of his brother, Jesse, in St. Joseph in April, but in Kansas City George Shepherd, the one-eyed former guerrilla who had been one of Jesse's trusted riders, scoffed at that possibility. Instead of a violent, melodramatic act, he predicted, "Frank will come in . . . he's lonely, afraid and discouraged. . . ."

Shepherd's prediction came true in the summer of 1882, when James contacted Edwards suggesting that he surrender to Gov. Crittenden.

The details of the negotiations for the surrender remain a secret to this day, but Frank wrote a long letter to Crittenden denying that he and Jesse were guilty of all the crimes they had been charged with and hoping for some sort of amnesty or pardon.[3]

Crittenden replied promptly. In a letter headed "Executive Dept. Jefferson City," he urged Frank to surrender, pointing out that he could not grant amnesty or a pardon but "if you abandon the life you are charged with leading, you shall have a fair, impartial trial. . . ."[4]

A short time before he appeared in Jefferson City, Frank had granted a secret interview to Frank O'Neill, one of the best political reporters in the Midwest.[5] It was a fascinating tale of his life as a hunted man: how he had ridden into Tennessee, his close calls, his association with Jesse, and his hopes for the future. As he told O'Neill:

"I am tired of this life of taut nerves, of night-riding and day-riding, of constant listening for footfalls, creaking twigs and rustling leaves

---

[1] *Noted Guerrillas or The Warfare of the Border* (St. Louis: 1877).

[2] *St. Louis Post-Dispatch,* June 24, 1923; *Nashville American* in *The St. Louis Missouri Republican,* April 22, 1882.

[3] Henry Huston Crittenden, comp. *The Crittenden Memoirs* (New York: 1936), pp. 256–59. Hereafter cited as Crittenden.

[4] Ibid., pp. 259–60.

[5] *St. Louis Missouri Republican,* October 6, 1882.

and creaking doors; tired of seeing Judas in the face of every friend I know—and God knows I have none to spare—tired of the hoofs and horns with which popular belief has equipped me. I want to see if there is not a way out of it. . . ."

Frank also disclosed to O'Neill that while Jesse was the most wanted man in the country, he had been living near Waverly, in Humphrey's County, Tennessee, casually racing his stable of "fine horses" including the well-known Jim Malone, and winning big purses.

"He [Jesse] was a great patron and lover of the race tracks," Frank said solemnly, "and spent most of his time there." [6]

Now Frank and Edwards walked across the lobby of the capitol building and entered Governor Crittenden's suite.

Crittenden was standing behind his desk as Edwards and James entered. Off to one side was a silent group of newspapermen and state leaders. Edwards said:

"Governor Crittenden, I want to introduce you to Frank James."

After Frank and the state's chief executive had exchanged greetings, Frank threw back his coat to reveal a pistol and cartridge belt. He slowly unbuckled the belt and handed it and the pistol to Crittenden.

"Governor Crittenden," he said, "I want to hand over to you that which no living man except myself has been permitted to touch since 1861, and to say I am your prisoner." [7]

The newsmen and state officials who had been told by Crittenden that he had a "Christmas box surprise" crowded about Frank to shake his hand and to interview him.

It was an incredible scene: the beaming governor, awed politicians and newsmen listening to the famous fugitive tell how crime does not pay and how he hoped there was a new life for him in the future.

It was decided to send James the following morning to Independence to await trial. Finis C. Farr, the governor's secretary, made the arrangements and escorted the outlaw and Edwards to a carriage which took them back to the McCarthy House.

Word had spread across the city; spectators milled about the hotel lobby, crowding about James to shake his hand and slap his back, while a large group stood outside hoping to catch a glimpse of Missouri's living legend.

The next day Frank's journey to Independence was a triumphant tour, worthy of a returned hero rather than an outlaw charged with the cold-blooded murder of an unarmed train conductor and passenger. Crowds lined the tracks and the train was stopped several times so that James could appear on the rear platform and wave.[8]

That night a reception was held in Independence's Merchant's Hall, "with the wealthiest, most popular and influential men waiting to shake his hand." [9] Bankers who only a few years ago had trembled when

[6] Ibid.

[7] St. Louis Missouri Republican, October 6, 1882; Crittenden, pp. 255–72.

[8] Crittenden, pp. 255–72; Sedalia Dispatch, October 6, 1882; St. Louis Republican, October 6, 1882.

[9] St. Louis Globe-Democrat, October 10, 1882.

they heard the names of Jesse and Frank James pledged to post a hundred thousand-dollar bail bond if necessary.

Even Governor Crittenden and his wife appeared. It was enough to make the St. Louis *Globe-Democrat* wonder editorially if it was the state that had surrendered, and not Frank James.[10]

A year later, in August 1883, James finally went on trial in Gallatin.

In one of the most famous trials in the history of America's Wild West, Frank was tried for the murder of Frank McMillan, a young stonemason, during the Winston train robbery in the summer of 1881.

His impressive defense counsel battery was headed by former Lieutenant Governor Charles Johnson and included several prominent Missouri trial lawyers.

Jackson County Prosecutor William Wallace, the unsung hero of the James-Younger saga, was joined by Daviess County Prosecutor William Hamilton and four of Gallatin's most prominent criminal lawyers. Wallace later revealed he had carried a pistol throughout the trial.

Wallace realized that his case, now drawing national attention, was legally weak. His strongest witnesses were former gang members Dick Liddil, Bill Ryan, and Clarence Hite. Then suddenly, on the eve of the trial, Hite died and Ryan refused to testify.

The state's case now rested on Dick Liddil. Under Wallace's quiet questioning, Liddil described how he had ridden with Jesse, Frank, Clarence Hite, and Wood Hite to rob the train at Winston. He swore that Jesse had killed the conductor and Frank the stonemason.

However, the star of the show was Frank James. Throughout his testimony he waved the Stars and Bars of the Confederacy and firmly denied that he had participated in the robbery or had killed the stonemason. He did not wilt under Wallace's blistering cross-examination; court buffs claimed he had won the day.

There was little chance of a guilty verdict. As the trial neared its end, Wallace discovered that the sheriff had selected the jury from a list supplied by the defense and was so outraged he threatened to quit the case. His assistants pleaded with him, pointing out that if he left the trial would fall apart, so he remained.

Almost a century later it is hard to believe that when Judge Goodman heard that Wallace was preparing affidavits pointing out that the sheriff had broken the law and asking for a mistrial, he summoned the prosecutor and told him that he would deny the motion—which had not yet been filed—"in order to prevent bloodshed." [11]

Three days were required for both sides to sum up. After less than four hours' deliberation, the jury acquitted James. However, his troubles were not yet over: he stood trial but was acquitted in Alabama for the Muscle Shoals stagecoach robbery.

Wallace had given his nephew his notes and transcripts of the trial. This book is therefore an excellent record of one of the most famous trials in the history of America's Wild West.

---

10 *St. Louis Globe-Democrat*, October 10, 1882.

11 William H. Wallace, *Speeches and Writings of William H. Wallace, With Autobiography* (Kansas City, Missouri: 1914), pp. 187–89.

THE TRIAL OF FRANK JAMES
FOR MURDER.

INTRODUCTORY.

In the town of Gallatin, Daviess county, Missouri, on July 21, 1883, begun the most exciting trial ever held in the West, the trial of Frank James, the noted outlaw, for the murder of Frank McMillan during the robbing of a Chicago, Rock Island & Pacific passenger train, at Winston, Missouri, July 15, 1881. The town was filled with people who had come from hundreds of miles around to attend the trial; a majority of them were friends of the James boys and the balance were against them, as there was no neutral ground. Many of those in attendance were known to be desperate men and it was fully expected there would be bloodshed before the trial was ended; there being many rumors of old feuds to be settled, of plots to rescue the prisoner, etc. Excitement was at fever heat. Many depredations had been committed in that part of the country within a few preceding years, most of which had been attributed to the James gang. In this same

5

town a bank had been robbed in 1868 and the cashier killed; supposed to have been done by the James boys. Frank James had surrendered about a year before to Governor Crittenden and placed in jail at Independence, Missouri, where he remained until the trial at Gallatin, where it was decided by the State authorities to try him, although there had been a number of indictments found against him at other places in the State.

THE CASE CALLED.

The indictment was returned by the grand jury of Daviess county in May, 1883, and by agreement of the attorneys, August 21, was fixed as a date for the trial. Court convened promptly at 10 A. M., on that day and the case of State v. Frank James was called. The State was represented by attorneys W. P. Hamilton, prosecuting attorney of Daviess county; William H. Wallace, of Kansas City, Missouri; J. H. Shanklin, of Trenton, Missouri; and M. A. Low, of Trenton; H. C. McDougal and J. F. Hiclin, of Gallatin, advisory counsel. The defendant was represented by Judge John F. Philips, of Kansas City; Wm. H. Rush, of Gallatin; Judge James H. Slover, of Independence, Missouri; Hon. John M. Glover, of St. Louis; Hon. Chas. P. Johnson, of St. Louis; Col. C. T. Garner, of Richmond, Missouri, and J. W. Alexander, of Gallatin. Judge —— Goodman on the bench.

The State announced ready for trial. The defense stated that several of its witnesses had not yet arrived and a continuance was had until 1 P. M. and at 1 P. M. another postponement was had until the next morning. After the announcement that the case would go over until the next morning, Judge Goodman made a short but pointed address to the crowd in which he told them what was expected of them during their attendance upon the trial; that order would be preserved at all hazard, and took occasion to very deliberately assert that the court was fully able to protect its dignity and the persons of its audience, and therefore "any person detected in the court room with weapons on, will be surely, swiftly and to the full extent of the law punished." The Judge further stated that for the accommodation of the populace the trial would be conducted in the opera house, and that to prevent inconvenience and provide for the safety of the audience the sheriff would issue tickets of admission not to exceed the seating capacity of the house. When court was convened in the opera house, the judge occupied a seat at the front of the stage; back of him were the press correspondents and a large number of ladies and the court officials. Just in front of the stage was a large space railed off for the attorneys engaged in the case, the jury and the bar. The jury panel having been called, the examination of the jury and making challenges occupied the time until the morning of August 25, when the trial was actually begun. The jury having been selected, the witnesses were all called and sworn, eighty-nine for the state and thirty-nine for the defense; and after having been sworn were all excluded from the court room.

OPENING STATEMENT.

Mr. Wm. H. Wallace made the opening statement for the state.

MR. WALLACE'S STATEMENT.

The court announced that time would be allowed each side to present or make its statement of the case to the court and jury, whereupon Mr. Wallace presented the case for the state. In brief, Mr. Wallace said that while criminal practice allowed him to make a statement of the magnitude of the crime, and set forth facts that would even augment the heinousness of the crime charged against the defendant, but, continued Mr. Wallace, I will not pursue this course, but merely put forth the facts that will corroborate the facts alleged in the indictment. Perhaps, remarked Mr. Wallace, this may be a mistaken course on my part. However, he thought it sufficient to refer only to the irrefutable and overwhelming testimony that would be produced against the defendant. There might be some of the jury who admired the exploits of the accused, his chivalric deeds, his expertness, and other characteristics that had made him famous, and such would regard it as a privilege for such a poor and obscure person as McMillan to be shot down by an individual of such great fame as the accused, but he, Mr. Wallace, would not tax the intelligence of the jury with such a suspicion, nor would it be right to attribute such a sentiment to any other intelligent and law-abid-

ing citizen.   A reader of yellow-covered literature
might get into a morbid state of mind that would permit such attributes to be attached to the defendant.

Following this, Mr. Wallace read the indictment,
charging Frank James with complicity in the Winston
robbery and the murder of McMillan.   He then, in
turn, graphically described how the train was signaled
and stopped; how, in turn, each step of the robbery and the tragedy of Winston was enacted.
The particulars were given in detail, every point minutely mentioned, and it was avowed that each in turn
would be proved beyond the possibility of a doubt by
the prosecution.   That was the purpose of the prosecution, Mr. Wallace said.

The story, as told in all the particulars, was a
repetition of the affair made familiar to the public
through the press.   Coming to the point involving
Frank's connection with the robbery and tragedy, Mr.
Wallace said that five men were engaged in the double
crime.   Evidence would be adduced to show that Frank
James, Jesse James, Wood Hite, Clarence Hite and
Dick Liddil were the parties.   Frank and Jesse James
and Wood Hite entered the cars, and Dick Liddil and
Clarence Hite had charge of the engine.   With this
assertion, Mr. Wallace next stated it was proper to
refer to the James band, its organization and the purposes of its organization.   Thereupon Mr. Wallace
related that the band was organized in Tennessee for
the purposes of robbery.   In 1877, Frank and Jesse
James, with their families, moved to northern Tennessee, and subsequently went to living in Nashville.

There the band was organized. It consisted of seven,
Frank James was the oldest member. Next was Jesse
James. Then followed a description of Jesse James:

Frank went under the name of B. J. Woodson
and Jesse as J. D. Howard.

Wood Hite was named as a member of the gang
and described.

Dick Liddil was next mentioned and described.

Bill Ryan was another.

Jim Cummins was another.

Ed Miller was another.

The three last, Mr. Wallace averred, were not
members of the band when the Winston robbery took
place.

Mr. Wallace gave a history of each individual,
and was interrupted by Colonel Philips, who objected
to the statement as setting forth matters not alleged in
the indictment; and evidence on such points would be
irrelevant and inadmissible.

The court said the question was whether a conspiracy could be proved when not alleged to make out
a crime charged. He was ready to hear arguments
now.

Colonel Philips presumed the question would
come up again and then could be argued and disposed
of; meantime he filed an exception to the court's ruling,
that the statement could continue in the vein as started.

Mr. Wallace continuing, told how the band came
to leave Nashville or that vicinity. Bill Ryan left
Nashville, where he went under the name of Tom
Hill, to visit the Hites' near Adairville. Enroute he

got drunk, threatened the life of a justice of the peace, was arrested, and the plunder on his person aroused suspicion. News of Ryan's arrest alarmed Frank alias B. J. Woodson, Jesse James alias J. D. Howard, and Dick Liddil alias Smith, and they left.

Then Mr. Wallace followed them on their journey; told how Clarence Hite joined the gang. As evidence Mr. Wallace set forth that a box of guns was shipped from Nashville to John Ford at Lexington, Missouri and thence reshipped to Richmond. John Ford was a brother of Bob and Charlie Ford, and is now dead. Another part related was that the James boys' families left Tennessee just after their husband, and among their traps was a sewing machine belonging to Mrs. Frank James, which was shipped to Pope City, it being her intention to meet General Shelby.

Then followed a statement setting forth that the gang rendezvous at Mrs. Samuels' residence near Kearney and at Mrs. Bolton's in Ray county, she being the sister of the Ford boys.

Mr. Wallace then came to the point and announced the fact that Dick Liddil would be a witness to these facts. A conspiracy, or such a band could only be discovered or broken up by one of its members. Liddil's, surrendered under promises of exemption from the consequences of his crimes, has accomplished this.

However, Mr. Wallace claimed that there would be testimony introduced, the testimony of respectable citizens of Daviess county, who had seen Frank in this county about the time of the Winston robbery. He was seen, known and recognized by him, and though he wore burnside whiskers at the time, they would swear to his identity now. All this formed circumstantial evidence, but an unbroken chain strong enough to award the punishment due the defendant for the outrage and crime against law and life at Winston.

THE TESTIMONY.

A PENSIONER'S STORY.

The first witness was John L. Penn who stated that he resided in Colfax, Iowa. He then told the story of the Winston robbery. He with several others, among whom were Frank McMillan, got on at Winston. They belonged to the stonemason gang. Old man McMillan got on too. It was about 9 o'clock. Just as they got on, three men entered the door. Westfall, the conductor, was putting checks in their hats. The party were standing up receiving their checks. The three men came in with a revolver in each hand. They rushed up to our crowd and said something, but just what, I don't know. Then two shots were fired, one going through Westfall. He rushed to the rear end of the smoking car, the three men following and firing. Westfall got out on the platform and fell off. The men then returned to the front end of the car, and as they passed us, or just as they went out at the front door, Frank McMillan and I went out the rear door. Just then two shots were fired. I looked through the glass of the door and a shot shivered the glass. I saw a man on the front end of the

car; he seemed to be watching and shooting through
the car every few minutes. Frank McMillan and I, on
the platform, sat down pretty close. Just then he
heard a man halloo in the car. At this time three or
four shots were fired. The train was going east, and
the man was at the front end, and the shot went through
the car. Frank heard the man call out, and said, "it
its father," and jumped up, and just then he was shot
above the eye and fell off the platform. I tried to catch
him, but couldn't. The train was going slow at this time.
The train slacked up near the switch, and at this time
some man cried out to move on, and the train pulled out
slow for three-quarters of a mile, when it stopped.
Then three men jumped off the train, like off the baggage car, on the south side, passed me on the platform
of the smoking car, went south of the track and disappeared in a hollow. There was shooting in the baggage car; several shots were fired. There were perhaps thirty to forty people in the car during the firing.
They got down under the seats as best they could. The
man who stood on the front platform shot through the
glass of the door; it was shut, as was the back door,
and the glass in the back door was pretty badly shattered. Witness stated that after the robbers had
abandoned the train, he, McMillan, the old man and
another, went back on the track to look for them, Mc-
Millan and Westfall. We found McMillan on the
south side of the track in the ditch dead. Before find-
ing him we met a hand-car with twelve men on it; they
helped us in our search. We found McMillan about
half a mile from the depot. Westfall was found before

we got there, on the north side of the track dead, and not very far from the section house.

THE CROSS-EXAMINATION.

The cross-examination was conducted by Governor Johnson. Witness did not remember the number of cars on the train. There was a coach after the smoker, and witness thinks a baggage and express car in front of the smoker. During the business, witness saw three men only. Witness remembers nothing by which he could identify the men. He recollected nothing as to their dress directly by which they could be identified. They were dressed in long linen dusters, had the collars turned up, and white handkerchiefs about their necks. They were not masked exactly, but masked so they couldn't be identified, by having their hats pulled well down over their faces. Witness was excited when he gave his testimony before the coroner, or agitated, and he believed he had the facts of the occurrence in mind better now than then. When witness took his seat on the rear platform, the three men, he thought, were in the baggage car, judging from the shooting. There was one man on the front platform at any rate. Witness stated no attempt was made to rob him or McMillan, or, as far as he knew, no attempt was made to rob any one in the car.

The cross-examination was all about the shots fired, and just when, and to show that they were not fired at anybody. Witness said that he thought they were fired to scare, and that when McMillan looked in the shot struck him, and shots were fired before and after he was killed. The design was to show that there was no intent to kill McMillan, or anybody else, and that the firing was directed against no one. Witness could not say which one of the three men fired the shot that killed McMillan. Witness roughly guessed that the whole transaction transpired within half an hour.

The cross-examination continued at some length, but developed nothing in addition to the prosecution excepting the point named above.

On re-examination witness said McMillan lived in Colfax, Iowa, had a wife, and was on his way home when he was killed. Witness's recollection was that the man who did the shooting through the car was a big man, and the same who killed Westfall.

THE ENGINEER'S STORY.

Addison E. Wallcott was the next witness. He was engineer on the train at Winston. The train left at 9:30; it was dark. He got a signal to stop shortly after leaving station. Somebody called out to go ahead. Witness looked around to see who gave the order, and two men jumped down off the coal in the tender. They had revolvers and ordered me to go ahead. And they told me to keep it going or they would shoot. They told me to stop at a tank in a hollow. They said they didn't want to hurt me, but would do so if I didn't obey orders. While going down my fireman and me went around the engine, jumped off and got on the third car, and there saw the express messenger and two ladies standing up. The rest were under the seats. I asked if they had left the train, and the baggageman and I went into the baggage car. The men who came on the engine were dark, good-sized men. It was so dark I could not see them plainly. Witness heard five or six shots in the baggage car. Witness did not remember the size of the train nor what it consisted of. The operation of the air brake was explained. The first stoppage was about two thousand yards from the station and the next two miles. Witness didn't know who applied the brake the last time.

The cross-examination developed nothing new, nor anything contradictory to the evidence given on the examination in chief. The witnesses stated the two men on the engine did not leave it while the firing was going on, and knew nothing of what was going on at the rear of the train.

THE BAGGAGEMAN'S STORY.

Frank Stamper was the next witness. Witness was baggageman. The baggage car and express car were together and next to the engine; the express agent was on the car. Witness related that train coming to stop, he stepped in the side door with his light, and he was grabbed by the leg and pulled out, and a man pulled a revolver on me and told me to stand still. The train then moved on, and running I got on it, and passing through the passenger coach and sleeper, the passengers asked me what was the matter, and I said, "robbers." The train consisted of a sleeper, three coaches, a smoking car and baggage car. Witness said the men came up to the side of the car on the north side, four or five, or six of them. They said "come out." No shots were fired until he got out, then there were shots in the smoking car and in the baggage car. Westfall was the conductor. Witness saw Westfall at the station last. Witness stated the train stopped the last time two miles from the station, and there the robbers left the train.

On cross-examination witness reiterated the story without any material change as to facts.

On re-examination witness said he had his light in his hand. He saw one of the men distinctly when he came up to the door and pulled him out. The man had a long gray beard, wore a gray vest and white shirt. He was the same man that stood guard over him.

On re-cross-examination, witness said the man was a rather tall and slender man. He was not masked. Not any of them were, that he noticed, and witness would have noticed it. There was no masking unless they wore false beards.

THE EXPRESS AGENT'S STORY.

Charles M. Murray resides at Davenport, Iowa, was on the train at the Winston robbery, and was express agent of the U. S. Ex. Co. When a short distance from Winston the train was stopped and the baggage master rushed to the door to see what was the matter, and was pulled out. I heard some firing, and there was some sample trunks there and I dropped behind

2

them. The train moved on and then stopped again. Then a man came in and demanded my money. He asked where the safe was, and I showed him; he demanded the key; I gave it to him, and then he directed me to open the safe. I did so and he got the money, or I gave it to him, I don't know which. He asked me repeatedly if that was all. He said they had killed the conductor, were going to kill me and the engineer, and ordered me to get down on my knees. I didn't. He told me again, but I didn't, and he struck me over the head and knocked me unconscious. I didn't come to until the baggagemaster came to my relief. Witness didn't know how much money or treasure was taken. Witness declared the packages taken, but could not tell anything as to their value; nor could he remember the number. Witness saw three men (robbers) all told, and two came into the express car.

During the examination of this witness, the state tried several times to have a description of the packages taken given, especially as to their value, and the defense objecting, the court over-ruled the objection very peremptorily, and Governor Johnson took exceptions just as shortly.

THE TECHNICAL TALE.

Dr. D. M. Cloggett, coroner of Daviess county at the time of the Winston robbery, described the wound on McMullen's body and stated he died from the wound inflicted by a pistol or pointed instrument half an inch above the right eye.

Dr. Brooks was called, and, just as he was taking the witness stand, an amusing incident occurred. It was discovered by the prosecution that Dr. Cloggett had given his testimony without being sworn; so he had to be recalled, and under oath repeat all he had said before.

Dr. Brooks was next called and corroborated the evidence of the preceding witness.

Charles Murray, the express agent, was recalled, and stated that all packages received on that trip by him were placed in the safe, and were taken therefrom by the men (robbers).

Recess until 1 :30 o'clock p. m.

AFTERNOON SESSION.

W. S. Earthman of Davidson county, Tennessee, was examined by Mr. Wallace. Nashville is in Davidson county, and witness is back tax collector. Witness resides seven miles north of Nashville on Whita's creek. Witness knows defendant; saw him first in 1879, and became well acquainted with him at a horse race. Knew him as B. J. Woodson. Woodson resided on Smith's place, and after leaving there didn't know where he went, but saw him about Nashville up to the fall of 1880. Never saw him after that.

"Did you know Jesse James ?"

Objected by defense as irrelevant. Objection overruled.

Witness replied that he knew Jesse. Saw him at Frank's place, got acquainted with him at a horse race. Witness was not as well acquainted with Jesse as with

Frank. Jesse went by the name of Howard, and doesn't recollect seeing him there later than the fall of 1879. Witness saw Frank and Jesse frequently together. He didn't know really who they were. Witness was here last June and saw defendant in court-yard, and they spoke. Frank, or Woodson, asked the witness if he had come up here to hang him.

"Do you know one Tom Hill ?"

Defense objected, and the state explained that while Hill was not named in the indictment, it was expected to show Hill was Bill Ryan and that his arrest caused the James gang to abandon Nashville, and it would be a link in the circumstances leading up to the Winston robbery.

WHAT CONSTITUTES A CONSPIRACY.

Governor Johnson briefly argued that the course pursued by the state was incompetent. The indict-ment charged especially a murder, and the defendant was here to meet that charge and not an irrelevant charge that a band of robbers existed here or there. Counsel apprehended that the existence of such a band in 1880 had nothing to do with the crime at issue. A specific allegation of conspiracy had not been charged in the indictment.

At this juncture, the court ordered the jury to re. tire, and said the question might just as well be argued now and settled.

Beginning the argument, Governor Johnson con-tended that conspiracy was a specific crime, the pun-ishment for which was especially provided for in the statutes. A conspiracy is a substantive offense, the corpus delecti, or offense charge must be proved before the circumstances of the consummated offense can be put in proof.

Col. Shanklin replied at length, elaborating his argument with frequent references to the books.

Governor Johnson was eloquent and argumentative in his reply.

In rendering his decision, the court confessed that his attention had been called to this question previous to the trial by a disinterested attorney; and he had given it careful consideration. The court averred that he thought the testimony admissible, and aptly illustrated his reasons therefor by several suppositious cases. The court overruled the objection, and decided to admit the testimony.

A BIT OF A DISCUSSION.

Col. Philips suggested that the testimony being offered should be carefully considered. It was doubtful in his mind that a conspiracy would be proved, but the state should be forced to produce its proof of the existence of a conspiracy before the introduction of evidence tending to affect the character of the defendant, or tending to show that he associated with men bearing a multiplicity of names.

The court understood the difficulties of the situation, but declared he could not direct the manner in which counsel introduced their evidence.

At this the jury was recalled, and the examination of Mr. Earthman continued.

Witness said he knew a man by the name of Tom Hill, who after his arrest was known as Bill Ryan.

Governor Johnson—"I object."

The court—"It appears this testimony at this time is incompetent until the connection of Bill Ryan or Tom Hill with the Woodson or James gang is established."

Mr. Wallace explained that the James gang robbed the Winston train, and that this James gang lived at Nashville, and that when Ryan was arrested they abandoned their field of operations about Nashville and came to Missouri, and he would trace them from Nashville, through Kentucky into Missouri, and into Daviess county.

Governor Johnson took objection to his client being called a robber. He was innocent until proven guilty. The theory of justice was against such an appellation. Moreover the court was not trying the James gang, or any band of conspirators.

The court said this was not the time for flights of rhetoric. He could understand a plain statement better.

Just what the court meant or whom he was knocking out, puzzled the audience.

Mr. Wallace declared he was authorized to speak of the accused as a robber and murderer, for the indictment so charged.

Colonel Philips next proceeded to score Mr. Wallace for using the term robber, and adjured the state to go to work and prove the conspiracy and make no more of it.

Colonel Shanklin thought the scolding of the defense without grace or without cause. The state wanted no directions from the defense as to its conduct of the case and could not be scolded out of its policy.

The discussion became so hot that the court had finally to order the wrangling counsel to cease.

TENNESSEE TALES.

Mr. Earthman, the witness, continuing, told of the arrest of Bill Ryan. When arrested he was armed and had $1,400 on his person. Ryan was afterward taken to the Nashville jail. This arrest was made on the 25th of March, 1881.

Witness did not know Dick Liddil. Ryan rode a gray horse to the place where he was arrested.

On cross-examination witness said he had known defendant for about two years. He was working on his farm. Woodson worked for witness during one summer, and was constantly at work. Woodson associated with good people, and witness never saw him with Bill Ryan or Hill.

Governor Johnson next asked what was his character there, and hastily withdrew it.

James Moffat testified: I have lived at Nashville ever since the war; am depot-master of the Louisville and Nashville Railroad; I knew B. J. Woodson at Nashville during the year 1880; I saw him frequently during that summer and fall; I remember Bill Ryan's arrest; don't think I ever saw Woodson there after that, but saw him just before; I knew J. B. Howard; he lived a square and a half from me; he had a wife and one child; I lived on Fatherland street, in Edgefield, or East Nashville, and he lived on Watson street; I think Howard was buying grain for Rhea & Sons; never saw Howard and Woodson together but once; it was a few days after March 30, 1881, that I saw Woodson and a Mr. Fisher, on Cedar street, talking; never saw Howard there after the arrest of Bill Ryan.

Cross-examined: Had only a pool-room acquaintance with Woodson, covering the summer and fall of 1880.

Re-cross-examination: The man on trial before me is the B. J. Woodson that I knew.

John Trimble, Jr., testified: I live at Nashville, Tennessee; I have been in the real estate and fire insurance business for ten years past; I rented the house 814 Fatherland street, in Edgefield, in the first part of 1881, about February 5, to a man named J. B. Woodson; I have not recognized the man since I have been here; he paid $8 per month in advance; in March he paid $8, and our books show no receipt of rent since; we sold the house about the twenty-first or twenty-second of March to J. B. May; we never received any notice that Woodson was going to quit the house.

Jas. B. May testified: I am a pressman, and live in Nashville, Tennessee; I bought a house from Mr. Trimble March 22, 1881; it is located on Fatherland street, and is No. 814; it stands by itself, has three rooms on one floor, with a side porch; I looked at the house before I rented it; saw a lady but no gentleman; this was a week before the twenty-second; didn't move in at once, because I wasn't ready; did not move into it till April, and then there was no one in it; never received any notice that the parties were going to leave; I went over to see if they wished to continue renting it, and found they had gone.

Mrs. Sarah E. Hite testified: I live near Hendersonville, Tennessee, with my father, Silas Norris, thirteen miles from Nashville. Have lived with my husband in Kentucky from 1874 until May last. I lived near Adairsville, Kentucky, which is about fifty miles north from Nashville. My husband had children when I married him. I know Wood Hite. He lived with us part of the time. There were seven children— four boys, named John, George, Wood and Clarence. We lived some two miles from town. Wood Hite was thirty-three years old. He is dead now. He died near Richmond, Missouri, so I was told. I think he was buried there. Wood Hite was about five feet eight inches high, had dark hair and light blue eyes. He had a light mustache, Roman nose, narrow shoulders, a little stooped. He was inclined to be quick in his actions. I last saw him in November, 1881. I had seen him before that in September. He said he was going West. I have seen the defendant. The first time I saw him was on March 20, 1881; he came to my husband's house on the morning of that day. Dick Liddil came with him and Jessie James came after him. Frank was riding. Jesse and Dick were walking. They did not tell me where they came from

They were armed. Jesse had two pistols and a rifle, Frank had two pistols, and Dick had two pistols and a gun. They stayed at our house a day or two. Clarence and Wood and George Hite were there, too. I saw them after that on the twenty-sixth of April. That day Dick, Jesse, Frank and Wood came back. They were still armed. Some men pursuing them came near the house. Jesse and Frank were excited at this, and commenced preparing themselves. Dick got at the front door, Jesse at the window, and Frank was in the parlor. The men rode on by. Frank James came that time on the twenty-sixth of April and left on the twenty-seventh. I don't know where they went. Clarence Hite was twenty-one years old, tall and slender, blue eyes, light hair, large mouth, and one or two teeth out. He is dead. He died in Adairsville the tenth of last March. Clarence was then living in Adairsville, but he would come out when Jesse and Frank and Dick was there. He left home in May, 1881. He was in Missouri in the summer of 1881. Wood Hite left home May 27, 1881. He and Clarence did not leave together, but left a few days apart. Next saw Clarence in September; stayed there till November, and I never saw him till he came home to die. Mr. Hite was related to Jesse James. His first wife was Frank James' aunt.

This witness was not cross-examined.

Silas Norris testified: I live at Mechanicsville, Sumner County, Tennessee. Sumner county adjoins Davidson county on the east. In the summer of 1881 I was living in Logan county, Kentucky. Adairsville is in that county. I was living within a mile and a half of it at the place of Geo. E. Hill, my son-in-law. Our two families had been together three or four years. I knew Jesse James. I first got acquainted with him in March, 1881, at Mrs. Hite's. I know Frank James. He was introduced to me by Jesse as his brother. I think Mr. Liddil was there also. Don't know where they came from. I didn't see any arms visible, but I saw some arms afterward. They stayed a short time and left. They came back, stayed a day or two, and went off for perhaps a week. Don't know where they went. I do not know where Samuels Station, Kentucky, is. When they came back the last time there were Jesse and Frank James and Dick Liddil in the party. Wood and Clarence Hite were away a portion of the summer.

Cross-examined: Old man Hite is probably sixty-five or sixty-six years old. He is still living.

DICK LIDDIL.

James A. Liddil called as a witness.

THE DEFENSE OBJECTS.

The defense at once objected to his testimony as incompetent, he being, as it was declared, an unpardoned felon.

It then transpired that Dick or James A. Liddil had served a term in the penitentiary for horse stealing, having been sentenced from Vernon county in November of 1877.

The prosecution admitted it, and, under the **great** seal (two bears) of the state of Missouri, and over the signature of Secretary of State McGrath, submitted the copy of a pardon for Dick, which the state deemed established his reliability as a competent witness.

The pardon was as follows:

DICK'S PARDON.

The State of Missouri, to all whom these presents shall come:

Greeting—Know ye that by virtue of authority in me vested by law, and upon recommendation of the inspectors of the penitentiary, I, Henry C. Brockmeyer, lieutenant acting governor of the state of Missouri, do hereby release, discharge and forever set free James A. Liddil, who was, at the November term, A. D. 1877, by a judgment of the circuit court of Vernon county, sentenced to imprisonment in the penitentiary of this state for the term of three and one-half years, for the offense of grand larceny, and do hereby entitle the said James A. Liddil to all the privileges and immunities which by law attach and result from the operation of these presents. Conditional, however, that the said James A. Liddil, immediately upon his release, leave the county of Cole and never return thereto voluntarily, and does not remain in the county of Callaway.

Witness June 30, 1877, etc.

A LENGTHY ARGUMENT.

The defense seemed to have anticipated the situation, and were prepared with a host of authorities **to** show that the law or text of opinions forbade the evidence of such as Dick Liddil.

Hon. John M. Glover of St. Louis was put up to present the law, and made a strong and exhaustive argument, replete with the citation of authorities. The points presented were about as follows:

MR. GLOVER'S ARGUMENT.

Quoting, Mr. Glover said: Every person who shall be convicted of arson, burglary, robbery or larceny in any degree in this chapter specified, or who shall be sentenced to imprisonment in the penitentiary for any other crime punishable under the provisions of this chapter, shall be incompetent to be sworn as a witness or serve as a juror in any case, and shall be forever disqualified from voting at any election or holding any office of honor, trust or profit within the state. 1 Wagner's Missouri Statutes 1872, page 465.

Section 1671, Revised Statutes, 1879: Pardon, effect of—When any person shall be sentenced upon a conviction for any offense, and is thereby, according to the provisions of this law, disqualified to be sworn as a witness or juror in any cause, or to vote at any election, or to hold any office of honor or profit or trust within this state, such disabilities may be removed by a pardon by the governor, and not otherwise.

Article 5, section 8, Constitution of Missouri, as to power to pardon being lodged in the governor.

Under the above section and article of the constitution the governor can remit any part of the punishment. Perkins v. Stephens, 24 Pick. 277; State v. Foley, 15 Ver. 64.

This paper is not a pardon. 1. It shows on its face it is a mere commutation under the three-fourths rule of section 21, page No. 989, Revised Statutes of Missouri, 1872. Which section has been supplanted in Revised Statutes, 1879, by section 6533, page 1283.

It is therefore merely a commutation under this rule.

An identical instrument with this is held not to restore competency in these cases. Black v. Rogers, 49 Cal. 15; People v. Bowen, 43 Cal. 439; State v. Foley, 15 Nev. 64; Perkins v. Stephens, 24 Pick. 277.

Liddil having been convicted, the infamy having attached, the same can only be removed by a pardon, and could not by an act of the legislature, because the disability is a part of the punishment. Evans v. State, 63 Tenn. 13; State v. Foley, 15 Nev. 64; Long v. State, 10 Tex. App. 197; Houghtaling v. Kelderhouse, 1 Parker's c. c. 241.

No part of punishment can be remitted by the legislature, as this would be exercising the pardoning power, which in Missouri is lodged in the governor alone. State v. Sloss, 25 Missouri, 291.

Hence the dropping of the disqualification to testify from the Revised Statutes of 1879, section 1378 can not operate to restore this witness to competency.

Section 1671, above cited, says the competency can be restored by a pardon alone.

THE STATE'S STATEMENT.

Colonel Shanklin of counsel for the state followed. He maintained that the executive of the state, under the constitution, was empowered to commute a prisoner's sentence, pardon him or conditionally pardon him. There was no partial pardon provided for. It was plain, the colonel claimed, that the paper in issue was not a commutation. It was, therefore, a pardon—the governor being empowered to do only the two things, commute or pardon.

With this, the colonel rested his case without reference to authorities.

Colonel Philips of counsel for the defense followed in a long, eloquent and able argument elaborating the law as previously presented by Mr. Glover.

The court retired in company with ex-Judge and ex-Congressman De Bolt, in the character of an *amicus curiae*, stating he wanted to consult regarding the question at issue. Returning, Colonel Philips spoke as recorded above, followed very briefly by Mr. Wallace, who merely cited authorities for the court to consider.

The court was in doubt about the matter at issue, and to reflect over it and not be too hasty, as he said, in deciding so important a question, ordered an adjournment until 1:30 o'clock.

AFTERNOON SESSION.

The court re-convened at 1:30 o'clock.

COMPETENT TESTIMONY.

The court at once proceeded to say that he had carefully examined the question as presented by counsel,

and in his opinion none of them had presented the case
so strongly that it warranted him in excluding the
testimony.   The court then took up the authorities cited
and reviewed them, and in turn failed to find their
pointed application to the case at issue.   The court
contended that the word pardon was not necessarily a
part or parcel of the pardon.   No special form was required, and words implying the same thing as pardon
were all that was necessary.   In regard to the paper at
issue, the court declared it neither a reprieve, commutation nor the remission of a sentence.   The governor
intended to do something, and that something in this
instance the court believed was the granting of a pardon.   The face of it proved that, as it distinctly set
forth, that the bearer went free, etc.   The court stated
that while the pardon was in effect granted, it did not
dispose of the preliminary proof, or proof to show that
the pardon in question was a correct and official instrument.

PROVING A PARDON.

Following this decision a discussion arose as to the
competency of the witness to prove or testify to the fact
that the pardon was genuine, or that the transcript in
court was a correct one of the pardon granted.

Messrs Glover and Philips argued against it, holding that the witness, so far as his status was established
before the court, was only competent to testify to material facts in the case on trial, and not to his own competency or any instrument making him competent.
Mr. Wallace held that he had been adjudged a com-

petent witness by the court, and as such could testify
as to all facts regarding himself or the matter at issue.
He cited authority to show that the testimony of the
witness regarding his own pardon was sufficient in law
without an exhibit of any instrument to that effect.

The court held he, Liddil, was competent, and in-
stanced the case of a witness under age who was questioned as to his competency.

Dick testified and stated he had been sent to the
penitentiary for grand larceny in 1874 from Vernon
county, and had been pardoned. He never was in the
penitentiary but that time. Witness said he had torn
up the pardon.

Colonel Philips cross-examined the witness, who
stated that he had been given the pardon by an officer of
the penitentiary. Witness never looked at it and did
not know its purport.

Colonel Philips here submitted that no pardon was
in proof. The witness did not know what the paper
was; he was merely handed a paper, and that was all.

The court proceeded to question the witness, but
he could not remember who gave it to him. He
thought it was a deputy warden, and it was handed him
in the warden's office.

To Colonel Philips the witness stated that he was
told his time was out and the paper was his pardon.
He never read it or knew its contents.

To the court the witness said he tore the pardon
up because it was of no use to him and he never showed
it to anyone. He tore it up about ten minutes after he

3

got it, and while on the way to the depot to take the
train.

The court apprehended the proof was sufficient.

The defense excepted.   The defense stated also
that it would put in proof that the conditions of the par-.
don had been violated.

Mr. Wallace admitted that Liddil had been to Cole
county.   He had been there twice, once with Sheriff
Timberlake and once with Police Commissioner Craig,
at the solicitation of the governor.   He was there under authority.

The defense stated it would offer such evidence.
The court said it would be expected.

DICK LIDDIL'S STORY.

Dick Liddil thus became a witness, and testified as
follows:

SECOND DAY'S TRIAL.

I am thirty-one years old.   Was born and raised in
Jackson county.   I know Frank and Jesse James.
First got acquainted with them in 1870, at Robert
Hudspeth's, in Jackson county, eight miles from Inde-
pendence, in Sinabar Township.   The Hudspeths are
farmers.   I was working for them, first for Robert
Hudspeth.   I saw the James brothers there a dozen
times or more from 1870 to 1875.   I saw them together
sometimes and sometimes separate.   I saw Frank and
Jesse James, Cole and John Younger and Tom Mc-
Daniel.   I have seen two or three of them there together—namely, Jesse James, John Younger and

James McDaniel; never saw all five together; they were generally armed and on horseback; they would stay around there maybe a day and a night, or two nights, or maybe not more than two hours; I supposed from what I heard and saw that they went together in a band.

Objection being made to the wide range of the testimony, the court ruled that the State must confine itself to showing the preparation for a perpetration of the robbery and murder at Winston.

Witness further testified: There was a gang known as the James boys; I belonged to it at one time: I joined four years ago this fall, in the latter part of September, at Hudspeth's; I saw Jesse James at Ben Morrow's one day; Ben lives in Fort Osage Township; I didn't go with him at once. I did afterward. The band was Jesse James, Ed. Miller, Bill Ryan, Tucker Basham and Wood Hite. That was in the fall of 1880, in Jackson county, of this state. From there we went to six miles from Independence. I left shortly after that. The others left—that is, part went and part remained. Jesse James and Miller told me they went to Tennessee. I went to Tennessee in the summer of 1880. I went to Nashville. First I went to the High Ferry pike. I went with Jesse James. There we found Frank and Jesse James and their families. We stayed there two weeks. We remained in Nashville nearly a year after that. The others came there in the winter of 1880—that is, Bill Ryan and Jim Cummings. Bill Ryan was from Jackson county. Bill Ryan, myself and Jesse James went there together. That was my

second trip. Ed. Miller was not there while I was
there. Ryan and Miller stayed with Jesse. Cummings stayed with Frank awhile. Afterward they
boarded with a lady named Kent. I last saw Ryan in
the last of February, 1881, about three weeks before I
left Nashville. I don't know where he went He got
up and left very mysteriously. I have never seen
him since. Jesse James lived for a while with Frank
on the High Ferry pike. Then he boarded with Mrs.
Kent, and then moved to Edgefield. He moved from
there over with Frank on Fatherland street some time
in February, 1881. Frank moved there the last of
January or the first of February, into a brown frame of
one story, with four rooms and a porch. The house
was No. 814. It was rented from Lindsay. While
Frank was living there, there were with him Jesse
James, Jim Cummings, and Bill Ryan. Frank and
Jesse and I left March 26, 1881. Bill Ryan had been
captured, and we took a scare and lit out. I had seen
Bill the day he was captured. He was going to
Logan county, Kentucky, to old man Hite's. I first
learned about his capture when I got a paper on Saturday describing Ryan's capture on Friday. We got
ready and left about dark.

We left on horseback. Frank had a horse of his
own. Jesse and I captured a couple. We were
twenty miles when those two horses gave out, and we
got a couple more. We went to old man Hite's. We
were armed. I had two pistols. Jesse and Frank had
a Winchester rifle apiece. It was forty miles from
Nashville to Mr. Hite's. We got there at sun-up.

At the house we found Mr. Hite, wife and daughter;
Mr. Norris, wife, and girl, and Wood Hite. We
stayed there a week. There were some officers from
Tennessee came after us. We went from there to Mr.
Hite's nephew's, three miles off—Frank, and Jesse,
and Wood Hite and myself. We stayed there a week,
and went back to the old man's. We were all armed.
We remained there only one night, leaving on Sunday
night for Nelson county, Kentucky, one hundred and
fifty miles off. Frank and Jesse and I went up there
on horseback. There was no one I knew when I got
there. We stopped at Johnny Pence's, Bud Hall's and
Doc Hoskins'. An arrangement was there entered
into for robbery by myself, Frank and Jesse James, and
Clarence Hite. Wood Hite came afterward. We
first agreed to take the express where the train crossed
the river. The river was high, and they had to trans-
fer by boat. The river went down, and we got there
too late, and we arranged to take a train here somewhere. This was talked over at Bob Hall's. Wood
Hite was there at his father's. This was the latter part
of April or first of May, 1881. Jesse's family at Nashville was a wife and one child. Frank's consisted of a
wife and two children, living at Fatherland street.
Jesse's wife came to Nelson county shortly after we
got there.

From there she said she was going to Missouri. I
never saw her after that till Jesse was killed. Jesse
told me she came to Kansas City. He told me he was
renting a house in Kansas City. He told me this in the
fall of 1881. I don't know about Frank's wife except

that Jesse told me she came out on the train to Gen.
Joe Shelby's at Saline. She brought a sewing machine with her and gave it to her mother. Jesse first
told me, and Frank told me afterward about it. That
sewing machine was shipped to Gen. Shelby's; so
Jesse told me. Jesse made some kick about Frank's
wife coming here, and Frank told me that it was all
right, and that he told her to come and give the
machine to her mother. This he told me on some
road somewhere between here and her mother's. He
objected because he said she told some things she
ought not to. Her mother was Mrs. Ralston, and she
lived some six miles from Independence. At Nashville
Frank James went by the name of B. J. Woodson,
Jesse was J. D. Howard, Ryan was Tom Hill, and I
was Smith, from Nelson county. Frank and Jesse
shipped two guns by Johnny Pence to John T. Ford,
at Lexington. They were a Winchester rifle and a
breech-loading shot gun. Jesse and I came here together on the cars to Kearney in May, 1881. We
came over the Hannibal and St. Joseph part of the
way. We went from there to Mrs. Samuels'. Frank
came out a week later on the following Saturday via
the Louisville and Indianapolis. Mrs. Samuels is
mother to Frank and Jesse James. She lived four
miles from Kearney. I had been to her house before.
Wood Hite came afterward. We found Clarence Hite
here, he having come out with Jesse's wife to Kansas
City, and then came to Mrs Samuels'.

Wood Hite was not at Hall's when the plan for
the robbery was made. The others left word where

they would meet him. Clarence Hite was twenty
years old. Wood was thirty-three or thirty-four years
of age. When in Missouri I don't think he wore
whiskers. If he did they were thin and light. His
name in the gang in Missouri I could not give. We
had to change names many times. I was Joe. Frank
was Ben in Tennessee and Buck here, and Jesse was
Dave in Tennessee. From Mrs. Samuels' I went on
the cars to Clay county, and went back on the cars.
My horse I bought of Hudpeth. He was a chestnut
bay, with several distinguishing marks. At Mrs.
Samuels' I found Frank James and Wood and Clarence
Hite. Jesse came along afterward. Jesse had bought
a horse from his half-brother, Johnny Samuels. We
started out in pursuance of an agreement about a week
after. We four started on horseback—Frank, Jesse,
Wood and myself. Clarence went on the cars to
Chillicothe. We were going there to take a train. I
rode the sorrel, Jesse rode a bay, and Frank and Wood
Hite rode horses that Wood Hite and I took from a
rack in Liberty. From Mrs. Samuels' we started to
Ford's, in Ray county, and got there about three
o'clock in the morning, and left there the next morning. The Widow Bolton, sister of Charley Ford,
lived there—a mile and a half southeast from Richmond. From there we went to Chillicothe, at a
moderate gait all day. We got dinner on the way. At
night we four stayed at a church on the prairie. We
got to Chillicothe about ten, stopping a mile and a half
from town in the timber. Wood Hite went in after
Clarence, and found him, and Clarence came out with

him. The roads were so muddy that we went back, Jesse and myself to the old lady, Wood and Frank to the Fords', and Clarence to Mrs. Samuels' also. We stayed there three or four days.

Shortly after this we started out again. Four went horseback and one on the cars, Wood going on the train. We came up to this county to look out a place to take a train. Frank was riding a roan pony. He took her at Richmond, and Wood Hite had a little bay mare, taken at the same time. Jesse and I had the horses we rode on the previous trip. The horses gotten at Liberty were turned loose at Richmond. We started that night, and camped out before daylight somewhere in the woods. We were to meet Wood Hite at Gallatin. We stopped and had dinner with a Dutchman in a one-story frame close to the road, with a large barn one hundred yards from it. He had a family of five or six children. He had a number of fine cows, and sold milk at Kidder. I left my leggings there and had to go back after them. I reckon this place was ten or fifteen miles from Gallatin. At that time I had short whiskers all over my face. Jesse was five feet eleven inches and a half high, round face, pug nose, dark sandy whiskers and blue eyes. He weighed 195 pounds and stood very straight. Frank James had burnsides and mustache. His whiskers were darker than his mustache. From that German's we went to Gallatin, first stopping in the timber to wait for Wood Hite. This was almost a mile from the town, on the road to Winston. I have never been to the place since.

We met Wood there. We started back. Jesse
got sick with toothache, and the creosote he used
swelled his jaw and his face and he had to go back.
Clarence went on foot, and Frank, Jesse, Wood and
myself went on and stopped with a man named Wolfenberger, some sixteen miles from there. I helped
him load up a load of wood next morning. We had
supper and breakfast there, and left next day. Clarence stayed somewhere else. Jesse was very sick and
we had to wait on him. We started for Mrs. Samuels',
and Jesse was so sick we had to stop at an old stockman's. Wood Hite took the train to the old lady's
and Clarence stayed with us. (Witness described the
stockman's place, as he described every other place
where they stopped, with great minuteness.) Jesse got
the stockman to take him in a buggy to Hamilton
depot. The others then started for Mrs. Samuels',
but Frank and I went to Mrs. Bolton's, in Ray county.
There was a week or ten days between the first and
second trip. Frank and I stayed at Mrs. Bolton's a
week, and then met Jesse, Clarence, and Wood at
Mrs. Samuels'. In about a week or ten days we went
on another trip. I rode the same horse as before; so
did Jesse. Frank was riding a mare he got close to
Elkhorn. We had a sorrel horse shod on the first trip
by an old man. I remember a dog and stool there.
The dog jumped upon and knocked down the stool,
and the horse started, knocking over the blacksmith,
and I had to bring the horse back to the shop. We had
some difficulty in making change. On the last trip we
all had horses. Frank rode the bay mare from Elk-

horn. Wood rode a dark bay, taken by Frank and I
from old man Frazier in Elkhorn. Frank rode the
sorrel I had started on.

We started at night. I assisted in robbing the
Winston train on this trip. We started from Mr. Samuels' at dark, coming northeast to Gallatin. We rode
till daylight, when we came into a skirt of timber, where
we stayed all night till sunrise. I don't reckon we
came over fifteen miles that night. Next day we scattered. Frank and Clarence went together, and I, Jesse
and Wood Hite together. We three ate dinner at a
white house on the road, with an old shed stable back
of it. There we met Frank and Clarence late in the
evening. That night we stayed in the timber where
we next met Wood on the former trip. We didn't get
supper that night. We left next morning. We left,
Frank and Clarence together, Jesse and Wood together
and I by myself, all going different routes. I got my
horse shod in Gallatin on the last trip we were here. I
can pick out the shop. It is off the square. It is an
old frame shop. There is another shop right below. I
had my horse shod all around. I also got a pair of
fenders on the square to keep my horse from interfering.
The saddler who sold them was a heavy man, with a
dark mustache and a dark complexion. We had quite
a little conversation over this trade. We were to meet
about a mile from Winston. I got dinner on the way,
and went on to meet the boys in a skirt of timber near
where the road crosses the track. We waited till dark,
hitched our horses and went up on foot to the train.

Wood and I went together, and met Frank, Jesse and Clarence at the depot.

The arrangement was as follows: that I and Clarence should capture the engineer, fireman and engine and start it or stop it as we might be directed by Jesse and Frank. Jesse, Frank and Wood were to get into the passenger cars and at the proper time rob the express car. We carried out the program when the north bound C., R. I. & P. passenger train came along. After getting outside of town Clarence and I got up back of the tender, and went over on top to the engine. We had two pistols. We kept quiet till the train stopped; then we hollered to go ahead. We shot to scare those fellows, who both ran onto the pilot. The first run was about two hundred yards, then a stop. About this time one of the boys pulled the bell rope and the engineer stopped the train and firing back in the cars commenced. Don't know how many shots. Jesse got into express car through the rear door and Wood and Frank tried to get in through the side door. The baggageman was standing in this side door and Frank seized him by the leg and jerked him out of the car and left him on the ground. He, Frank, dived into the express car and he or Jesse hollowed to us to go ahead. The engineer pretended he could not move the train as the brakes were down. We then struck him with a piece of coal and told him we would kill him if he did not start the train. He then threw open the throttle and started it under a full head of steam. The engineer and fireman then got out of the cab and hid in front of the engine. We, firing a number of shots to frighten them, did not aim to hit them, as we could have easily killed them, being most of the time within a few feet. I then started back to the express car, but Clarence called to me and I returned to the engine. Frank came out and shut off steam, and as she slacked we jumped off while it was running. Frank and Clarence got off first. I went back after Jesse who was still in the express car. Jesse jumped first, and I followed. We got $700 or $800 that night in packages. It was all good money. We all got together then, except Wood, who had been knocked down as Frank pulled the baggage-man out of the car, and we never saw him. Frank talked to me about the robbery afterward. He said he thought they had killed two men. Jesse said he shot one, he knew, and that Frank killed one. He saw him peep in at the window, and thought he killed him. From there we went to our horses, taking our time. We all unhitched, except Clarence, who cut his halter-strap. From there We went to Crooked River. The money was divided in a pasture, just before daylight. Jesse divided, giving us about $130 apiece, before we got to Crooked River. Wood and I then went to Ford's, the others went toward their mother's. I stayed at Ford's about a week, and then went to Mrs. Samuels', but found no one but the family there. Jesse and Frank came to the Fords' a week later, and then all five of us went to Mrs. Samuels'. We left in a wagon. All the horses had been previously turned loose.

We went to Kansas City, crossing on the bridge. Jesse and Charley Ford got out at Independence. Frank

and Wood Hite went to Doc Reed's, about four miles
from Ralston. Clarence and I went to McCraw's, fifteen miles east of Independence. Three or four weeks
after I saw Frank James in Ray county, in September
or October. He was at Widow Bolton's. He came
there one night and left the next night for Kentucky
with Charley Ford and Clarence Hite. They went to
Richmond, missed a train, and took a buggy to the R.
and L. Junction and went to Kentucky. I have never
seen him since. We were all armed with pistols at
Winston. I had on a plaid suit; Frank had a bluish
suit, all alike. I don't remember Jesse's suit. He had
a dark striped coat and pants, and had on a big duster.
Clarence had a dark suit, all alike. Wood had pants
and coat of different cloth. I saw the guns that were
shipped. I saw them at Mrs. Samuels'. Frank and
Jesse had them. We didn't have them at Winston.
The robbery was in 1881, in July. Either Frank or
Jesse designated the meeting place at Gallatin, because
no one else knew anything about the country.

At the close of Liddil's direct examination a recess was taken for fifteen minutes, when Liddil's, being
recalled to the stand, further testified in reply to questions put by the defense, as follows:

By Mr. Philips: I went back to Jefferson City
with Sheriff Timberlake in 1882, in January or February. I was there shortly after that with Mr. Craig, of
Kansas City. I saw Governor Crittenden both times,
first at the depot and the other time at his office. I
don't remember telling the Governor at either of those
times that after the Winston robbery Frank James up-

braided Jesse for killing any one, or reminded him of the agreement before the robbery that no one should be hurt or killed.

At this stage of the proceedings *Governor Thos. T. Crittenden* was, by consent of counsel, called out of time, in order to save him the trouble of staying here till his name could be reached in the usual order, and testified in behalf of the defense as follows:

By Mr. Philips: Liddil did make such a statement to me as propounded just now. I think it was the second time he was at Jefferson City. It grew out of asking him why they killed an innocent man engaged in his duties. He said that it was not the intention to do it; that the understanding was there was to be no killing; that Frank had said there was to be no blood shed, and that after it was over Frank said, "Jesse, why did you shoot that man? I thought the understanding was that no one was to be killed, and I would not have gone into it if I had known or thought there was to be anything of that sort done." To which Jesse said, "By G—d, I thought that the boys were pulling from me, and I wanted to make them a common band of murderers to hold them up to me."

THIRD DAY'S TRIAL.

On August 27th the trial of Frank James, for murder in the first degree, was resumed at eight o'clock. Dick Liddil, being cross-examined, testified as follows:

By Mr. Philips: When I left Jackson county I went to Vernon county somewhere along in 1875 or 1876 and worked for my father, and some other parties also.

Q. What time were you tried there?

Objected to and the objection overruled.

I don't remember the date of the trial, witness continued. The party associated with me on trial was named Frakes. I was in the penitentary for that offense thirty-one and a half months. I left in June, but can not give the year. I went to Hudspeth's in Jackson county. I first saw Jesse James at Ben Morrow's, in 1879. I also saw Ed Miller and Wood Hite. I think this was in the latter part of September, 1879. I saw Bill Ryan and Tucker Basham at other places. Frank James was not there at that time. Up to 1879 I had not met Frank James. I joined the gang in 1879. We scattered out at this time. I went to Ft. Scott and stayed there about three months. I went the latter part of October or the first of November. We had been in some trouble and thought it best to scatter.

Q. What trouble?

To this question counsel for the state objected, as being an endeavor to investigate another and distinct offense. The point being raised that witness had a right to decline to answer if he should criminate himself, the Court informed witness of his privilege.

Mr. Philips here stated his intention to investigate the Glendale robbery, which occurred October, 1879, and was therefore, so far as any question of privilege was concerned, barred by the statute of limitations.

Mr. Wallace averred that this offense was not barred, and the Court remarked that the statute did not run against robbery.

To this Mr. Philips retorted that he didn't know whether the Glendale affair was a robbery or a larceny, which called forth the observation from Mr. Wallace that if the defense went into the Glendale matter the State would take up the robbery at Blue Cut.

Witness further testified: "From Fort Scott I went to Carthage; then came up to Six Miles, and went over to Mrs. Samuels', and from there, in July, went to Tennessee. Jesse James and Bill Ryan went with me to Tennessee."

Witness here detailed the course taken en route to Tennessee.

On this trip we did not see Joe Shelby or stop at his place. I never saw Shelby but once in my life, and that was in November, 1880. I was at his house then one evening and came back next morning again. We crossed the Mississippi at Cape Girardeau, went to old man Hite's in Logan county, Kentucky, and went to Tennessee to Frank James'. From 1874 I didn't see Frank till I saw him in Tennessee at his place, three miles from Nashville, on the High Ferry Pike. From Frank's we went back to old man Hite's, and then I went back to Frank James' place in August, and stayed four or six weeks. From there we went to Atlanta. We left on Saturday night by rail, returning Sunday morning a week later. We next returned to Missouri. We arrived about the first of November, 1880. Jesse James only came with me. Bill Ryan had come out in September previous. We came out after Bill Ryan. We didn't know but what we might do something. We went back without doing anything.

We went the same route. Bill Ryan, Jim Cummings, Jesse James and myself were the party that went back to Tennessee. Jim Cummings was five feet eleven inches high, very slender, with sandy hair and whiskers and blue eyes. He was about forty or forty-one years old. Mr. James (the defendant) and he are about one age. I never heard about his being a married man. First met Jim Cummings on the first of November, 1880, at Ford's, near Richmond, in Ray county. On this trip south we saw Gen. Joe Shelby at his house, or rather about one hundred yards from his house, getting out hemp seed. I and Cummings were ahead and the others were behind, we having previously separated to meet on Shelby's place. We rode up to the barn and then I went on foot to Gen. Shelby. We were not all together at the time we met Shelby.

Q. Did not Shelby on that occasion state to Jesse James that there were a couple of young men who had been arrested for the Concordia bank robbery, and that he didn't believe that those men had anything to do with it and asked Jesse if he knew anything about it, and didn't Jesse James turn to you and say, "There is that man that hit the Dutchman over the head and knocked him down," to which you made no reply? A. There was never any such conversation between us.

Witness continuing said:

I went to Nashville, part of the way on horseback and partly by rail. I got there first and the others arrived two weeks later. Frank James was still living at

4

his place until the last of January or first of February, 1881, when he moved into Edgefield. I had not seen Ryan for three weeks before his arrest, and have not seen him since. He was arrested for a breach of the peace, in which he drew a pistol, and was put into Nashville jail. We left as soon as we heard of Ryan's arrest. We left March 26, and went to old man Hite's on the morning of the twenty-seventh. We borrowed the horses on which we made this trip. We didn't ask their owners' permission to use them, they being asleep. [Laughter.] Clarence Hite was the first one to tell us about the officers from Tennessee being on our tracks. Mr. Norris told us about seeing a posse of men fixing to go out somewhere. That same day (Sunday) we saw three men coming riding by the house. We thought they were coming after us, and Jesse and Frank and myself fixed ourselves. Frank went and fixed himself a place in the parlor by the window. I was in the hall behind the door, and Jesse on the opposite side of the hall near the door.

I decline to answer about any expeditions in 1879 on the ground that I do not desire to commit myself. I decline to answer who went with me. The defendant was not with me. From Hite's, in 1881, we went to Logan county, Kentucky, where I stopped first at old Dr. Haskin's, and afterward at Bob Hall's, and then started to Missouri. At Bob Hall's we made the arrangement about coming to Missouri. We went to bid Johnny Pence good-by. By "we" I mean Frank James, Jesse James and myself. We went on horseback from Hall's to Louisville. I decline to answer where I got

my horse. Jesse James went with me to Louisville,
and I came to Missouri with Jesse James.   The arrangement was that we were to come out here to take
the express where it crossed the river at Kansas City,
the river being high so that trains could not cross.
There was no other definite object right at that time.
From Mrs. Samuels, on the last of May or first of June,
we learned that the river had fallen, and this project
was abandoned.   I was in Clay county or Ray in June,
and made one trip to Jackson county.   The Chillicothe
trip was some time in June and only took four or five
days.

Here the witness repeated the details of the Chillicothe trip, telling how they went into a church because
of the rain, and had no supper or breakfast, and how
Wood Hite went after Clarence, who had gone ahead
by rail to bring out food, which was eaten in the woods.
The rest of the cross-examination of Liddil may be ac-
curately described by saying that Mr. Philips took the
witness over every step of ground referred to by him
in his testimony in chief without eliciting anything
which tended in any way to contradict that testimony.
If anything Liddil's testimony to-day was more full
and particular to dates, places, persons and descriptions
than on Saturday.   He told how he had since paid a
visit to Gallatin, recognized some of the persons referred
to in his direct testimony, such as Mr. Hamilton, the
saddler, who sold him the fenders for his horse, and
Mr. Potts, the blacksmith, who shod his horse.   He detailed facts and circumstances without the slightest hesitation or confusion, and freely admitted that he was

here now under guard of Marshal Langhorn, of Kansas City, ever since leaving that last named town. His
testimony was given in an easy, fluent, even, matter-of-
fact way, and in conversational tone. He was at no time
embarrassed, and probably made but one slip all morning, when he described Woolfenberger's house, where
the gang ate shortly before the Winston murder, as being southwest of Gallatin, whereas it is southeast. The
State's counsel let the defense ask all the questions they
wanted without objection, and witness did not seek to
evade telling anything unless it had a tendency to criminate himself.

A little flash of feeling passed between Mr. Philips
and the witness towards the close of the cross-examination. Witness was asked about eating at a Mrs. Montgomery's, and answered that he knew nothing about
Mrs. Montgomery, and was not with any parties who
ate there, so far as he knew. He then turned to Mr.
Philips, and asked what time the question was supposed to refer to. The defendant's counsel tartly remarked that it would be time for witness to cross-ex-
amine him when the time came, when the court
administered a sharp rebuke to counsel, stating that
witness had a right to ask the question of counsel, and
that counsel must observe due courtesy towards witness.

Liddil re-described the train robbery at Winston.
He said that he and Clarence Hite were on the engine
all the time except the time he went back over the coal
to see if the brakes were on, and the time he went into
the express car after Jesse James, after the thing was
ended. The baggage or express car had solid doors.

Jesse came out of the forward door when the train stopped and they all got off, and Frank came through the same door when he came over the tender to shut off steam. Witness heard firing back in the rear cars while he was still on the tender to the number of six or seven shots, and before he did any shooting himself. Witness did not fire a shot until after the engineer and fireman had run out on the pilot, when he and Clarence Hite fired two or three times each to bring them back. Witness did not hear any shooting at all after Frank James came over the tender. The shooting I heard was just after we started and before the first halt. If he heard a shot after the first halt he didn't remember it.

After the robbery witness and Wood Hite went to the Ford's, getting there the Saturday night following the Friday of the robbery, where they were joined by Jesse and Frank James and Clarence Hite. I was at Nichols' house right after this, with the other four. We got there at midnight, and only stayed a few minutes to eat all the cold grub they had. Nichols and his wife were present. I don't think we were in the house, but that we sat around the platform of the well. I was also at Joe Hall's. Jesse and I stopped there one night to get some buttermilk. I don't remember any one coming down to the fence to see us. Nichols' place is about half a mile from Mrs. Samuels'.

Witness further explicitly denied ever seeing Jim Cummings during the summer of 1881. He denied also that in September, 1881, in company with Jesse James, Wood Hite and Jim Cummings, he met Joe Shelby in a lane near Page City, when Shelby was on horseback

and in his shirt sleeves, and declared he had not seen
Shelby except the time at his house and last Thursday
at Kansas City. He denied that at Page City Shelby
had asked where Frank James was, or that Jesse James
had answered that Frank's health was such that he had
been south for years, or that Shelby then asked witness
when he had seen Frank, and that the reply had been
that he had not seen him for two years. No such conversation ever occurred.

Witness also emphatically denied telling Joe B.
Chiles, at Kansas City, that Frank James was not at
the Winston robbery, but stated that he had a conversation with Chiles, in which Chiles said he had a pass
from Governor Crittenden, and that he had been riding
around on it, but that he had never looked for the
James boys; never had tried to find them, and did not
want to. Witness admitted that at or about the time of
his arrest in Kansas City, he might have told Major
McGee that he (witness) was not at Winston. It
was not probable he would go around telling everybody
he was there.

Witness also denied in toto telling Frank Tutt,
coal oil inspector at Lexington, on the same occasion,
that he didn't know where Frank James was, and that
he had not been with the party for years, on account of
Jesse and Frank having had trouble. Witness denied
having heard Jesse James on another occasion tell
John Samuels (Frank James' half brother) that Frank
was in Tennesee or Kentucky, and had gone south on
account of his health, but he said he heard them asking
for Frank, and that Jesse said he would be at Mrs.

Samuels' in a few days. Witness also declined to answer the question, so far as inquiry by Mrs. Samuels was concerned on the ground that it would criminate him. Liddil declined to tell when or where he last saw Wood Hite, or when he first heard of his death, and declined also to answer whether Wood Hite was dead or not. He was in Ray county when he first heard of it. Was at Mrs. Bolton's at the time, with her brothers, Wilbur, Captain, Charley and Bob Ford. From Mrs. Bolton's he went to Kansas City. He remembered Mrs. Bolton's house being raided in January, 1882, and crept out that night through a door. Hid next day in a field, and went to Kansas City about ten days later, but first went to Bill Ford's, uncle of Charley and Bob. There he first met Sheriff Timberlake, about a quarter of a mile from the house, in a pasture. Had been negotiating for a surrender with Governor Crittenden through Mrs. Bolton, who had brought him word to surrender to Sheriff Timberlake, the condition being that he was not to be prosecuted, but was to give evidence and assist in the capture of the James brothers.

Court here took a recess till 1:30 P. M.

On the reassembling of the court after recess Dick Liddil again took the stand, and testified that he had been in jail in Alabama for eight months, but had been released on his own recognizance to come to Kansas City, and there bailed by Messrs. Craig and Timberlake to come to Gallatin. I was turned out on April 28, 1883, stayed in Huntsville, Alabama, a week, went to Nashville, and came on to Kansas City in June;

have since been out West in Kansas and the Indian
Territory; Mr. Wallace and Mr. Craig and those
gentlemen paid my expenses; got back to Kansas two
weeks last Friday.   While last at Kansas City I
boarded at the court house in care of a Deputy Marshal.   I had passes to travel on the railroads.   Mr.
Longhorne has charge of me.   He has served a writ
on me two weeks ago.   I have not been put in jail
under it, and have not given any bond.   I paid my own
way from Alabama, Bob and Charley Ford having
sent me $100 when I was there.   I had only enough
to get to St. Louis, and came the rest of the way on
my carpet-sack and pistols.   Have been to St. Louis
since on a pass furnished by Mr. Wallace.   I redeemed
my carpet-sack and pistols.   Capt. Craig got them for
me.   I have not been engaged in any business since
my return from Alabama.

Re-direct examination by Mr. Wallace: At
Winston we all had two pistols except Wood Hite,
who had but one.   And leaving the train we all loaded
up, Frank and Jesse, Clarence and Wood and myself.
The defendant loaded up and said he had fired several
shots, he and Jesse both.   I saw him loading his pistol.
On one of these trips Frank had the little bay mare
from Elkhorn, and on the second trip the horse I had
shod was the Matthews horse.   When I saw Sheriff
Timberlake I told him I had sent a party to see the
Governor.   I don't know that I told Mr. Timberlake
full details at that time, but I told him shortly after.   I
think it was after Clarence Hite was captured, in February, 1882—two or three weeks after I had given my-

self up. Jesse never had a horse after the Winston robbery. I never was with him when he was on horse-back after that. In Kansas City, during the weeks immediately after the Winston robbery, the defendant and his companions when they went anywhere had to walk.

By Mr. Philips: At the time of the Winston robbery the defendant wore long burnside whiskers and a mustache.

William Earthman was recalled and testified: At Nashville Frank James wore whiskers long all over his face, the whiskers being a little darker than his hair. I arrested Bill Ryan, not because he was drunk and carried a pistol, but because he said he was a robber and an outlaw against the state and country.

J. Thomas Ford testified as follows: I live in Ray county; am the father of Bob and Charley Ford. Have lived in Ray County, two and a half miles north of Richmond. In 1881 Mrs. Bolton, my daughter, lived half a mile east of Richmond. I know the defendant. I saw him in 1881. I heard of the Winston robbery. I saw the defendant a short time before that, between the first and tenth of July. He was alone. I went down there and ate dinner with him at my sister's. He went by the name of Hall. The defendant is the man I saw on that occasion.

Cross-examined: My son, Charles, in 1881, lived at the Harbison farm, where Mrs. Bolton kept house for him. Wilbur was there that year till August. Charley and Cap rented the farm in March, 1880, and Mrs. Bolton kept house for them. Cap went to Rich-

mond, Missouri, and Wilbur took his place. **They**
had all previously been living at my house. Mrs.
Bolton lived with me for five years prior to moving to
the Harbison place. Had seen Mr. Hall (the defendant) in the May previous to July, 1881. My son John
told me who he really was the Sunday evening in May.
I knew at that time that the officers of the law were
trying to find Frank James. I told my wife, but never
told any of my children that didn't already know it. I
have seen Jesse James two or three times. First saw
him in 1879 or 1880, when he came to my house. I
know Dick Liddil. Think he first passed my house
once with Jesse James in 1879 or 1880, when they
stopped and got their supper. Afterward I saw Wood
Hite under similar circumstances in the fall of 1879 or
1880. It was in 1879 and not in 1880. I never knew
Clarence Hite. Had often seen Jim Cummings in
Clay and Ray counties. He lived five or six miles
from me. I remember also seeing Wood Hite and
Jesse James at my place in September, 1881. Know
James C. Mason, a neighbor of mine. I never told
him shortly after Jesse James was killed that Frank
was not in the Winston or Blue Cut robbery, or that
he had not been in the county for a long time, or that I
never knew anything about their being at my son's
house. I always tried to keep from saying anything
about them, because I thought it policy to do so. I
never made any such statement to Wm. D. Rice either.

Re-direct—By Mr. Wallace:

When Frank James told me he hadn't seen his
mother for five years it was at my son's, the last time I

saw him there. My brother married Jim Cummings'
sister. When I saw him the defendant wore "side-
burn" whiskers and a mustache.

By Mr. Glover: Frank James said either he
hadn't seen his mother for five years, or was trying to
see her, or hadn't been in the county for five years. I
haven't talked with Liddil since the winter of 1882.
He was at my house twice since his surrender. He
came there once before with Jesse James, some time
in the summer of 1879. The last time I ever saw
Wood Hite he was in company with Dick Liddil, in
July or August, 1881. I never saw him, alive or dead,
after that. I heard he was killed at the house where
the boys were farming.

Elias Ford, otherwise Capt. Ford, testified: I
have been staying in Kansas City the last few weeks,
but am now staying at Richmond. I know defendant.
First saw him about the first of May, 1881, at Charley
Ford's. When I saw him there were present Frank
and Jesse James. I can't say about Liddil or Wood
Hite being present or not. I walked with defendant
that day. He went by the name of Hall. Jesse introduced him under that name. First saw Jesse in September, 1879, at my father's, with Ed Miller. I have
seen Frank James often since. In June and July;
about the first of July, 1881, with Jesse, Dick Liddil,
Clarence Hite and Wood Hite. Saw him next again
about August 1. The same party were there then.
They were riding. Frank was there a week or ten
days. He had side whiskers and a mustache. I have
a brother, J. T. Ford. I know of a box shipped to

him at Richmond, I couldn't see where it was from. It had a couple of guns in it. I opened it at John Ford's store, in Richmond. The guns were a double-barreled shot-gun and a Winchester. Jesse took the rifle off. I don't know who took the shot-gun. I know Jim Cummings. I got acquainted with him in 1871 or 1872; last saw him in the fall of 1881 at Charley Ford's house. I know him well.

The cross-examination of this witness, Elias Ford, afforded no matter of interest till he was asked if he did not help to bury the body of Wood Hite in the brush near the Woods pasture in Ray county, which question the state's counsel objected to, and the court sustained the objection.

Defendant's counsel then asked witness whether Dick Liddil didn't kill Wood Hite, which involved a similar objection and ruling. The court also ruled that defendant need not answer a question as to whether he did not keep concealed the body of Wood Hite all day till it could be buried. The argument over this point was sharp and bitter. Defendant's counsel gave as their reason for putting the question that they desired to show that Liddil had killed Wood Hite, and then gone and given himself up, and given away the rest of the gang to secure immunity for that crime.

The court adhered to its previous ruling, that the questions asked were improper, and that a witness' conduct could not be shown by proof of special bad or immoral acts. Liddil's credibility might be attacked, but not in that manner.

Witness further stated that he had been working for Captain Craig, of Kansas City, in looking after the James boys, and that he quit looking for them in October of last year. Since then he has been staying at his father's.

Re-direct examination—By Mr. Wallace: The Winston robbery was in July, 1881. Have not seen Jim Cummings since 1880.

Re-cross-examination: I heard of Jim Cummings being in the neighborhood about June 18, 1882.

Mrs. Martha Bolton testified: I live at Richmond, Missouri. Am the daughter of Thos. Ford, and a sister of Bob and Charley Ford. I know Frank James. First saw him at my brother's in May, 1881. He came there one night with Jesse James. I first saw Jesse James in 1879 at my father's. Ed Miller was with him. At the May, 1881, visit Jesse stayed all night and Frank stayed a week, reading Shakespeare and other books in his room. I saw Dick Liddil, Wood Hite, and Clarence Hite there. They all went away together with Frank James. At that time Frank wore side whiskers and mustache, and went by the name of Hall. I saw him again two or three weeks after, in company with Dick Liddil. They went away together. He was gone two or three weeks, and came back again and stayed till the fourth, fifth and sixth of July, before the Winston robbery. After that I saw him and Jesse and Clarence Hite come there about the last of July. Wood Hite and Liddil were there already. That time they remained two days, and left together. I next saw Frank James about the first of October. He

came with Charley Ford and Clarence Hite. Dick
Liddil was already there. They all left my house
together for Richmond. Never saw Frank James or
Clarence Hite after that. I know Jim Cummings.
He was once at my house in Richmond; that was in
1879, I believe. I did not see him the summer that I
have described seeing the other men I have named. I
have heard that Jim Cummings was there in the spring
of 1881. Never heard of his being there in the summer or fall of 1881.

Cross-examined: Liddil was in the house January 6, 1882, at the time of the raid, when he escaped, I
didn't ask him how. Wood Hite is dead. He died
December 5, 1881. He died about one hour before
sunrise that morning. The question of how Wood
Hite came to his death, or what was done with his
body, or where he was buried, were all peremptorily
ruled out by the court.

Witness continued: The raid on my house was
made about the sixth of January following the fifth of
December on which Hite died. Liddil gave himself
up alone the twentieth of January, 1882. I went to
Jefferson City to see the Governor on business, between
January 6 and 20. Bob Ford sent me there on business. I went there to make arrangements for the surrender of Dick Liddil. Dick surrendered on condition of immunity from punishment, and that he would
testify against the rest of the band. I know James C.
Mason. He lives about three-quarters of a mile from
me. I never told him, shortly after Jesse's death, that
Wood and Clarence Hite, Jesse James, Dick Liddil

and Jim Cummings were in the robberies, or that I thought Frank was trying to lead an honest life, and was different from Jesse, or that Frank would move to different places when Jesse would go to where he was, and when the detectives would come after Jesse, Frank would have to leave, or that Jesse James, Wood Hite, Clarence Hite, Dick Liddil and Jim Cummings were at my house just before and after the Winston robbery, and that Frank James was not. I did testify before the Coroner's inquest over Wood Hite's body, but I did not state at that inquest that I had not seen Frank James for two years, or that he had not been at my house or my brother's in that time.

An attempt by the defense to get witness to talk about the killing of Wood Hite, or of her conduct on the day of his death, was emphatically sat down on by the court.

FOURTH DAY'S TRIAL.

Here the jury entered the court room, and Mrs. Bolton, taking the stand, was informed by the court that she need not answer any self-criminating questions. In answer to questions by Mr. Glover, the witness said: "On Sunday, December 5, 1881, Bud Harbison and William Jacobs were at my house. They reached it in the afternoon. We had dinner that day between 12 and 1 o'clock."

Q. In what room of your house was Wood Hite killed?

Objected to as being a collateral matter, and that if it were to be gone into Dick Liddil would enter his appearance to the charge within thirty minutes. The court overruled the objection.

A. He was killed in the dining-room. I don't know how long after that his body was taken upstairs. I refuse to answer whether his body was taken upstairs. I had nothing to do with his killing. [Counsel for defendant here admitted this to be a fact.] I do not know who took the body upstairs or how long it remained there. I didn't go upstairs to see it, was not in the room afterward, and haven't been in it since. I don't know when the body was taken upstairs. I was there that night. I didn't see anyone that evening but my own children. I don't know who took Wood Hite's body down-stairs. I saw no coffin there that day. I did not see the body carried out. I don't know when the body was taken out. I didn't tell William Jacobs nor Bud Harbison nor any one that Wood Hite's body was up-stairs. He was buried about two hundred yards from the house. His body was covered with a sheet when I saw it after it had been exhumed. Hite's body had been out there about five months before I saw it at the time of the inquest. In the winter time my dining room and kitchen are all in one.

Here the court ruled again that Liddil's connection with the killing of Wood Hite, or his whereabouts on the day of Hite's death, were not to be inquired of by this witness.

Witness further testified: Wood Hite was killed in December, and I left that house in February, as I understood Wood Hite and Jesse James were cousins.

At the close of this testimony Mr. Wallace vigorously protested against the manner in which the examination of Mrs. Bolton had been conducted by the defense, and flung down the challenge that if Liddil's connection with the Wood Hite killing was to be inquired into, he (Wallace) would enter Liddil's appearance to answer that charge, and it might be inquired of before the jury now trying Frank James.

Elias Ford, otherwise Captain Ford, being recalled, the court notified defendant's counsel that while they might show this witness' connection with the Hite killing, they could not show the connection of any other witness with that matter.

Witness then testified: I was at Mrs. Bolton's on December 5, 1881. Wood Hite was killed in the dining-room of that house about 9 o'clock. I got there about ten minutes after the shooting. I didn't see the body taken upstairs. The body stayed up-stairs till about 9 o'clock in the evening. I refuse to answer who took the body out and buried it, on the ground that it would criminate myself. I saw the body taken out that night. Four persons carried the body out. I know where the body was buried—about one-quarter of a mile east of the house in the brush. There was no coffin. He was wrapped in a blanket and placed in a trench three feet deep, and covered with earth and some stones and brush. He was only partially clad in his clothes. He wore a gray suit when he was killed.

Re-direct—By Mr. Wallace: Dick Liddil was shot and wounded at this time and was a long time recovering from his wounds.

5

This admission was jerked out suddenly, and was in before the jury before any one could prevent it. The prosecution kicked about it most vigorously.

Miss Ida Bolton, a thirteen-year-old girl, in a blue dress and straw hat, testified: I know Frank James. I see him now. I knew him well. I saw him at Uncle Charley Ford's, a mile and a half east of Richmond, Missouri. I lived there with him (Charley Ford) two years. During the second year I saw Mr. James, who went there by the name of Hall. I saw him five or six times. The first time I saw him was in May. Jesse James was there, too, going by the name of Johnson. That summer I also saw Dick Liddil, Clarence and Wood Hite. Liddil went by the name of Anderson, Clarence Hite by the name of Charley Jackson and Wood Hite by the name of Grimes. After the first visit I saw defendant there two or three weeks later, and again saw Frank James there later in the summer. He wore side whiskers. I last saw him there in October, 1881. Clarence Hite and Dick Liddil were there. When defendant left that time, Clarence Hite and Uncle Charley went with him. I know Jim Cummings. I saw him in 1880, in the fall. That is the last time I saw him.

Cross-examined—By Mr. Glover: I came here Friday. Mr. Ballinger brought me and paid my expenses. Have talked to Mr. Hamilton and Mr. Wallace about what my testimony would be. I have not talked it over with my mother, Mrs. Bolton. The last day I saw Frank James was the ninth or tenth of October, 1881. He was dressed in black coat, vest and pants. Saw Clarence Hite the same day. He wore dark clothes and a drummer's hat. I saw Dick Liddil that day, too. They left that day at 5 o'clock on foot, all walking together. Uncle Charley Ford went with them. Cummings had not been there that year. In the summer of 1881 Jesse James came there. He was there the first day of May. He was there between May and October of 1881, but I don't remember the time. He came in the night. The first time Dick Liddil came, in the summer of 1881, Jesse James was with him. Dick wore a gray and Jesse a black suit. Dick had a mustache, but no whiskers, and Jesse had whiskers about an inch long. Dick had whiskers in the winter. Frank James was there from May 1 to May 6, 1881. Dick Liddil was there the first part of June. Clarence Hite was there some time in July. Wood Hite was there off and on all through the summer. I remember he was there in September, about the sixteenth or seventeenth of the month. I don't remember the day of Wood Hite's death, but remember the place. It was in 1881. He was killed in the morning about 7 or 8 o'clock. Uncle Bob Ford and ma and Dick Liddil were present when he died. I didn't see him taken upstairs. He was buried in the night. I don't know who took him out or who buried him, or how he was buried, or where. I left the house in January, 1881, after the time an armed posse raided the house. Mother and I moved away from the house in March. I remember mother going to Jefferson City to see Governor Crittenden and her return. Dick Liddil left about a week after her return. The last time Jesse James left there was during the Christmas holidays of 1881. I saw Cummings there in the fall of 1880. I first saw him in 1878. Never saw him but twice. I have never heard of his being in that country in 1881.

Willie Bolton, a light-haired boy of fifteen, and brother of the last witness, testified: I know the defendant. I first saw him in May, 1881, about a mile east of Richmond, at the Harbison place, when Cap and Charley Ford were living there. Saw Frank James four or five times that summer. He had side whiskers at that time.

Cross-examined: I remember Wood Hite's death. He was killed about 8 or 9 o'clock on the morning of December 2, 1881. I saw the body that night. I heard the shooting at the time, went to the house from the barn, where I had been milking. I did not go into the room where the shooting occurred. I don't know when or by whom the dead body was taken upstairs. His coat, vest and pants were removed and a horse-blanket put on him. He was then taken down and buried in the Wood's pasture. In a conversation with A. Duval, in the presence of W. D. Rice, near the Ford residence, in Ray county, on August 17, 1883, I did not say I knew Frank James at our house as Mr. Hall, but did not know him to be Frank James, but that I intended to swear it was he anyway. I testified before the coroner on the occasion of the inquest over Wood Hite. Don't remember any conversation with W. D. Rice after that inquest. I did not tell him my mother had made me swear the way I did at the inquest.

Brief proof was here made by the state that the different members of the Ford family had been brought into court on attachment.

James Hughes testified: I live at Richmond, Missouri; have been living in Ray county since 1830. I have seen the defendant since I have been here. I saw a gentleman that resembled him very much last fall a year ago at the depot in Richmond. I conversed with him. I think the defendant is the man. I saw him at the depot in September or October, 1881. I went to the train. There were three gentlemen wanting to get off on a freight train to the R. and L. Junction. The train didn't come, and the party I refer to asked if there was any other way to get to the junction. I looked at my watch, and said it could be made by taking a hack. The prisoner and the two gentlemen who were with him got a 'bus at Mr. Swash's livery stable and went in the direction of the junction.

Cross-examined: I can not remember how the party I speak of was dressed, or how he wore his whiskers.

Thomas Ford, or "Old Man Ford," was recalled to show that he was brought into court by attachment. He last saw Jim Cummings in the fall of 1881. Have never seen him since.

Cross-examined: I saw Cummings during 1878 and 1879, when I lived in Clay county. I dont remember the precise time at which I saw him. I don't think I saw him in 1879, but I am satisfied I saw him in 1880.

I saw him five years ago last winter at my house in Ray county and then again in 1880 at my house in Clay county.

The court here took a recess till 1:30 P. M. Joseph Mallory was the first witness called after recess, and testified: I have lived in this county about forty-three years. I remember hearing of the Winston robbery. I then lived eight miles west of Gallatin and four miles northeast of Winston. I think I have seen the defendant before at Mr. Pott's shop getting his horse shod. It was Thursday morning prior to the robbery at Winston. He and another gentleman were there together. The other was a slender man of ordinary height, a little humped in the back. They were getting a horse shod —a small bay nag. The defendant was holding the horse. I and he conversed there about most everything relative to Garfield's assassination, and so on, and defendant said he was going up to Nodaway to run a race there at the fair. Mr. Potts said they came from Caldwell, and they themselves said they came from Ray county.

Cross-examined—By Mr. Rush: Never saw any other strangers get horses shod at that shop. The other man present when the horse was shod was clad in a dark suit, but not of a solid color. Mr. Whitman and a Mr. Wm. Hughes were also there. I remember when the horse was shod the man went to pay Mr. Potts and said, "This is all the change I have got," pulling out some silver. The man that held the horse had whiskers on his face and chin about three or four inches long, of rather a light color. After I left the blacksmith shop I saw the two men going west. I did not see the defendant after that till I saw him in jail here. At that time I could not identify him on account of the dim light. I believe now that he is the man I saw at Mr. Potts' shop.

Jonas Potts testified: I live in Daviess county, about four miles northeast of Winston. I have seen the defendant, Frank James. I saw him once at Independence, and before that at my shop some time in the latter part of June, 1881. He was at my house twice on or about the last of June, and again on either the thirteenth or fourteenth of July. I shod a horse for him. There was another man with him with full mustache and whiskers, which I think were colored. I met this other man here the other day. I knew him the moment I saw him. On the first time the horse shod was a sorrel horse of good size with a blaze on his face. On that occasion my dog ran against the shoe-box and scared the horse, and he ran out of doors. This was shortly before noon. We had some little conversation when it came to paying. There was fifty cents short, and the other man (James) said he would play me a game of seven-up whether it was $1 dollar or nothing. I told him I had no time, or he couldn't say that twice. As it was I had to send out and get change. On the other visit there came a slender fellow with the defendant. A slender man, tall, light-complexioned, with light whiskers and mustache, and a couple of black teeth. The other man called him Clarence. They came a little after sun-up and had us get them breakfast, and I shod a little bay mare for the defendant. I

had considerable talk with the parties when they called
the first time.   Mr. James did most of the talking both
times.

Cross-examined: Mr. James came both times
with a different companion each time.   At the first
visit Liddil wore a heavy mustache and short whiskers
all around his face.   James had side whiskers that
were darker than his mustache.   Liddil wore a light
plad suit, rather worn, and a black hat.   He had on
boots, and the other man also.   Mr. James' companion on the second visit wore light, grayish clothes.   I
would judge him to be five feet ten inches, slim, with
light complexion, blue eyes, light mustache, burnside
whiskers about an inch long.   Frank James was dressed
on this second occasion in a dark suit with a gold
speck in it, and had his whiskers like they were on the
previous visit.   On this second visit Frank James
talked a long time with Squire Mallory.   This was
about the thirteenth and fourteenth of July, 1881.
The Winston robbery was on the fifteenth.   I had
never seen Liddil before, but was under the impression I had seen Mr. James at the Kansas City Fair,
when Goldsmith Maid trotted there, and at the Hamilton Fair.   First saw Mr. James after his arrest at Independence.   Went down there with Loss Ewing, of
the Rock Island Road.   He furnished the money,
except what little I spent in a saloon.   At that time I
didn't come to any conclusion at all, but it was such a
dark place that I didn't have a good chance to see
him.   When I got a good look at him, I was perfectly
satisfied he was the man.   Loss Ewing introduced me

to him. I shook hands with him and don't think I did any talking. I didn't tell the defendant on that occasion that I had shod a horse for him once. Subsequently saw the defendant in the Gallatin jail. Did not then fully make up my mind that he was the man. In June, I saw him in the court room and in the court house yard, and made up my mind that he was the man. I don't remember telling Marion Duncan, about a month after Jesse James' death, that I had seen Jesse James' picture, and that he was one of the men for whom I had shod a horse. I remember being slightly in liquor on that occasion, and that he was trying to pump me.

Q.   Where did you get your liquor?

A.   At Winston, I suppose, where you got yours. [Laughter.]

Witness added: I know John Dean. If I ever told him anything I don't know it. I never told John Dean after I had been to Independence that I had never seen Frank James before. I don't remember telling G. H. Chapman after I had been to Gallatin that I had no way of telling whether Frank James was the man whose horse I had shod. I never made a similar denial to Robert Simpson, turnkey of the Independence Jail. I will explain my wife's shaking her head when Mrs. Annie Winburn asked her if Frank James was the man who ate at our place, by saying that she shook her head because she didn't want to tell; because there were too many sneaking round and listening. I never said on Saturday last in the court house yard in the presence of F. W. Comstock that from

what I had heard of Liddil's testimony, he might
have had a horse shod at my place, but that I had no
recollection of the transaction. I never said any such
thing.

By Mr. Hamilton: I don't know any man by the
name of Comstock, unless it be a man who was introduced to me who owns a sorrel horse. At the shop,
when I shod his horse, the defendant gave me his name
as Green Cooper, and said that he lived in Ray county
and was a cattle dealer. I believe I have seen the
little bay mare I shod on the trip in a livery stable at
Liberty. She had on a pair of shoes in front that I
thought I fitted up. I think I can recognize my work
when I see it. I saw this mare about a month or six
weeks after the Winston robbery. I was going through
the stable, when a boy showed me the mare telling me
not to go too near her, as she was a kicker and was
Jesse James' mare.

Re-cross-examined: I believe those were the
shoes I fitted up for the mare. I heard from some
source such a mare was reported to be there, and I
went there to see her. The defendant gave his name
as Green Cooper on the first visit. I may have told
Squire Mallory of this name. Don't think I ever told
Mr. Hughes.

G. W. Whitman testified: I live in Daviess
county, four miles northeast of Winston. Have seen
the defendant. I saw him at Mr. Potts' shop on the
fourteenth of July, 1881. He got a mare shod there
on Thursday morning. There was a man with him
with light whiskers and just a patch on his chin. He

had a small-sized mare. It was a bay mare, about fifteen and one half hands high. The defendant was getting her shod. I was there about an hour and a half. Mr. Mallory and Mr. Hughes were there, too. Squire Mallory and defendant did all the talking, except that as the two strangers left, the defendant, in reply to a remark of mine, said he thought Mr. Potts had done a good job. I have since seen the defendant at the June term of court and recognized him as the man I saw the morning in July, 1881.

Cross-examined: When the horse was shod defendant wore lightish whiskers, rather short all around his face except the chin.

Re-direct: He had a mustache, too. I am positive he is the man.

Frank R. O'Neill testified : I live in St. Louis, and have been connected with the St. Louis *Republican* as reporter for nearly the last ten years. I know the defendant. First saw him in October, 1882, before he gave himself up. Had an interview with him and published the same by consent. Stated in that interview that he went to Nashville in the fall of 1877, being then in ill-health ; that he farmed and drove for the Indiana Lumber Company, and lived a hard, laborious life for four years ; that he was well known in Nashville as B. J. Woodson ; that there he met Jesse, whom he had not seen for two years ; that he left Nashville. He also talked about Cummings and described him as a man easily frightened. Cummings went away and they were afraid he had gone to give the boys away. Ryan was arrested shortly after. What the defendant had done since that time was passed in the interview by mutual consent. He spoke of Cummings as a lazy man who drawled in his speech. He said, too, that Jesse, Jim Cummings and Dick Liddil were all at Nashville at the time he was; that after Ryan was arrested he and Jesse left. He said he went unarmed while in Nashville, and that he never had any trouble there except on one trifling occasion, and that he numbered several of the officials among his friends. When armed he carried a Winchester and a pair of Remingtons. Defendant had read the interview as printed. He noticed no error.

Witness was here asked where the interview took place, but begged to be relieved from stating further than that it occurred in Missouri. The defendant's wife was present. Witness declined to state who were present besides those named, and was given till morning to decide whether he would answer touching the place and time of the interview and the names of the parties present threat.

Mrs. Jonas Potts testified: I live eight miles from here. I have seen the defendant at my house the thirteenth or fourteenth of July, 1881. The Winston robbery was the fifteenth of July. The man who came with him had light whiskers and blue eyes, and had a stoop in his walk. I think we talked, amongst other things, about the Talbott case. He remarked that a mother never forsook her children. When they left the breakfast table the taller one, or defendant, said, "Clarence, make out your breakfast."

Gen. Jamin Matchett testified: **I reside** in Caldwell county, Missouri. I remember the Winston robbery. Was living three miles from Winston at the time. Believe I saw Frank James at my residence on July 14, 1881. A Mr. Scott was with him. Scott was five feet eight or nine inches high, brown hair, a few freckles and a very ill-formed mouth, with irregular teeth ; somewhat slim. They came to my house about 11 o'clock. One of the party rode a bay, the other a sorrel, with two white hind legs. They first inquired for some one on the premises. I came down stairs to the front door. They wanted to know if they could get dinner. I said I would see my wife, who objected somewhat as she was washing, to which they remarked they were in no hurry, and I then told them that they could be accommodated. We watered the horses, which they tied to my shade trees in the orchard and then inquired for feed. I stepped into the field and brought bundles of oats. One of them inquired if they were fresh cut, and being told they were, said they didn't want to feed any green food, and I gave them a blunt ax and they cut off the green part. When they rode up I noticed they were wearing heavy goods for that time of the year, and had gum coats or blankets strapped to their saddles. One gave his name as Scott from Plattsburg, Clinton county, and the other, **the defendant, said his name was Willard, and had been in Clinton county about eight years, and came from the Shenandoah Valley. We talked some about the Shenandoah Valley, Virginia.**

I inquired of Willard where he had been between the Shenandoah Valley and this section, and he never answered me, but said, "What do you think of Bob Ingersoll?" We discussed Bob for some time, till we differed so that I went to my library for a volume of his lectures, which I gave Willard, and he read some till he fell asleep. At dinner we talked about Clinton county. I asked some questions about Lawson, which Willard answered, and then later I asked about Greenville, Clay county, once called Clintonville, which Willard did not answer, but said, "What is your judgment of the Talbott boys?" We then discussed the Talbott boys, and Willard expressed himself with indignation at boys doing crimes of that kind. Willard wanted to pay for the dinner, and I declined at first, but finally took fifty cents. In conversation with Scott he observed he would take me for a minister of the Christian church, and I answered that I was. He said he thought if he ever united with the church he would join the Christian church, and referred to his wife as a Presbyterian. Willard acquiesced in that, but said there was no man ever lived like Shakespeare, and declaimed a piece and remarked, "That's grand!" which observation I indorsed. Finally Scott said something about going, and I invited them, if they ever came that way, to call again, which they said they would be pleased to do, that they were going to Gallatin, where Willard said he had not been for ten years. I recognize the defendant. When he stopped at my house he had whiskers on the side of his face. I am not certain about the chin. He had a tolerably fair mustache, and his whiskers were darker outside than near the skin.

Cross-examined: I am this confident the defendant is the man who stopped at my house that if he hadn't paid for the dinner I would say, "Mr. Willard, I would be pleased to have the amount of that board bill." [Laughter].

Ezra Saule testified: I live two miles northeast of Winston. I have seen the defendant here. I saw him on the line of the railroad, about one-fourth of a mile south of the track in the country, nearly two miles from Winston, between 4 and 6 o'clock on the day of the robbery. I live about forty or fifty rods north of the road. The meeting was half a mile from my house in a secluded place in the woods. I had started out for berries and to fetch my cows. It was a low place, heavily wooded on three sides and scattering on the other. I saw him under suspicious circumstances, and talked to him about an hour. We talked about the weather and Kansas. He pretended to be buying fat cows for that market; said he had lost a cow, and had been looking for her. He said he had a partner. I saw no partner, and on the saddles were packages like blankets or gum-coats. He said his partner was thirsty and had gone to D. C. Ford's for a drink. In about three-quarters of an hour a man came up from the opposite direction, whom I took for the partner.

This partner appeared to be twenty-two years old, as I described him next day to Squire Jeffries, five feet eight or nine inches high, slender, hollow-stomached, with shoulders that leaned forward, and a general kind of a consumptive mien. His beard was a little yellow fuz, and he looked as if he was trying to raise a mustache. Before seeing the man I struck on an old road not traveled for twenty years. There I found a horse hitched, saddled and bridled, and twenty yards from that was another. They were both bays, or rather one was a sorrel with white stockings on her hind legs, and then I saw this man. By and by his partner came up, and was much more sociable and communicative than the one first met. Next day I went to the trestle work on the railroad, where I discovered four horses had been hitched, and then I found another, and here is a little trophy I found (producing a halter-strap.) I also saw a halter-strap picked up there by another man, which looked as if it had been cut off or broken through. I recognized the defendant as the man I saw that night.

Cross-examined: I thought I had found a horse-thief, and that he had a partner. The next time I saw this man was in the court house here in February, 1883. I was here in response to a subpœna. I do not take more interest in this case than any citizen should. I shall not be disappointed if he is acquitted. I don't know that he was armed, but from the way in which he handled a coat on the ground, it seemed as if there was something heavy in the pockets, and I kind of imagined there might be some bull-dogs there, but I didn't see them. I noticed that the whiskers of this man were darker on the outside than near the skin. I mistrusted they were dyed.

FIFTH DAY'S TRIAL.

George W. McCrow, first witness for State, testified: I live in Port Osage Township, Jackson county. I know Dick Liddil; have known him for the last five years. I remember hearing of the Winston robbery. There was a man left a wagon at my house some time after that robbery. The man was a stranger. The wagon has never been claimed, and is there yet. I know Lamartine Hudspeth. He lives six or seven miles from me. I know a sorrel horse that he owned before and after the robbery. I can not describe the horse particularly.

Cross-examined: I have seen other sorrel horses at Hudspeth's. I am a brother-in-law of Mattie Collins, wife of Dick Liddil.

W. R. McRoberts testified: In the spring and summer of 1881, I was agent for the Wabash, at Richmond, Missouri. The express books were kept by W. L. Stewart. I know his handwriting; have seen him write every day for thirteen months. I find an entry of the shipment of a box from Lexington, Missouri, on May 18, 1881. The entry is in Stewart's handwriting. The entry reads: "W. B. 118, May 18, Lexington; one box, 40 pounds; J. T. Ford; back charges $1.95; our charges 35 cents; total, collect, $2.30."

Miss Ella Kindigg testified: I live nine miles west of here, and four miles from Winston. I have seen Dick Liddil here. I will not state positively

6

that I have seen him before, but I saw a man with features like him on July 15, 1881, on the day of the Winston robbery. He had dark hair and whiskers. He came there about 11:30 A. M. and stayed to dinner. There was no one with him. The house is a low frame, with trees all round, standing about 100 yards from the road that runs west. My mother and brother were there, and two of Mr. Mapes' girls. The oldest is a simple girl, eighteen or nineteen years old, with sore eyes.

Cross-examined: The party I saw at our house had on a linen duster.

Mrs. Samuel A. Kindigg, mother of the last witness, testified: I have seen a man called Dick Liddil here in court. He looks like a man that took dinner at my house on the morning of the Friday on which the Winston robbery occurred. The man who called at our house was five feet nine inches high, with dark hair, light eyes and chin whiskers. His whiskers were just started out. I don't remember whether he had a mustache or not. The day I saw Liddil here I asked him if he had ever seen me before. He said that he had, and had taken dinner at my house.

Cross-examined: I did not need to have Liddil pointed out to me. I knew him when I saw him. My conversation with him occurred last night as I was passing along the sidewalk.

Wm. Bray testified: I live at Hamilton, Missouri. In the summer of 1881 I lived two miles west of Hamilton, in a story and a half house, with a little stable back of it. I have seen the defendant. I saw him, or a man that looked like him, at m_ house some two or three weeks before the Winston robbery. Was not home at the time, but found the defendant and three others there when I came home. One of them was sick with the toothache.

This was a low, heavy-set man, with about a week's growth of sandy beard, and the other was a smaller man, with a large tooth. Have seen Dick Liddil since, but will not say that he was there, but believe him to be the man that was out in the stable most of the time. The day they called at my house I took the man with the toothache to town and he had his tooth pulled.

Cross-examined: The party with the toothache was almost five feet eight or nine inches high. The defendant wore burnside whiskers of tolerable length, say two or three inches long, of light sandy color.

R. E. Bray, son of the foregoing witness, Wm. Bray, testified: I have seen the defendant. I saw a man that looked like him at my father's house some two or three weeks before the Winston robbery. There were three others with him. Three went away on horseback, and a low, heavy-set man, with the toothache, with my father in his buggy. I was told Dick Liddil was here, and when I saw him I thought he was one of the men who stopped. I don't know that I would have recognized him if I had met him on the road.

Mrs. William Bray testified to seeing the defendant at her husband's house some ten days or two weeks before the Winston robbery. Three other men came with him. One of the men was a spare-built man with light hair, large teeth, slight mustache, and little or no beard. The heavy-set man had sandy beard of two or three days' growth. The defendant looks to me as like one of the men that was at my house. I talked to the defendant that day about the sickness of the heavy-set man. He thought his sickness was caused by the use of creosote for the toothache. The defendant told me they stopped the night before at A. Mr. Wolfenberger's, where they pulled and ate cherries in the morning.

Cross-examined: The man called Liddil came to the house with the heavy-set man that was sick and asked for a vessel to carry water out to him. I gave him either a pitcher or a quart cup. In the meantime the heavy-set man got off his horse and got in the shade, so that his companion had to call out for him. He called him Dave, and Dave answered him. After that two others came up. They all had dinner at our house. They spent most of the time out of doors in the shade, in their shirt-sleeves. The defendant that day wore burnside whiskers, tolerably long, and a little thin mustache. I don't think he had any chin whiskers. He had a dark coat, grayish pants and black hat. Think I would recognize the defendant more easily than I would the man called Liddil should I meet him in the road.

Re-direct: I would recognize the defendant more easily because he sat facing me at the table, and I talked with him. On three or four occasions when he came in the house I remember talking with him about physicians, and he said the sick man was anxious to go to Cameron to see a doctor there. They went south as they left.

Mrs. David Franks testified: I have seen a man at our house eight miles west of here, that represents the defendant from the face, upon July 13, 1881. There were three men at dinner there that day. One was a tall, slim man that wore burnsides. Another was slender and lightly complexioned, while the third was heavier.

Cross-examined: The defendant's hair was dark brown and his whiskers blacker than his mustache. He had a face tanned by riding in the wind, and wore dark clothes and boots. This was two days before the Winston robbery. One of the other men wore a light checked plaid and a dark hat.

Re-direct: I guess we live about three miles southeast of Mr. Jonas Potts' blacksmith-shop.

Frank Wolfenberger testified: I live eight miles southwest of Gallatin. I have seen the defendant here in court. Saw him before at my home, in the latter part of June, 1881. Three other men were with him. I recognize one of them as Dick Liddil. Another was a heavy-set man of about five feet ten inches. The other was not so tall, and round-shouldered, and in walking let his shoulders come in together forward. He had a slouchy gait. He had light whiskers, very short. The other heavy man had whiskers all round, that looked as if he had let them all start growing at the same time. It was evening when I met them. They had been helping themselves to feed, and then

went from the barn to the house. We washed for
supper, and defendant and Liddil blackened their
boots. The sick man said he would wait till morning,
and the slouchy one didn't think he would black his
boots at all. The sick man retired early, and in the
morning asked me to examine his mouth, which I did.
In the evening previous the defendant asked if we had
any opium. I said no, but as my wife had been sick I
had some morphine. I fixed two doses in one. The
defendant observed, "I reckon it is not poison," and
the heavy man took it. At the supper-table the
slouchy man's name was called. The defendant's
name was McGinnis, and the sick man's name was
given as Johnson.

The defendant said he was married and so was
the sick man, and the others were single. The defendant seemed to know all about fair horses, but more
about runners than trotters. In the morning Liddil
helped me to load my wood. The slouchy man produced a bottle of stimulants and offered it to me, but I
declined. Then they sampled it lightly themselves.
The arrangement with the defendant had been that if
the sick man was not able to leave I should take him to
Kidder in a buggy. The prisoner gave me fifty cents
to buy quinine with, but I still owe him that sum, as he
had left before I returned with the quinine. Since I
first saw the defendant in the Gallatin jail I went in
there by myself, and after some preliminary talk with
the defendant, I said: "I guess I had the pleasure of
entertaining you and three other men one night." He
looked at me slightly and then down and said: "I

have no remembrance of it." Said I: "I guess I
did. You and three other men, and one was quite
sick." He looked up in a kind of study and shook his
head and said: "I don't remember. I have no recollection of it." I have since seen Dick Liddil and
recognized him as the man I saw at my house.

Cross-examined: The defendant when at my
house wore burnside whiskers about three inches long,
and a light mustache. Liddil at that time had a
beard all over his face, about three or four week's
growth. His mustache was not so long as now.

Re-direct: I am positive the defendant is the
man who was in my house on that occasion.

Mrs. James Lindsay testified: I live at Chillicothe. I am a sister of the last witness. I saw the
defendant at my brother's in June, 1881, about two
weeks before the Winston robbery. Three others
came with him. I recognize Liddil as one of them.
He had a good appearance. Had a mustache and had
not recently been shaved. Another of the three, who
was sick with neuralgia at the time, had a beard all
over his face. I first saw the defendant, who rode up
to the gate, and said that they had a sick man with
them and asked if they could be entertained for the
night. The fourth man was rather green looking. I
remember the defendant having a conversation on
some religious topic with my sister-in-law. He
seemed to be a very religious man. I am sure the
defendant is the man I saw that day.

Cross-examined: The man I saw at my house
had burnside whiskers and a mustache. In the morn-

ing after Frank James was out eating cherries under the trees and Liddil was with him. I would have known either the defendant or Liddil if I had met them on road before the surrender. I never forget a face. I remember seeing Mr. Johnson here at the June term. I do not remember seeing Mr. Philips. [Mr. Philips was not present in June.]

Dr. Wm. E. Black testified: I live at Gallatin, Missouri; have seen the defendant since the surrender; had a few words in the jail with him; I talked with him in jail at Independence; he spoke of the merits of different actors; I believe he said he had seen Keene play Richard III, at Nashville, and also seen Lawrence Barrett, McCullough, and, I think, he spoke of Ward as a favorite actor with him, and that he delineated the Shakespearean characters he played better than any one he knew, being a young man; he also spoke of Miles.

D. Mathews testified: I live in Clay county, Missouri, near Kearney, four and a half miles from Mrs. Samuels; I lost a horse on June 19—before the Winston robbery—a sorrel, with a blazed face and white hind feet; I got him some time in August after the robbery; he was at a farmer's by the name of Miller, in Ray county.

Cross-examined: This horse was fifteen and a half hands high. The blaze was two inches wide and extended from his eyes down over his nose. I recovered him through a reward I had offered for him.

Wm. R. Roberts testified: I live in Clay county. I remember the Winston robbery. I took up a bay

mare about the end of July or first of August. She
was taken up on my farm in Clay county and I turned
her over to Sheriff Timberlake, who told me that he
was going to take her to Liberty. To the best of my
recollection I took her up about a week after the Winston robbery.

Cross-examined: The mare had a small star in
the forehead and a white left hind foot.

Mrs. Lindsay was recalled and testified that Mrs.
Wolfenberger was a sister of hers and could not at-
tend at this trial on account of sickness. I said I saw
Mr. Johnson here in June, but I was frightened at the
time. I know I have seen him, but can not say when.
I noticed my mistake as I left the court room.

Court took a recess for dinner at this point, and
the State announced its expectation of closing in a few
moments after recess.

After recess Frank R. O'Neil, of the *Republican*,
was called to the stand, and, having stated that he had
counseled with no one touching the questions submitted last evening for his answer to-day, was informed
by the court that the law did not regard communica-
tions to the press as privileged. Mr. O'Neil, at the
suggestion of Mr. Shanklin, of the State's counsel,
submitted a paper to the court containing a statement
of his position. This paper was afterward read by
witness in open court. It is simply a disclaimer of any
attempt to obstruct the process of justice, but states
that after giving his pledge of confidence to the defendant before the surrender, he afterward, to some
extent, acted as adviser for the defendant, and should

on that account be excused from answering. Witness
further declined to state whether any of the parties present before the surrender with the defendant and himself were called as witnesses for the defense in this
case. The court reserved its decision on the question
of compelling witness to answer.

James R. Timberlake testified: In 1881 I lived
in Clay county, and was its sheriff. I know Mr.
Roberts. At that time he lived in the northeast portion of the county. I went out to his place and got a
bay mare with a star on her forehead shortly after the
Winston robbery. I kept her at Liberty for ten or
fifteen days, and then the owner claimed her. The
owner was named Graham. He afterward traded her
to a livery man named Reed, who kept her at his
stable, which is next to mine.

THE STATE RESTS.

Mr. Wallace here announced that the state rested.

THE DEFENSE.

Governor Johnson arose and said the state had
surprised the defense by so suddenly resting its case.
In justice to the defense, he asked the court for an
adjournment so they could have a consultation, to pre-
pare testimony, make it compact, and otherwise pre-
pare. He asked, therefore, an adjournment until to-
morrow morning.

The court remarked that as counsel had mani-
fested no disposition to delay the court, and he therefore granted the request.

"I will adjourn the court until to-morrow at 8 o'clock."

SIXTH DAY'S TRIAL.

The court was opened promptly at 8 o'clock to an audience of four men in the auditorium, sixteen ladies on the stage, two representatives of the press, the jury, prisoner and court officials, while not one of the counsel for either state or defendant was present.

Business begun by calling old man Ford for further cross-examination, and he denied ever having said to Ann Duvall or anyone else that he did not know or had never seen Frank James.

MR. W. M. RUSH'S ADDRESS.

The case for the defendant was presented by Mr. Rush. He began by returning thanks for the maintenance of health on the part of all concerned in the case so far, as health was a great factor in an intelligent and wise consideration of so important a case. The speaker then enlarged upon the importance of the case, and declared it the greatest that had ever engaged the attention of a jury in Daviess county. At the outset Mr. Wallace had declared his purpose to establish a conspiracy, and to follow the band of conspirators from its organization in 1879 in Nashville, up to and even into the Winston robbery. He had done this to a certain extent, but by the testimony of Dick Liddil —and his nature and character would be exhibited to the jury in all its immoral enormity.—Whatever corroboration other witnesses had given the continuous story of the state—these witnesses and their characters would be exposed for the contemplation of the jury. Coming to the facts alleged to be proved, Mr. Rush averred Frank James was not at the Winston robbery. The only witness who placed him there was James A. Liddil, and his testimony was of such a character that, unsupported, it could not be credited. Moreover, in turn, the speaker alluded to the Bolton and Ford witnesses, and said that people capable of aiding in such a tragedy as was enacted there, and with the ghost of recent death in their house, 'were able to entertain guests and make merry with neighbors, had such blunted moral sensibilities that the truth was not in them, or they would lie for a purpose, and that purpose was manifest. Referring to the witnesses in this section of the country, the speaker promised to show by witnesses present at the blacksmith shop and other places purported to have been visited by "the gang," were mistaken in identifying any one of them as Frank. Moreover, a witness on the train would be introduced to show Frank was not on the Winston train, and that the man seen in the woods a few hours before the robbery, by Ezra Sule, was not Frank James. Coming again to Dick Liddil's evidence, the defense claimed his story in court and his tale to Governor Crittenden did not agree, and that lying thus in any one particular his testimony was unworthy of belief. The speaker then took up the impelling motive of the interested witnesses in this case, and the nature of the prosecution. Dick Liddil's motive was that of revenge, superinduced by cowardice. He killed Wood Hite,

feared Jesse and betrayed the band. He agreed to
swear them into prison or to the scaffold, and he is
merely fulfilling that agreement. The Boltons and
Fords had the motive arising from the fact that Bob
Ford had assassinated Jesse James, a brother of the
defendant. The motive of the prosecution was revenge. The officers of Kansas City had been cheated
out of the reward offered for his apprehension by the
surrender of the defendant. Referring again to the
Liddil, Boltons and Fords, he declared a conspiracy
existed among them to down the defendant. As to the
witnesses, one and all, in this region of country, the
speaker in answer to their alleged identification of the
defendant would say they had seen a man, but the defense would prove that man was not Frank James.
The speaker here enlarged upon the character of the
defendant. For fifteen years he had been hunted
through a country grid-ironed with railroads and with
a web of wires overhead to ascertain his whereabouts.
Yet he lived quietly and led a laborious life at Nashville from 1879 to March, 1881. The defense admitted
this and confessed he left because of Bill Ryan's arrest. This was not the first time he had been forced
to abandon his home, because Jesse, with outlawed
companions had driven him out in the world. He,
Frank James, was an outlaw, made so against his protest and against his appeals. The speaker then referred
to the civilization that denied James citizenship and kept
him from his home. He referred to the fact that
other men, poor Bill Poole among the number, had
been warned away from here, and returning had been

shot down from behind.   The civilization that **permitted** a party to sneakingly surround his mother's
home, maim her and kill an infant brother in cold
blood, warned him not to trust himself near people
capable of such deeds of violence.   He had been
refused amnesty; had had governors refuse him clem-
ency.   This was not the place for him, and the defense
was prepared to prove he was not in Missouri in 1881,
nor at the Winston robbery.

THE FIRST WITNESS.

Samuel T. Brosius was the first witness called
and testified as follows:

I live at Gallatin; have lived here for the past two
years.   I am a lawyer by profession.   I was on the
train that was robbed at Winston.   We were about on
time at Winston.   There was a commotion on the front
platform of our car, and two men commenced firing as
I thought at the time, directly through the car.   As the
two men came in they called out, "hold up" or "show
up," and I looked squarely into the face of the smaller
of the two men to see that he noticed me; I held up my
hands.   As soon as the shooting commenced I saw
that the conductor was hit.   The two men continued to
advance through the car till the larger of the two came
up and nearly passed, when the conductor commenced
sinking.   He caught him, and the other man then came
up on the other side.   They hustled the conductor out
on the platform, then came back, and passed me
again, going out at the front end of the car.   There
was firing on the outside after they passed out.   The

larger man was full-faced, with beard all over his face, and would weigh one hundred and eighty to two hundred pounds. He was perhaps a full half-head taller than the conductor. I do not think the defendant is the man.

Cross-examined: Think I was erect a full half minute of the time during which the men were in the car. I noticed that the bullets all hit in the ceiling. The big man did not have on a duster. I could not swear to a stitch of clothing that either of the two men had on. The smaller man was dark-complexioned and had whiskers three or four inches long. Plenty of people have heard me tell about what I saw. They would tell me that I was too scared to notice anything, and I would assent to that to avoid further inquiry. I don't remember telling parties who came to me after the robbery for a description of the robbers that I could not describe them. Believe I told somebody that the muzzle of the robber's revolver looked pretty large and that I thought that it was an eight-inch navy revolver. I did not tell Mr. T. B. Gates, the day after the robbery, that I could not recognize either of the men, and that I was under the seat. I don't believe I could recognize either of the robbers right now if he was brought into the court room and placed before me. If any citizen ever said that I told him that I was under the seat, he lied.

Re-direct: I don't remember a conversation with Mr. Eli Dennis in which I stated that the shooting was done so quick and there was such confusion that I couldn't tell how the men looked or anything about it.

I don't remember telling Mr. Robert L. Tomlin on the first of August, after the robbery, that one of the robbers looked as though he was fifteen feet high, and that I was so excited I couldn't tell how the men looked at all. If I had such a conversation I made the statements to avoid inquiry, as so many people were asking me about it. I did not tell my law partner, Mr. Gillingham, in the presence of C. L. Ewing and A. Ballinger, that I was so badly excited I could not remember anything as to how these men looked. When I described them before, it was as I did to-day—that they both had whiskers all over their faces.

Re-cross-examination: I am certain the defendant is not one of the men I saw on the train.

Re-direct: I went to Nashville with the following note from the defendant:

Mr. Brosius, go to see Mr. Clint. Cantwell by all means. He lives in sight of the Jeff Hyde property. Remember me kindly to all the family.

Respectfully,

(Signed)   B. J. WOODSON.

May 3, 1883.

I did not go to Nashville to get testimony to support an alibi. Did not see the accused until three weeks after my return. I am not interested in this trial. If the defendant is guilty I want him punished.

Fletcher W. Horn testified: Live in Nashville, Tennessee. I am now connected with the detective force of that city. I know B. J. Woodson. I believe I got acquainted with him in 1877. I first formed his acquaintance in the summer of 1877, and last saw him in March,

1881. He resided most of the time in the White's
Creek settlement. He was either farming or hauling
logs for the Indiana Lumber Company. Then I saw
him as often as once a week. Saw him last in Nashville, about the twenty-sixth of March, the time that
Bill Ryan was arrested. When I knew him he wore
sandy whiskers, short on the sides, and fuller on the
chin, say four or five inches long. He was a hard-
working man, who conducted himself as a gentleman.
His associates were men of standing and position. I
have seen Dick Liddil there in 1879 or 1880. I knew
him as Smith. Met him in Bosse's saloon at Nashville.
Never saw Liddil and the defendant together. The
next time I was introduced to him by Squire Adams,
on the corner of Dedrick and Cherry streets as Dick
Liddil. This was after he had been in Alabama. I
knew Jesse James as J. B. Howard. Remember his
buying a blooded horse in partnership with Taylor, the
blacksmith. Afterward he bought the horse "Jim
Malone." He owned the horse "Jim Scott." In 1877
I saw Howard and Woodson together once or twice in
the pool room. Believe I knew Jim Cummings, but
am not positive. Did not know the Hites. Never saw
B. J. Woodson in company with Liddil or Cummings.
Never saw Liddil and defendant together. I saw very
little of Liddil, and that only by accident. Was sub-
pœnaed here for the state. Was present in June on
transportation furnished me by Squire Earthman.

Cross-examined: Did not know Woodson and
Howard were the James Brothers, or I would have
tried to take them.

7

As far as I know Dick Liddil deported himself well while in Nashville. The defendant has since alluded to me as a "Falstaff." Never saw any of the men I have spoken of in Nashville. After the arrest of Bill Ryan, I went with Mr. Sloan to Mrs. Hite's, and sat round while he asked questions. Mr. Sloan professed at that time to be attorney for Frank James. I wrote a letter to Thomas Furlong, in St. Louis, asking transportation for Mr. Sloan as a witness for the state; also for Mr. Moffatt, Wm. Earthman, Mrs. Hite and myself. I made this request for transportation for Mr. Sloan after I knew he was attorney for the accused. Mr. Sloan did not request me to get him transportation.

Re-direct: The letter is dated July 29, 1883. As far as I saw, Liddil conducted himself as a gentleman, though I didn't see him as frequently as I did the defendant.

Raymond B. Sloan testified: Am an attorney at law. I live in Nashville. I knew the defendant by the name of Woodson some time during the winter of 1876–77. That winter I discovered he was living in the old Felix Smith house, that had never had a light in it since the war. I have crossed the ferry with him and seen him driving a four-horse team or sometimes mules. I had no intimate personal acquaintance with him. I last saw him in Nashville, March 26, 1881. Once that day I saw him at Jonas Taylor's blacksmith shop, and then again near the Louisville depot. He had light sandy whiskers all over his face, short on cheeks and longer on the chin, and a mustache. I don't think he showed evidence of shaving any part of his face. He was dressed in a light colored coat, raw-hide boots, pants within his boots, and a soft black derby hat. I remember seeing the defendant after that. I once was a witness in the various continuances and hearings of an assault and battery case. I never missed him from his place till after March 26, 1881.

Cross-examined: I remember telling you in the Maxwell House, at Nashville, that I thought I was the last man in Nashville who had seen Frank James. That I saw him on horseback shaking hands with a man, and saying, "good-bye. I may never see you again." I did not know that from February 5 to March 26, 1881, Woodson or James was not doing anything, or that he was living in Nashville with Jesse James. I went up to Mrs. Hite's as attorney for Frank James, and reduced her statement to writing. I knew Horn was a witness for the state. Mrs. Hite didn't sign it; and Horn signed a statement that she acknowledged it to be true. I took Horn along, because I considered it would save me a trip to Gallatin if he came here. He could contradict Mrs. Hite if she made a contrary statement. I remember telling you at the Maxwell that perhaps you had better see a man named Sullivan, who pretended to know a great deal about this matter. I was Frank James' attorney at the time. I remember observing to you that the papers said I was Frank James' legal attorney before I knew it myself.

Re-direct: I was engaged as the defendant's local attorney August 8, and saw Mrs. Hite on August 13. Think I saw Mr. Wallace at the Maxwell a day or two after, say about August 17.

Mrs. Elizabeth Montgomery testified: I live a mile and a half east of Winston. I remember the Winston robbery. Some strange men ate at our house that night. The clock struck seven before they finished. The younger man was the taller and light complexioned, with burnside whiskers. The older man had dark whiskers and mustache, and dark clothes. One horse was a bay and the other a shade lighter. They had some bundles tied to their saddles.

Q. Is the defendant one of those men? A. I think not, but I can not be positive.

Cross-examined: I think both horses were bay but one was lighter than the other. The bigger man had whiskers all over his face, chin and all.

Miss Missouri Montgomery testified: I live a mile and a half east of Winston. Am a daughter of the last witness. I remember the night of the Winston robbery, and remember two parties coming to our house that evening about six o'clock on horseback. They remained there half an hour, I suppose, and got their suppers at the end of the house in the open air. I don't think I saw the defendant there. I wouldn't say positively. I don't think he resembles either of them in the least.

Cross-examined: The older of the two had whiskers all over his face of a brown color. He was a rather heavy set man, and wore dark brown clothes. I never saw Jesse James. The other man was tall and very slim; had light hair and no whiskers, except a little on each side. Neither of them had a large blaze-faced sorrel horse.

John L. Dean testified: Am a farmer and live seven miles southwest of here. I know Jonas Potts. I remember a conversation with him at his shop November 20, 1882. He said he had been to Independence to see Frank James, and that he had never seen him before. I remember on another day that two men came up to Potts' shop in a carriage and wanted to get a neck-yoke fixed, and that Potts left the shop, and when he came back was somewhat excited, and said they were the men he had shod horses for before the Winston robbery. The larger of the two men was a low, heavy-set, dark complexioned man, with heavy whiskers. The other was about my size, with fair complexion and no beard at all.

Cross-examined: I told Mr. Rush what I knew about this matter. I don't remember talking to Mr. Rush about this case at Winston in April or May last. I don't think Potts was in liquor when I talked to him.

Marion Duncan testified: I am a farmer and live about three and a half miles southeast of Winston. I know Jonas Potts. I remember conversing with him about Jesse James along in the fore part of the winter of 1882–3. I don't remember any conversation with him before that. Remember Potts' saying to me that Jesse James was at his shop; that he had seen his picture at Winston, and he was the very man he had shod a horse for.

Cross-examined: Mr. Potts had been to town that evening and was pretty boozy in that conversation.

Gus A. Chapman testified: Know Mr. Potts. I remember him saying to me after his return from Gal-

latin jail, where he had seen the defendant, that he
didn't know if he had ever seen him before and could
not tell.

Wm. E. Ray testified: I know Frank Wolfenberger. I saw him in Winston after Frank James had
been brought here. Did not hear him say that he did
not think he would be able to recognize him.

Here the defense offered in evidence the record of
the trial and conviction of Dick Liddil for horse stealing in Vernon county in 1874, which after objection
was admitted to be read to the jury. Recess till
1:30 P. M.

Joseph O. Shelby, usually alluded to as "Gen.
Joe Shelby," was the first witness called after recess.
He testified as follows:

By Mr. Philips: I have for thirty-four years
resided in Lafayette county. I live nine miles from
Lexington and nearer Page City. I remember Jesse
James, Dick Liddil, Bill Ryan and Jim Cummings
coming to my place in November, 1880. I was spreading hemp at the time, working some twelve or fifteen
men, and when I returned home that evening I found
four men with horses in my yard. Jesse James was
there. Young Cummings I knew before, and this man
Liddil passed as Mr. Black at that time. In the morning I had a conversation with Jesse James in the presence of Dick Liddil, in which I said that a couple of
young men had been arrested for supposed complicity
with the alleged bank robbery at Concordia, and that I
didn't think they had anything to do with it; and I asked
Jesse James if he knew anything about that affair to tell

me, and he said, pointing to Dick Liddil, "There is
the man that hit the dutch cashier over the head."

I remember in the month of November, 1881,
meeting Liddil and Jesse James in my lane, and when
I asked Jesse who was ahead of them he replied, Jim
Cummings and Hite. I remember meeting Jesse James
and Liddil again in the fall of 1881, and of asking
Jesse where Frank was, and of his announcement that
Frank's health was such that he had been south for
years, and that when I asked the same question of Liddil he announced that he had not seen him for two
years. I reckon I know Cummings better than any
man except the Fords and his own people. I knew him
in the army and since the war. He has been at my
house a dozen times. He was with me in the Confederate army. I have not seen Frank James since 1872.
I believe he sits right there now. With the permission
of the court, can I be tolerated to shake hands with an
old soldier?

The court. No, sir, not now.

Witness. I did not see him in jail. I have not
seen him since 1872. I am correct about it, sir, when
I say that the four parties to whom I have alluded by
name did not include Frank James, who was not with
them. With regard to the arrival of Mrs. Frank James
at Page City in the spring of 1881, I have this to say.
It seems a lady arrived at Page City. I can not talk
dates, like any other farmer, and Mrs. Scott, a widow
woman, whose husband was captain of the 3d Loui-
siana, and who died at Wilson's Creek, sent her son over

for me, and stated there was a lady there who wanted to see me.

I went at once. Mrs. James said to me: "I am in distress. This man Liddil and others are committing depredations in the south, and they are holding my husband amenable for it, as he has been charged with being connected with them. I have come over on purpose to ask you to intercede with the Governor." I told her there was no necessity for that, and no hope of success. I told her further that Governor Woodson had talked to me at the Planter's House. For Hardin I had no respect at all. She wanted me to interfere in her husband's behalf with the governor. I told her it was folly to do so, and advised her to go home to her father. I think I remained half an hour talking to her. She remained at Mrs. Scott's all night. She didn't stop at my house. She could have stopped there if she had desired As to the sewing machine, I don't know what time the sewing machine arrived there. She simply gave Mr Birch, the agent at the depot, directions for shipping it, and I don't know where she directed it to be shipped at all. I was only assisting a woman in distress, and if she had been Gennison's wife, the most obnoxious man in the country——"

Here the court stopped the witness short with a severe reprimand. The fact was, and it was rapidly becoming patent to everybody in the court room, that Mr. Shelby was drunk. A sample of this testimony will be given verbatim a little further on.

Continuing, the witness said: Mrs. James left orders with the agent for the shipment of the sewing machine. She was a lone woman, with a little child, and crying, and any man who would have faltered in giving suggestion or aid ought to be ashamed of himself. I had known Frank James since 1862. I know him now, the first time I have seen him for twelve years. I got acquainted with him in our army.

Cross-examined—By Mr. Wallace: This sewing machine you didn't see at all?

"Nobody knows better than yourself that I didn't see it."

The Court. Answer the question in a straightforward manner.

Witness. I did not.

"You didn't have anything to do with it at all?"

"Nothing in the world."

"Sir, you are just as sure of that as you are of anything else?"

"Yes, and I am just as sure of anything else."

To the Court: "I would like to know if the Judge is going to permit a lawyer to insult an unarmed man, who is a witness in this case?"

The Court. Every witness comes in here unarmed, sir.

By Mr. Wallace: What are your initials?

"If you are desirous of knowing go to this bank here and you will find out."

The Court. Answer his question.

Witness. Joe O. Shelby is my name.

"Then your initials would be J. O. S."

"Go to the banks in this town and you will find it Joe O. S."

"Look at the way-bill and see if that has 'J. O. S.'
as the consignor of that sewing machine! There may
be a great many J. O. S.'s, who in that section have
those initials beside you."

"You had better go and inquire."

The Court. I won't have any more nonsense of
that kind. You will have to answer questions as they
are put.

Witness (to court). You are not protecting me
at all.

Mr. Philips. I simply suggest to the court that
under the circumstances this examination had perhaps
better be deferred.

Witness. Not at all. Better let it go on. Now
is the time for it to go on.

The Court (to witness). "General Shelby, you
are a man that I respect and a man with a state-wide
reputation as a gentleman. We did not expect such
demeanor in this court room. I must admonish you
that I can not permit this to go on any further."

Witness. "I want to know from the court, if,
after having said what he (Mr. Wallace) has, he is to
charge me with receiving a bill of lading as J. O. S."

To this there was no reply.

Mr. Wallace. "I ask you if when Mrs. Frank
James came there with a sewing machine to be shipped
to Mrs. B. J. Woodson, you did not yourself become
the consignor and ship it thence to Independence for the
purpose of keeping any one else from getting track
of it?"

"No, sir, I did not."

"I ask you ii this 'J. O. S.' doesn't indicate that?"

"No, sir, not at all. She arrived there as I related. I gave her a note to Mr. Russell, agent of the Missouri Pacific at Independence, to take it and send her up to Independence."

But it would be wearisome to follow the witness word for word. He testified further: I saw Dick Liddil. I was not brought into court to see if he was the man; neither you nor anybody else can bring me in anywhere. Nobody knows better than yourself that I was not brought in to look at Mr. Liddil. The man I saw was Mr. Black, alias Liddil, the thief.

The Court. I want no more epithets of that kind in the court room.

Witness. Very good, Judge. He has forced it on me. If I am guilty of a misdemeanor, correct me or punish me for it.

The Court. I shall do it.

Mr. Wallace. You saw Liddil down at Capt. Ballinger's house, afterward, didn't you?

"You don't propose to invade the household of Capt. Ballinger, a soldier of the federal army?"

"It is very wrong for a rebel soldier to make remarks about what occurred in a federal soldier's home?"

Mr. Wallace. The war is over.

Witness. I don't like to allude to a visit to a gentleman's home. That is indelicate and improper.

"Did you see Liddil there?"

"I did, sir. I saw him like a viper, curled up in rocking-chair."

"You saw him again at the hotel the other night, or was that a drummer that you took for him?"

"No, sir; by no means.

"Were you not about to kill the drummer, thinking he was Dick Liddil?"

"I have lived thirty-four years in this state and never killed anybody yet."

"Answer the question."

"I was not."

"This gentleman was seated at the table opposite to me, and he dropped his knife and fork and looked at me. I have his card in my pocket. He is a Michigan man, not one of your people at all, but a better man than yourself for instance. He was staring at me. I am not in the habit of staring at men on the street, especially ladies anyway, and I must have made some casual remark about it."

"Did you get your pistol out?"

"No, sir!"

"Didn't the marshal of Lexington see you draw your pistol?"

"No, sir; he is a liar, or anybody else, if he says so."

The Court. I want no more such remarks as that, Gen. Shelby, or I will fine you $50.

In this way the testimony proceeded. Witness testified that Dick Liddil had partaken of his meals, and fed his corn to Liddil's horse. That was in 1880, and Jesse James was with him and Cummings and Ryan. Did not know that Jesse James was wanted by the officers? Knew it was asserted that he had been guilty of misde-

meanors. Never told any officer where they could find
him, but did once notify the Chicago and Alton and Missouri Pacific people that if they were under the apprehension that George Sheppard had killed him they
were being misled, and that he was not dead. The
last time Jesse was at my house was at Page City, in
the fall of 1881, where I saw Frank James in 1872,
which is the last time I saw him. He was bleeding at
the lungs, and Dr. Orear was attending him. I don't
know that he was an outlaw then, or that he is one to-
day. I don't know that he was then fleeing from the
officers.

He was at my house some sixty or eighty days that
time, and everybody knew it. When the four men
came to my house, as I have already stated. I told
them I could only accommodate two of them for the
night. Bill Ryan and Jesse James stayed all night
with me. The others stopped with a man from Illinois
named Graham, who had been in the Federal army.
I am certain that Ryan was not pointed out to me as
the man who hit the Dutch cashier over the head.

As witness started to leave the court room he
asked permission to go over and shake hands with the
defendant. This the court refused saying:

"You can call on him some other time." Whereupon Shelby nodded to the accused as he walked out,
and said:

"God bless you, old fellow."

Frank Tutt testified: I reside at Kansas City.
Prior to living there I lived at Lexington, Missouri. I am
a coal-oil inspector. I know Dick Liddil. I remem-

ber meeting him in front of Gardener's saloon at Kansas City just after the Ford boys had been pardoned, after the trial at St. Joe. Mr. James M. Crowder was present at the time. On that occasion Liddil, when asked where Frank James was, said he didn't know the whereabouts of Frank, and that he and Jesse didn't get along well together, and he hadn't seen him for years.

Cross-examined: I had been pursuing the James boys for a couple of months, but never caught any of them.

James S. Demastus testified for the defense, as follows: I reside in Richmond, Missouri; am a justice of the peace there. I remember the testimony of Mrs. Bolton at the Wood Hite inquest. I understood her to testify that she had not seen Frank James for about two years, and then at her father's. She was then living at the Harbison Place, and had been there about two years.

Cross-examined: She named Wood Hite, Dick Liddil, Clarence Hite and Jesse James as members of the gang. The answer as to how long since she had seen Frank James was given in an examination conducted by Mr. Farris, a juror, after the formal examination, and as much for curiosity as anything else.

Here Mr. Philips said that Gen. Shelby was at the door, and desired to make a statement. The court's permission being given, Gen. Shelby said:

"Before I say anything more I desire to say that if anything I said offended the dignity of the court yesterday, I regret it exceedingly. As to other parties, I have no regrets to make."

Here ensued a running colloquy between witness and the court, in which the court severely censured witness for coming into court yesterday in a condition unfit to testify, and fined him for that offense $10, which the witness paid and left the court.

James C. Mason testified: I reside in Ray county; remember Captain Ford stating to me that he didn't think Frank James was at Winston or Blue Cut; that he had settled down and left the boys; remember also a conversation with Mrs. Bolton, when she said that Frank James was trying to lead an honest life, and was a different man from Jesse; that Frank would go away and try to settle down, when Jesse would come to live with him, and the detectives would come and he would have to leave.

Here a wrangle came up over a question said to have been propounded to little Willie Bolton by the defense. A reference to the official report showed no such question had been asked, whereupon Willie Bolton was recalled in order that the defense might bring their impeachment battery to bear.

W. Bolton being recalled denied ever telling James C. Mason shortly after Jesse James' death that he had never seen Frank James, or that the others had been at his mother's house, and had said that Frank James had quit them. He didn't remember ever telling Mason anything at all about the outlaws.

James C. Mason, resuming the stand, testified that Willie Bolton had made at the time and place

stated the statement which he just now denied having
made.

Annanias Duval testified: I live in Ray county
and know Mr. J. T. Ford.   I know all of the family.
Know Willie Bolton.   Had a conversation with John
T. Ford, in which he said he never saw and didn't
know Frank James, and did not know that he was anywhere in this country.

Cross-examined: Never heard the Fords say that
any of the gang were there.

W. D. Rice testified: I reside three miles south of
Richmond, Missouri, and half a mile from J. T. Ford.
I remember a conversation with Willie Bolton a day or
two after the Wood Hite inquest, in which he said he
had told a story before the coroner's jury, and that his
mother had made him do it.

Cross-examined: Believe this was before Frank
James had given himself up.

James Duval, recalled for the State, testified in
answer to Mr. Wallace: The horse my brother lost
was a sorrel.   We got him from Mr. Sawyer, and I
found him in February, 1883, in charge of Bob Hall, at
Samuels' Station, in Nelson county, Kentucky.   The
horse was lost November 10, 1880.

John T. Samuels, called for the defense, testified:
I am a farmer.   I am a half-brother to defendant.   I
live three miles northeast of Kearney with Mrs. Samuels.   Have lived there with her twenty-two years continuously.   It was in 1876 that I last saw the defendant
before the Winston robbery.   He was married then.
Last saw him in January last.   Never saw him from

1876 up to that time. I was at home in the summer of
1881. Was not absent at any time during that summer. Saw Jesse James during that summer about the
first of May at my mother's. He was in company with
Dick Liddil. He told me he came from Kentucky.
My mother and father were home when Dick and Jesse
arrived. I heard my mother ask Jesse where was
Frank, and he replied he had left him in Kentucky, and
that he was in bad health and was talking of going
south. She then asked Liddil the same question and
received a similar answer. Jesse James was at our
house two or three months that summer off and on. I
last saw him there about the last of July or first of
August that summer. During that time I saw at our
house Dick Liddil, Clarence and Wood Hite, and
Charley Ford, and no one else. The James boys and
Wood Hite are cousins.

Continuing, the witness said: Wood Hite was
rather tall, with high forehead, long nose, fair complexion, and beard on his face about one and a half
inches long, also a mustache. Jesse was a large man,
full-faced, with beard all over his face—a sandy beard,
which I don't think was darker than Wood Hite's.
Clarence was square built, delicate, and fair complexioned, with bad front teeth, so decayed that they would
be quickly noticed. There was a striking family resemblance between Frank James and Wood Hite. I
saw Jim Cummings at my mother's house that summer
in the last of June, 1881. His sister lives two and a
half miles from my mother's. I next saw him July 1

8

at the same place. He came there the first time with Jesse and Dick Liddil. He was by himself the last time. These parties were there several times that summer. I did not know of my own knowledge where the defendant was that summer. Cummings was rather tall and slim, with light hair—as tall as Frank James, and about thirty-six years old. Last saw him in July, 1881.

Cross-examined: I heard that all these men were outlaws. Saw in the papers that they had robbed trains and killed men. They came and went armed. We fed Dick Liddil, though not related to him or Cummings. I knew that Cummings was charged with horse-stealing in Clay county. Never told of his presence there. Kept his presence there and that of the others a secret. In 1876 I saw him in company with Jesse and their two wives. Saw him in 1875 and 1874. When I first saw Jim Cummings in 1881 he was on the porch of Mrs. Samuels. The other time he came to my window at night. I tended a crop that summer. Charley Ford first came there in July, 1881.

He was there also immediately before the Blue Cut robbery, when they left in a wagon, to which Charley Ford's black pony and another horse was hitched. I was there then. The other horse was Dick Liddil's. I don't remember whether that wagon left in July or August. Think Charley Ford's first visit was in the last of July. He was never there until after the Winston robbery. First saw Jim Cummings there the last of June. First told Mr. Johnson from this stand that Cummings was there in 1881. I talked to Messrs.

Johnson and Philips, of the defense, day before yesterday. Mr. Philips asked me about Jim Cummings. I
had also told Mr. Garner, of the defense, about Cummings. I have heard Wood Hite called Father Grimes
because of his stoop shoulders and old ways. He had
whiskers all over his face—dark whiskers, darker than
Jesse's. Jim Cummings had a complexion perhaps as
red as mine, with little eyes. I don't know anything
about his education. He could carry on a conversation
as well as some other men. Never heard him quote
any Shakespeare. There was left in the wagon Dick
Liddil, Charley Ford, Clarence Hite, Wood Hite and
Jesse James. There were not six men, and the sixth
man was not Frank James, as far as I know. They
were armed with revolvers. They had guns at the
house, two Winchesters and a shotgun. Liddil had a
shotgun and Jesse a Winchester. I don't know whether
there was a suit of woman's clothes there. They got a
woman's dress from my mother. I don't know what it
was for.

Mrs. Zerelda Samuels, a gray-haired lady of 55,
with a shortened right arm, and dressed in black, testified: I have lived for forty years in Clay county. I
am the mother of Jesse and Frank James. Frank was
forty years old last January. I have lived three miles
from Kearney. I have other children—Mrs. Palmer,
Mrs. Nicholson, Mrs. Hall and John T. Samuels.
Jesse was killed two years ago next April (this with
tears). I was home during the summer of 1881. Jesse
was at my house during 1881. He came there either
in May or June—in May, I think. Before that he had

not been home for some time. The first time he came
Jim Cummings and Dick Liddil were with him—no,
only Dick Liddil. I asked Jesse where "Buck," or
Frank, was, and he said he had left him in Kentucky
in bad health. I said, "Son, you know he is dead,"
and I turned to Liddil and he said they had left him
in Kentucky. They left my house after the Winston
robbery. I don't know the time. During that summer
the parties that met at my house were Charley Ford,
Dick Liddil, Clarence and Wood Hite and Jesse
James. My son Frank was not there that summer.
I have not seen Frank for seven years till I saw him at
Independence. The last time before that I saw him
was when Mr. Broome was sheriff of Clay county, and
they came to my house and shot at him. I saw Jim
Cummings that summer. His relations live three or
four miles from my house. One of his sisters married
Bill Ford, uncle of the Ford boys. Liddil and the
Hites were often at my house that summer previous to
the Winston robbery. I did not know that summer
where Frank James was. I thought he was dead. I
am fifty-five years old. Was fifty years old when I lost
my hand.

   Cross-examined: I remember the wagon leaving.
There were in it Jesse James, Charley Ford, Wood
Hite, Clarence Hite and Dick Liddil. Jim Cummings was there in June. I didn't see him but that
once. Johnny Samuels told me he was there one night
at his window. The party that left in the wagon took
food and clothing, and a dress, apron and bonnet that

I furnished, so they could pass off one of the gentlemen for a lady, so you couldn't catch them.

Allen H. Palmer testified: I live in Wichita county, Texas. Am a cattle man. Have lived in Texas twenty years. First lived in Grayson county. The last years in Wichita county. I married Frank James' sister about thirteen years ago. I was not at home all the time of the summer of 1881. I think I left home in May, between the first and tenth. I was dowr below Fort Worth working on a railroad, freighting. I had three children then. I returned about August 1, or not far from the first. When I got home the first of August I found Frank James home with my family. I don't know what time he came there. I could not state how he was dressed at the time. I only stayed at home but a few days, and I left him there. It was September before I was home any more. When I got back he had gone. I next saw him yesterday.

Cross-examined: Wichita Falls is on Wichita River, terminus of the Fort Worth and Denver. In 1881 there was no road nearer than Gainesville. In 1881 I lived in Clay county, eighteen miles northwest of Henrietta, on a ranch. My closest neighbor was a widow lady named Bogar, about half a mile off. She visited my family occasionally. She had two daughters and a son, a young man grown, who was attending to a bunch of cattle and visiting at my house.

Wichita Falls is ten miles from the ranch I had then. A family named Wicker lived two miles from me. The family consisted of three boys and one married daughter, and her husband, Beckler. My next

neighbor was six or seven miles off, called Harness, W.
T. and I. H.   They are now at Henrietta.   Frank
James had a horse when I got to my place—a dark bay
horse.   I didn't ask him when he came or where from.
I don't know any Clarence or Wood Hite, or Dick Liddil.   I didn't ask where he came from or where he
was going.   I hadn't seen Mrs. Samuels since 1879,
when I was in Kansas City in jail and she came to see
me.   The last time I saw Jesse James was the year of
the railroad strike (1877).   In 1881, in the summer, I
worked on the roads in Texas, hauling from Fort
Worth.   Hauled on the Missouri Pacific, which was
building there from Fort Worth to Cleburne, and from
Cleburne to Alvaredo.   My name was not on any of
the rolls, but we were paid in money every few days.
Don't remember who I worked for, or with, or whom I
loaded with.   We were working between Cleburne
and Alvaredo, on the Missouri Pacific, I think it was
called.   Frank White, at my house, stayed mostly upstairs.   He ate with the family.   I think he was unwell
at the time.   He said that his lungs were affected.

Re-direct: He was talking of surrendering if it
could be fixed up in Missouri.   When I was in jail at
Kansas City I had been arrested in Texas for the Glendale robbery.

Re-cross: I think it was to Governor Crittenden
that he talked of surrendering.

The court at this point took a recess till 1:30 P. M.

The first witness called after recess was *Mrs.
Allen H. Palmer*, who testified: I live at Wichita
Falls, Texas; I am the wife of the last witness; have

been living in Texas about ten years continuously; have
lived in Sherman, Clay and Wichita counties; lived in
Wichita county since last fall; the defendant is my
brother; he is older than I am; in the year 1881 I
saw the defendant at my house in Clay county; he
came there in June, in the first part of the month; he
spoke of coming from Tennessee, and of having lived
there. My family consists of a husband and two children. He stayed there till the first of July. He was
gone and came back again by the first of August, and
was gone off and on till September. The first time he
was gone three or four weeks. My husband came back
the first of August. My brother was there at that time.
I dont know where my brother went while he was
gone. He remained in Texas a little over three
months. I saw him off and on. He was there all of
June. He went away the latter part of June or first of
July, and was gone until the latter part of July, and
from then off and on until some time in September he
was at my house. I remember talking about him being
anxious to have his friends negotiate his surrender to
the Governor of Missouri. When he left Texas he
started for California. I didn't then know where his
wife was. Since then I never heard of him until the
surrender. During this three months he was in Texas
his health was not very good. While Frank was there
my husband was home once. I can not say for how
long—say four or five days. At that time my husband
was working on the railroad near Fort Worth. He
returned August 1, and Frank was still there. I
heard Frank speak of Jesse; that they got scared and

left where they were living.   When they left Tennessee
Frank came to my house.

Cross-examined: Frank got to my house the first
of June.   He told me he. came from Tennessee.   Of
my own certain knowledge I don't know where he came
from.   He went away in June and stayed away all of
July till the latter part.   After he came back he stayed
off and on till September.   I don't know where he was
in July.   He finally left in September.   I couldn't give
the date, but it was along in the first of the month.
I think the negotiations for the surrender were spoken
of in the early portion of his visit.   He spoke of friends,
but didn't say friends in Missouri.   He said he would
like to have his friends negotiate his surrender, as he
would like to be pardoned.   I don't know anything
about Jesse wanting to surrender.   I never saw Dick
Liddil till this week.   I know nothing of Clarence or
Wood Hite.   Frank came to my house on horseback
on a bay horse.   He hobbled it and turned it out on
the range.   He didn't tell me where he got the horse.
He stayed at my house in all of the three rooms at
different times.   If any one came he would go upstairs
or out of the room.   We lived in a remote part of the
county where there are few visitors.   We had a few
visitors during the time.   Mrs. Bogar was there visiting
once.   She didn't see Frank that I know of.   When
she was there Frank would sometimes be upstairs and
sometimes down cellar.   Mr. Harness, a stock man,
now living at Henrietta, was also a visitor while Frank
was there.   He was originally from Cooper county, Missouri.   We saw him coming and Frank went into another

room. In speaking of the surrender, he said he wanted to surrender; wanted a trial and to become a common, peaceable citizen.

Q. Wanted a trial for what? For the Winston robbery. A. No, sir.

Witness continued: I don't know of his mentioning the name of any one who had been negotiating with Governor Crittenden.

Re-direct: He told me that he left Tennessee because Bill Ryan had been captured; that he got frightened; that his health was bad, and he came to my place to see if it would improve his health, and he wanted to to try and negotiate with the governor for surrender.

Bud Harbison testified: I reside in Richmond, Ray county, Missouri. In coming from Richmond to the Harbison place, where Mrs. Bolton lived, the road passes right in front of my house without any fork or division, till the town is nearly reached. I was home and farming in 1881. Have frequently seen men passing my house on the road. Remember meeting a party of two or four at the creek on the road. Never saw defendant until I saw him in the court house yard. Could not say that I recognized him as one of the many parties passing my house in the summer of 1881. Saw Dick Liddil or Mr. Anderson at Mrs. Bolton's in February, 1882. I remember being at the house on Sunday early in December from 10 to 11 A. M. I talked with Bob and Wilbur Ford and Mrs. Bolton. I believe I saw nothing and heard nothing unusual that day.

Cross-examined: I couldn't identify any one of the four men whom I met at the creek on the road. I don't pretend to identify Dick Liddil as one of them. Did not recognize Wood Hite as one of them. I saw him after the exhumation of his body. He might have been stoop-shouldered. Had short whiskers and a little mustache, and would weigh 140 or 150 pounds. I don't know whether defendant is one of the men I saw at the creek or not. I was on the Wood Hite jury of inquest. If Mrs. Bolton said anything about Frank James I don't remember. I remember telling you that if she said anything about Frank James being there that he was there in May, though I could not be positive as to whether she said anything about it or not. I believe she said that he might have been there twice. She spoke of him as going by the name of Hall. She was asked about the James boys, and she said that she knew them, but when or where she had seen them, or what year I don't remember.

Samuel Venable testified: In 1881 I was working as a carpenter for Mr. Weston till July. I know where Mrs. Hamilton's is, about a mile north of Gallatin. I remember the circumstance of the Winston robbery. I remember that Mrs. Hamilton's house was raised after I quit Mr. Weston, which was a few days before the Winston robbery.

This testimony was evidently introduced to contradict Liddil where he speaks of a house in the locality indicated as having two stories, he thought, though he couldn't swear to it.

At this point the defense announced that if they were given fifteen minutes' recess they could probably

get along with one more witness. The court ordered
the recess asked for.

At 3 o'clock the defendant, *Frank James*, took
the stand in his own behalf, and was duly sworn. The
examination was as follows: By Mr. Philips: "Mr.
James, you are the defendant in this case?"

"Yes."

"Begin your statement of the history of this case,
where the prosecution began, with the time of your departure from Missouri for Tennesee some years ago.
Just state when that was?"

"That was in the winter of 1876, if I remember it
correctly."

"State where you went and where you stayed."

"Well, sir, it is quite a route to follow it all round.
I ranged across southeast Missouri directly into Tennessee, crossing the Mississippi river, I think, perhaps
about between the first and fifth of January, if I am not
mistaken."

"State what time you arrived at Nashville."

"I didn't arrive at Nashville until July, 1876. I
think I went directly then from Nashville out into what
is known as the White creek neighborhood. The first
place I went to there was the widow Harriet Ledbetter's who lives over on White creek. In the meantime
I rented a farm, which, however, I could not get
possession of until January 1, 1878. I remained at Mrs.
Ledbetter's during that fall. I put in a crop of wheat
and moved there and lived in the place known as the
Jesse Walton place. I lived on this place one year,
that was up to 1878. Next year I rented a place from

Felix Smith, on White creek also, but nearer to White's creek than the place I have just mentioned.

"I remained there a year, and made a crop in the meantime—a general crop, as farmers raise—corn, oats and wheat. The next year I lived on what is known as the Jeff Hyde place, on Hyde's ferry, about three and a half miles from Nashville. I remained there a year. During that year I didn't farm any. I was working for the Indiana Lumber company. That I think was in 1879."

"What kind of work did you do for the Indiana Lumber company?"

"I was working in the woods, logging, as they term it, and I worked off and on all that summer at that business, driving a four mu'e team, and after that time, I don't remember just what month, I think it was in 1880, I moved into Nashville. During that time, as it was very hard work logging, I got several strains and my health became impaired, and I found I would have to go at some other business. Thinking I could not stand working ten hours a day for three years as I had, I concluded to move into Nashville and go into some other business. During that time this gentleman who has been spoken of before, Mr. Ryan, was captured. Well, of course, I was apprehensive, and not knowing what sort of a man he was and only having a short acquaintance with him, I concluded that perhaps for the sake of his liberty he would be willing to sacrifice my life. So I concluded to leave, and did so."

"When and where was the first time you met your brother Jesse and the man Ryan?"

"My first meeting with my brother Jesse was entirely accidental; I was farming, as I stated, on the Walton place, and I had gone into the store of B. S. Rhea & Son, and while I was sampling oats and talking to one of the clerks, Jesse James walked out of the office, came up to me and says: 'Why, how do you do?' I spoke to him; didn't call any name of course. He was going by; he asked me where I was living, and I told him; he went out home with me, and told me he was living in Humphreys county, which is, I suppose, one hundred miles west of Nashville, if I am not mistaken. I am not positive about the distance. He had been buying grain for this firm of B. S. Rhea & Son. That is where I first met him. That, I think, was in the spring of 1878—perhaps in February or March. We generally sow oats there in February—in the latter part of February or first of March."

"Where did you first meet Ryan in Tennessee?"

"The first time I ever met William Ryan, I think, perhaps, was in the fall or winter of 1879. I am not positive as to that date, but it occurs to me now, as well as I recollect it, that it was in 187—no, it must have been in 1879. I am pretty certain it was."

"Where did you meet?"

"I met him at my house. He had returned there with Jesse James, my brother, I suppose, though I can not state that of my own knowledge. However, he came there one Sabbath with Jesse James, but his wife and children were boarding in Nashville at that time. He had gone to Jesse James'. Previous to this Dick Liddil had arrived at my house."

"What time did he come down there?"

"What I mentioned about being apprehensive was the second time. The first time I ever met Dick Liddil in Tennessee was, I think, in 1879. I am not positive what month. He and Jesse James came in together. No one was with them when they arrived at my house. Liddil was there off and on until that fall. He was then making trips to and fro, but where I have no idea. I never saw Ryan, Jesse James and Liddil together any great deal in Nashville. When they were out of my sight my impression is they were together, but of course when they were out of my sight I could not state what became of them. When I left Nashville, in consequence of Ryan's arrest, my first purpose was to protect my life so as to be able to support my family, and secondly to get shut of those parties who were around me. I could not prevent it. Of course I had no control of things, and that was the reason I left there and went to Logan county, Kentucky, to George B. Hite's, who had married a sister of my father's for his first wife. I could not state when his first wife died. I do not remember the date we arrived there, nor just how long we stayed. I think, however, we arrived in the latter part of March, or the first of April, as well as I recollect the circumstance now. As to the officers coming there, if my memory serves me right it was on a Sunday that it was reported they were at Adairsville, one and a half or two miles from the Hite's place, detectives looking for us, and they had followed us from Nashville.

"That Sunday morning three men were noticed coming toward the house. Our lane ran for quite a distance south of the house past the farm, and there was a little lane came up directly to the house. Some one saw them coming from a distance and said: 'Yonder come three men.' My brother, being a somewhat excitable man, said: 'No doubt those are the men that were in Adairsville.' The detectives, as they supposed. I said, 'I reckoned not; that I could not see what anybody could be following us for.' 'Oh, yes,' Dick says, 'you know Jessie and I borrowed a couple of horses, and I expect these men are from back down in Nashville.' I said, 'I guess they won't come here.' We went down stairs, and I said, 'Don't shoot anybody; for heaven's sake, don't kill anybody!' They came down and went I don't know where. I went into the parlor and looked out of the window to see if they came up the lane directly in front of the house. I kept looking, but they didn't come, but went off. I thought perhaps it was some one going to church—neighbors, perhaps—so I went back up-stairs. However, the men went on by, and Wood Hite followed them on a mule, and reported that they had gone in a roundabout way to Adairsville, and they were the same men that we suspected of being detectives. I could not state positively whether I remained at Mrs. Hite's ten days or two weeks, but it was in the neighborhood of that time.

"The Hite family was composed of George B. Hite, Mrs. Sarah Hite, her daughter Maud, old Mr. Norris and his wife. That is all who were there then. Of course, he had other children who were not there at

that time. Wood Hite's name was Woodson Hite. I
would suppose him to be between thirty-three and
thirty-five years of age. I think I was perhaps two
years older than he. He was five feet nine and one-
half or ten inches high. Can not say whether his eyes
were black or gray. His hair was light and his whiskers darker, rather dark sandy. He was a little stoop-
shouldered, had a large, prominent nose and high forehead, and would weigh one hundred and fifty pounds
whereas I only weigh one hundred and forty. There
was very little difference in our height. There was a
striking family resemblance between us. My attention
was first called to it the first time Dick Liddil and
Jesse James came to our house. The next morning
after breakfast Jesse looked at me and says, 'Why, Dick,'
he says, 'he looks like old Father Grimes.' I said:
'Who is old Father Grimes?' He says: 'He is your
cousin, Wood Hite,' and Dick laughed and said; 'Yes;
he is.' Clarence Hite was slender. You would call
him a stripling, very loose in his movements, light complexioned, and, I believe, light-haired, with no whiskers
at all. When I saw him in Kentucky he looked just
like a green boy. I suppose he would be five feet
eight or nine inches high. From the Hite's we went to
Nelson county, Kentucky, the county which has Bardstown for its county seat. We first arrived at Richard
Hoskin's, an old gentleman who lived in the 'knobs,'
for it is a very broken country. There I separated from
Jesse James and Dick Liddil, and can not tell where
they went. I know a man in Nelson county named
Robert Hall.

"I was not at his place in company with Dick Liddil and Jesse James.   There was no agreement entered into between Jesse James, Dick Liddil and myself, or myself with any other parties, to go to Missouri for the purpose of robbing the express at the Kansas City ferry; but, on the other hand, I tried to persuade them not to come to Missouri.   Jesse and Dick had been talking of coming to Missouri ever since we left Nashville.   Liddil had left his wife here and seemed very anxious to get back.   I am not certain who was his reputed wife, but I believe it was Miss Mattie Collins. That is what I heard.   I told Jesse and Dick not to come to Missouri, because it would endanger the life of our mother.   I said: 'You know already what has been done there.   You know there is no protection for my mother and family in the state of Missouri, let alone for you, and I would never go there.'   My advice to Dick Liddil was to go to work somewhere and then he would have much more money at the end of the year than if he put in his time galloping around the country.   But Jesse said they would go anyway.   So I separated from them in Nelson county, Kentucky.   As a matter of fact I was not at Hall's in connection with Liddil and Jesse James.   I remained there perhaps till the tenth or fifteenth of May, though I don't just remember the date. I then went to Louisville.   Robert Hall took me in a buggy.

"From there I went to Texas.   On the trip from Nashville to Hite's I rode a horse I got from Dick Liddil in 1879, as well as I can recollect.   That is the

9

horse he speaks of having sold to me, and its description corresponds with that of the horse referred to by the witness Duval.   I gave that horse to Mr. Hall for his services in driving me in a buggy to Louisville.   From Louisville I went to Texas by rail, going to Memphis over the L. & N.   From there I went to Little Rock, where I think I changed cars and went to Texarkana, on the Iron Mountain.   Thence I went to Dallas by a road whose name I don't remember.   It occurs to me like the International.   From Dallas I went up into northern Texas.   Mrs. Palmer is my sister.   I got to her house about the first of June, 1881.   I remained there five or six weeks.   I don't remember exactly where I learned of the death of President Garfield.   I think I heard of it while I was there, and I left my sister's between that time and the tenth of July.   The nearest postoffice to my sister's place was Henrietta, and that was eighteen miles away.   After leaving my sister's I went into the Indian Nation, and I think I was gone ten or fifteen days.   I went on horseback.   My sister's place is about thirty miles from the line of the Indian Nation, but the way I went I reckon it was about one hundred and twenty miles.   I know I got down in that country about the time I heard of the Winston robbery, so I talked round and went to Denison.

   "I can not state whether I read of the Winston robbery in a paper or whether somebody told me. After that I went back to my sister's in Clay county, and remained there through August and a part of September.   I left my sister's I am satisfied between the tenth and fifteenth of September, 1881. I know as I returned on that trip I heard of the Blue Cut robbery. When I left Tennessee I gave my wife directions to go to Gen. Joe Shelby's, in the state of Missouri, and see if there could be any arrangements made with the governor for my surrender. If I could have a fair and impartial trial accorded me I felt perfectly satisfied I could be cleared beyond a doubt. I told her if anything could be done in this behalf to communicate with me in northern Texas, otherwise to go to her brother, Samuel Ralston, in California. I think he resided in Sonora, Tuolumna county. She went there. I didn't do much in Texas, as I felt the need of rest, for the three and a half years of hard work in Tennessee had told on my health. I would sit and read or lounge about the house. I was not engaged in anything while I was there. When I left my sister's in September I returned to the neighborhood of Denison and the Chickasaw Nation, and remained there perhaps two or three weeks. Then I returned to Kentucky, going by way of the M., K. & T. to St. Louis, and the K. & O. to St. Louis and on to Samuel's depot. I received no answers in 1881 to my petition for leave to surrender.

"Otherwise my wife would not have gone to California. On my return to Kentucky my wife met me in Nelson county. She arrived there some time in the latter part of October, 1881, with one child, now five years old. From Samuel's depot we went across to Georgetown, in Scott county, Kentucky. There we took the Cincinnati Southern train to Chattanooga, and stopped at the Stanton house, where I registered as J.

Ed. Warren and wife. From there we went over the
E. T. V. & G. railway to Bristol. Changed cars there
for the Norfolk and Northwestern, which carried us to
Lynchburg. I remained there a couple of weeks, de-
tained by the miscarriage of a trunk which I had expressed from Louisville to Georgetown when I had
gone across the country in a buggy. At Lynchburg
we stopped at the Arlington on Seventh and Clark
streets, if I am not mistaken. My intention was to go
into North Carolina somewhere, and remain there. I
went from Lynchburg over the Virginia Midland to
Danville, and then over the Richmond and Danville to
Jonesboro, North Carolina, where I stopped at the
McAdoo house, registering as before. Then there was
a little town called Salem, thirty or forty miles from
Jonesboro, at the foot of the mountains. That seemed
to be a secluded place, and I thought I would go into
business there, as I had experience in mill work, and
there were any number of mills there, but the place
seemed full of diphtheria. There was a great deal of
sickness there. They had just been putting in water-
pipes, which a great many people supposed to be the
cause of sickness. So I went back to Jonesboro, the place,
by the way, where, I think, Gen. Joseph E. Johnston surrendered, and I got my family and went from there to
Raleigh, North Carolina. As soon as I got into the
town I saw it was dead. There wasn't a manufacturing
establishment in it to amount to anything, although it
had fifteen or sixteen thousand inhabitants. I saw that
was no place to stop and I went to Norfolk, stopping
at the Purcell house and registering as Warren. I

didn't like that place so my wife says, 'Suppose we take a trip up the James river.'

"I says, 'very well, all right.' We went up the James River with Captain Gifford, on the Ariel, and, arriving at Richmond, stopped at the Ford House. There I found the town all yellow-flagged for the small-pox, which scared me, as I didn't want to lose my wife and child. So we went to Lynchburg, which was a healthy place, and rented a house there. I was quite feeble all winter and very sick. I stayed there until about the tenth of May. While at Lynchburg, I noticed the assassination of Jesse James. I was taking the New York *Daily Herald* at the time. I had been out walking, and when I got back to the house I saw my wife was excited, and she came rushing to me with the paper and says 'Jesse James is killed.' I says, 'My God, where and how and who killed him?' That was the third of April. After that I paid close attention to my papers. I remember reading in the New York *Herald* how Governor Crittenden, when asked what hope there was for Frank James, he replied, 'wherein as none of his friends have ever asked anything, I will not state anything about it.' That gave me hope. I said to my wife, 'possibly if you return to Missouri and show a willingness on my part to let the past be buried, and that I am willing to surrender myself up, and be tried and meet every charge they can bring against me, I may have a fair and impartial trial.' She went. I left Lynchhurg, May 10, 1882, returning as I went to Nelson county, Kentucky. I remained there until I effected my surrender, and came to Missouri, October

5, 1882. I shipped no arms from Samuel's Station to Missouri. As to what Jesse James and Dick Liddil did I am not able to speak. I was not in Missouri from 1876 to the time I passed through going from Texas to Kentucky.

On cross-examination witness said: "I went to Tennessee in a wagon. Mr. Burns was with us."

THE TRIP TO TENNESSEE.

"Us, who do you mean by us?"

"I mean Jesse James and the others."

"Where did you separate?"

"In southeast Missouri."

"And not in northern Tennessee?"

"No."

Witness continued: "There were two wagons. One was mine and one was Jesse's. I do not know where Tyler Burns is. He lived when he went south with us in Hell's Corner, Jackson county. We got to Tennessee with a little money in July, 1876. When I left Tennessee I had about $300, a $200 bill and change."

"Was that all the money you could command?"

Colonel Philips objected, as this matter was not referred to in the examination in chief.

FRANKS FUNDS.

The court not being positive about this matter, believing a defendant as a witness was subject to different rules of evidence from ordinary witnesses, sent out for the authorities. The court decided the question might be put, and the witness answered:

"I had other means; my wife had some money. She had between $600 and $700, which came from the sale of six mules, a wagon and general farming utensils. When I left Nashville, I left from the town, not from the farm."

"I remember an interview with Frank O'Neill, and when a part of the interview was read he could not remember having said it. The portion read made him say he had lived continuously on a farm while in Tennessee.

"I did not tell Mr. O'Neill that I had left the Smith place to become a wanderer again."

"I can't state how long ago I became acquainted with Dick Liddil. I had seen him before seeing him at Nashville. I had seen him at Hudspeth."

"I think when he came to Nashville it was in July, 1879.

JIM CUMMINGS.

"Dick Liddil never came to Nashville with Jim Cummings. I did not regard the interval when I said to Mr. O'Neill that Jim Cummings and Dick Liddil came to Tennessee in the fall of 1880. Under my oath, I say Dick Liddil came there in July, 1879, and Cummings came in the fall. I can't remember when he left, exactly."

The court here put a stop to further examination about Cummings, as his name had not been brought out on the examination in chief.

"Mr. James, you say it was your purpose to get rid of these men; why did you go to Kentucky with them?"

"I went because I wanted to go there to see friends and to help in getting rid of these people."

"After getting into Kentucky I kept with them and went to Nelson county for the purpose then of keeping Jesse from going back to Missouri, fully realizing the result would be what it has been, and to prevent another hand grenade raid on my mother's family and the children of the whole family. I was at Hall's, but made no agreement.

"Did you not say to Mr. O'Neill that you were in Missouri in October, 1881?"

"I did. He asked me if I had been in Missouri. My answer meant that I was in Missouri passing through."

"I did not leave Ray county in October of 1881 with Clarence Hite and separate from him at Independence.

The State here took up the trip from Nelson county to Georgetown and thence to Chattanooga and so on, and it was retold without a single break.

"When at Hite's I had pistols. I had no gun. I owned one. My wife had it. I told Mr. O'Neill that when I went armed, I carried two pistols and a Winchester, and I did so. When in Nelson county I had two pistols.''

"Were you at peace in Nelson county?"

"I decline to answer that question."

The court—"You can do as you please."

Continuing the cross-examination. Mr. Wallace was particular as to the places and dates on which the defendant stopped during his tour out of Kentucky and to Lynchburg.

The witness was surprisingly accurate, and missed nothing from the story first told. While in Lynchburg witness rented a house from Mr. Winfrey, near the water works. He gave the names of several residents there, but did not know the name of the butcher from whom he bought his meat.

Returning from his trip, from Kentucky to Texas, Mr. Wallace got him to Denison, Texas, where he stopped with a friend, whose name he refused to disclose, saying he was engaged in negotiating for his surrender, and he would not give a man away who had protected him when every other man's hand was lifted against him. At Denison he bought a horse on the street, and from whom he did not ask or know, and started for his sister's, Mrs. Palmer's, twelve miles to the west. He was closely questioned regarding this trip and answered: "The first day I traveled forty miles and stopped at a ranch, but don't know who owned the ranch and can't describe it. The next day rode to within three or four miles of Montague, on the Gainesville and Henrietta road. Don't know whether south or east or west of Montague; stopped at a house one story high and near a creek. I remember it was near a creek because it had rained that day, and I rode my horse in to wash off the mud. The next evening I got to my sister's, and asked, six miles from where she lived, just where she resided. I inquired at Harness Bros. I heard that my sister gave that name in her testimony. Witness was then questioned as to when he left there, and said it was the first of July or thereabouts, and went to the Indian nation, riding 120 miles. He could not remember the name of any one with whom he stopped on the journey, and could not describe a place at which he stayed. He declared he went to Colbert station, Indian Territory, to meet his mysterious friends, so as to get a letter from his wife regarding her negotiations for his surrender. Getting home, and hearing of the Winston robbery about this time, he returned to his sisters.

Mr. Wallace pressed him closely about his Texas visit and tours, and could extract from him only three places he had stopped at, though three months in the State, and he could give the name of but one man he met—a cowboy named Hoynes, with whom he camped one night near his sister's.

Mr. Wallace asked if his memory was better when traveling through Virginia, that he could remember dates, hotels and places, than when in Texas. He said it was because he had his wife with him, and when in Texas he was alone and anxious.

When questioned about the time he was at Calvert station, witness, as a matter of fact, became confused

and though explaining that Calvert was in the Indian
Nation, could not tell with whom he stopped, with the
exception of this mysterious friend, whom he had previously said lived in Denison. On re-examination,
witness was placed right to a certain extent as to his forgetfulness of places in Texas by saying that the country
was scarcely settled, and had been given over to cattle
grazing, and he had not taken much account of his
surroundings. The defense rested its testimony with
the introduction of Frank, and the court adjourned
until to-morrow.

EIGHTH DAY'S TRIAL.

REBUTTAL.

The trial commenced by calling back to the stand
Mr. D. Brosius, the lawyer, who was on the robbed
train and who had declared the defendant to be not
one of the men, the purpose of recalling him being to
question him as to whether he had not at stated times
and places told divers persons that the whole affair on
the train occurred so quickly that he could not describe
any of the men and didn't even know what they looked
like. His answer to all these questions were in substance that he had always declared he couldn't give a
description of men as he could not now, and that being chaffed and joked with on all hands after the robbery he might have stated that the robbers were
fifteen feet high and that they had revolvers four feet
long.

Boyd Dudley, an attorney, testified that Brosius told him just after the robbery that he saw but one man, who was fifteen feet high, and that he thought that there were others.

On cross-examination, witness stated his office was with Circuit Attorney Hamilton, who was prosecuting the case.

Wm. M. Bostaph testified that on the morning after the robbery Brosius told him that he could not describe either of the robbers as to their complexion or dress, but believed they had slouched hats pulled down over their faces.

A. M. Irving testified that Mr. Brosius told him the story about a robber fifteen feet high.

Eli Dennis testified that Brosius told him the robbery was so quick and there was so much confusion that he could not describe the robbers or tell anything about them.

W. D. Gillihan testified to about the same effect. After Frank James was brought to Gallatin, Brosius told witness that he could not say whether the prisoner was one of the robbers or not.

George Tuggle, R. L. Tomlin and T. B. Yates, all testified to Brosius' story about robbers fifteen feet high and revolvers four feet long, thus affording a powerful illustration of dangers of imagery in describing an occurrence.

Mrs. Sarah E. Hite was recalled. She testified: I knew Wood Hite since 1878, and was in the same house with him about four years. He was very untidy in his toilet, and not at all literary in his tastes.

Frank was always neat, and he and Wood did not resemble each other.

On cross-examination, the witness described Wood Hite as she did on a previous occasion, saying that his forehead was not high, nor were his ears large. In other respects her description agreed with that of Frank James. Witness stated that in the spring 1881, Jim Cummings and Frank James were not on friendly terms. Jesse came to the house one morning to kill Jim Cummings. He seemed much excited, and said he was going to kill Jim Cummings. Jim was at the Hite place alone in February, 1881, and was not there since. I don't know whether they became friendly or not after that.

Silas Norris testified that he knew Wood Hite four or five years, and that he did not to any general extent resemble Frank James, being somewhat smaller. He would take Frank to be six feet high. He never noticed any striking resemblance between the two men, though he never saw Frank James but once before coming here.

Major J. H. McGee testified: I was in the smoking-car on the train that was robbed at Winston. I sat close by the conductor when he was shot. There were three strange men in the car when the conductor was killed.

A long argument as to the admissibility of such evidence as this in rebuttal, it being clearly evidence pertaining to the case, resulted in two or three contrary decisions from the court, which at last determined to admit the evidence.

Witness resumed: Two of three men were engaged in shooting, and one was engaged in cutting the bell-rope. I saw two of them come in at the front door of the car, but did not see where the third came from.

Cross-examined: Heard pistols and heard the exclamation, "down! down! down!" I saw one man standing near me at the middle of the car with pistols, and one near the conductor, both shooting. The conductor pulled the bell-rope, and then one of the men cut it. I saw all three of the men and sized them up, but I couldn't tell whether the defendant was one of them or not. I saw no pistol in the hand of the man who cut the rope, nor did I see him doing anything else after shooting Westfall. The man who shot him walked with the other two to the front end, and going out on the platform shut the door and I saw no more of them.

THE INSTRUCTIONS.

Thereupon the court ordered the submission of the instructions, and Mr. Hamilton, of counsel for the state, read the instructions for the state, as follows:

INSTRUCTIONS FOR THE STATE.

State of Missouri against Frank James.

The court instructs the jury on behalf of the state as follows:

First—If the jury believe from the evidence that defendant Frank James, in the month of July, 1881, at the county of Daviess, in the state of Missouri, willfully, deliberately, premeditatedly, and of his malice afore-thought shot and killed one Frank McMillan; or if the jury believe that any other person then and there will-fully, deliberately, premeditatedly, or of his malice aforethought, shot and killed said Frank McMillan, and that defendant Frank James was present, and then and there willfully, premeditatedly and deliberately and of his malice aforethought aided, abetted or counseled such other person in so shooting and killing the said Frank McMillan, then the jury ought to find the defend-ant guilty of murder in the first degree.

Second—The term willfully, as used in these instructions, means intentionally, that is, not acciden-tally. Deliberately means done in a cool state of the blood, not in a sudden passion, engendered by a lawful or some just cause of provocation, and the court instructs you that in this case there is no evidence tending to show passion or provocation. Premeditately means thought of beforehand any length of time however short. Malice does not mean spite or ill will as understood in ordinary language, but it is used here to denote a con-dition of mind evidenced by the intentional doing of a wrongful act, liable to endanger human life; it signifies such a state of mind or disposition as shows a heart regardless of social duty and fatally bent on mischief. Malice aforethought means malice with premeditation as before defined.

Third—If the jury believe from the evidence that the defendant, Frank James, with Jesse James, Wood Hite and Clarence Hite, or with any of them, and oth-ers at the county of Daviess, in the state of Missouri,

in the month of July, 1881, made an assault upon one
Charles Murray, and any money of any value then in
the custody or under the care of said Murray by force
and violence to the person of said Charles Murray, or
by putting said Charles Murray in fear of some immediate injury to his person, did rob, steal, take and carry
away; and if the jury also believe from the evidence
that the defendant, Frank James, in the perpetration of
such robbery with malice aforethought as before defined,
willfully shot and killed Frank McMillan, then the jury
ought to find the defendant guilty of murder in the first
degree.

Fourth—If you find from the evidence that the
defendant, Frank James, at the county of Daviess, in
the state of Missouri, in the month of July, 1881, shot
and killed Frank McMillan, and that such act was done
neither with the specific intent on the part of the defendant to kill any particular person, nor in the perpetration
of a robbery, yet if you further find that defendant was
then and there recklessly, intentionally and with malice,
firing with a deadly weapon, to wit, a pistol, into or
through certain cars of a railway train containing a number of passengers and those in charge thereof, and while
thus firing, said McMillan being on said train, was shot
and killed by defendant, then you will find defendant
guilty of murder in the second degree; or should you
find from the evidence that at said time and place said
McMillan was shot and killed by any person or persons
whomsoever, and that such act was done neither with
the specific intent on the part of such person or persons
to kill any particular person, nor in the perpetration of

a robbery. Yet, if you further find that such person or persons were then and there recklessly, intentionally and with malice, firing with a deadly weapon or weapons, to wit, a pistol or pistols, into or through certain cars containing a number of passengers and those in charge thereof, and that while thus firing said Frank McMillan, being on said train, was shot and killed by such other or others, and that defendant was present, then and there recklessly, intentionally and with malice, aiding, abetting, assisting and counseling such other or others to fire into or through said cars, then you will find defendant guilty of murder in the second degree.

Fifth—The jury are instructed that by the statutes of this state the defendant is a competent witness in his own behalf, but the fact that he is a witness testifying in his own behalf, may be considered by the jury in delivering the credibility of his testimony.

Sixth—The jury are further instructed that to the jury exclusively belongs the duty of weighing the evidence and determining the credibility of the witnesses; with that the court has absolutely nothing to do. The degree of credit due to a witness should be determined by his character and conduct; by his manner upon the stand; his relations to the controversy and to the parties, his hopes and his fears; his bias or impartiality; the reasonableness or otherwise of the statements he makes, the strength or weakness of his recollections reviewed in the light of all the other testimony, facts and circumstances in the case.

Seventh—In considering what the defendant has said after the fatal shooting, and previous to the time of his testifying in this case, and with reference to any material matter in issue, the jury must consider it all together. The defendant is entitled to the benefit of what he said for himself, if true, as the state is to anything he said against himself in any conversation proved by the state. What he said against himself in any conversation the law presumes to be true because against himself, but what he said for himself the jury are not bound to believe because said in a conversation proved by the state; they may believe or disbelieve it as it is shown to be true or false by all the evidence in the case.

Eighth—The jury are instructed that the testimony of an accomplice in the crime for which the defendant is charged is inadmissible in evidence, and the degree of credit to be given to the testimony of such accomplice is a matter exclusively for the jury to determine. The jury may convict on the testimony of an accomplice without any corroboration of his statements, but the testimony of such accomplice as to matters material to the issue, if not corroborated by facts and circumstances in proof should be received by the jury with great caution.

Ninth—If the jury entertain a reasonable doubt as to the defendant's guilt, they should find him not guilty, but to authorize an acquittal on the ground of doubt alone; such doubt must be real and substantial, and not that there is a mere possibility that the defendant may be innocent.

Tenth—If the jury find the defendant guilty of murder in the first degree, they will simply so state in their verdict, and leave the punishment to be fixed by the court.

If they find the defendant guilty of murder in the second degree, they will so state in their verdict, and will also assess punishment at imprisonment in the penitentiary, for such term not less than ten years, as the jury may believe proper under the evidence.

INSTRUCTIONS FOR THE DEFENSE.

Colonel Philips excepted to the court's announcement of the order of speaking, on the ground that it was inequitable and unjust. Then he proceeded to read to the jury the instructions for the defense, as follows:

The State of Missouri against Frank James:

First—The defendant is on trial for the killing of one James McMillan, and for no other offense. To authorize the jury to find him guilty under the first count of the indictment, the jury must find from the evidence that defendant, Frank James, shot and killed the said McMillan; and if the jury entertain a reasonable doubt of the defendant's doing the specific act of said killing, they must acquit him under the first count of the indictment.

Second—The court instructs the jury that under the second count of the indictment the defendant is charged with making an assault in connection with others upon one Charles Murray, and robbing him of certain money, the property of said Murray, and that in perpetration thereof they shot and killed one Frank McMillan. Before the jury can find the defendant guilty under this count they must find and be satisfied beyond a reasonable doubt from the evidence that the defendant made such felonious assault on said Murray and stole from him money as charged in the indictment, and also that in the perpetration of said felony he shot and killed McMillan, or that the defendant, acting in connection with one or more of the parties named in the indictment was present aiding, counseling and abetting them in committing said assault and robbery; and that some one or more of said other persons so named in the indictment did shoot and kill said McMillan, and that said killing was so done in the prosecution of said felony.

Third—It is not sufficient to authorize you to find the defendant guilty under the second count of the indictment, that you should believe that the defendant was present at the time and place of the alleged homicide and felony, and that he had gone there with others for the purpose of robbing the said Murray, or that one Frank McMillan was then and there killed by some one of the party engaged in the robbery of said Murray. But you must be satisfied beyond a reasonable doubt either that the defendant himself shot and killed said McMillan or that some one of the party with whom he was acting, as alleged in the indictment, and in the prosecution of the purpose for which the party was assembled, shot and killed said McMillan. If, therefore, the jury should believe from the evidence that some one of said party so engaged in the alleged attack and robbery, aside from and independent of the common design and not in the prosecution of the purpose for which the party assembled, or after robbery of the said Murray was committed, shot and killed said McMillan of his own motive, without the concurrence of defendant, then the defendant can not be convicted under the second count of the indictment, and the jury in such case must return a verdict of not guilty as to the second count.

Fourth—The jury are the sole judges of the weight of the evidence and of the credibility of the witnesses who have testified therein ; and if the jury believe that any witness has willfully sworn falsely to any material fact they are at liberty to discard and disregard the testimony of such witness. And in determining the credibility of any witness the jury may take into consideration his or her moral character as disclosed by the evidence developed on the trial ; and if, on account of his or her moral turpitude or criminal acts, if any, the jury regard him or her as untrustworthy of belief and credit, they are at liberty to disregard and reject the whole of such testimony, although a part of his other testimony may be corroborated by other evidence in the case.

Fifth—Whilst the law admits as a competent witness for the state one who confesses that he was engaged in the crime charged and an accomplice therein, yet the jury should receive his statements with great caution and circumspection, unless corroborated by other testimony, and corroborative testimony should be, as to material facts, tending to show defendant's presence at and participation in the homicide.

Sixth—This instruction embodies the usual statement that the burden of proof is on the state, and defendant is presumed innocent until proven guilty beyond a reasonable doubt.

Seventh—In order to justify the inference of legal guilt from circumstantial evidence alone, the existence of the inculpating facts must be absolutely incompatible with the innocence of the accused and incapable of explanation upon any other reasonable hypothesis than that of his guilt.

Col. Shanklin here interposed a plea for the defense, urging the court to grant the defense twelve hours in which to deliver themselves of their eloquence, and claimed while the state had ample time in ten hours, the defense had more lawyers. This generosity on the part of Col. Shanklin was so appreciated by the court that the extension of time was allowed the defense.

The arguments of counsel were begun on the morning of September 3 and closed at noon on September 6. Nine speeches were made in all; the following gentlemen for the prosecution: W. P. Hamilton, J. F. Hicklin, J. H. Shanklin and Wm. H Wallace. Arguments were made in behalf of defendant by John M. Glover, Col. C. F. Garner. Jas. H. Slover, Judge John F. Philips and Charles P. Johnson.*

---

*It being impossible to here print all of the speeches made in the case, the publisher has selected one from each side of the case, which is here given in full.

THE ADDRESS TO THE JURY BY JUDGE JOHN F. PHILIPS IN BEHALF OF DEFENDANT WAS AS FOLLOWS:

May it please the court, and you gentlemen of the jury:

In view of the malign criticism of certain newspapers in the state as to the propriety of my appearing as of counsel in this case, it is not improper, in justice to truth and my position as a member of the Supreme Court Commission, that I should detain you for a few moments in explanation.

There is nothing in the constitution of this state to prevent me from appearing here as counsel. There is nothing in the act creating the commission to render it unlawful or improper.

Long before the commission was created, or I had any expectation of connection with it, and long before the prisoner at the bar had surrendered to the governor of the state, he applied to me, through a mutual friend, to know whether, if he should come in and throw himself upon "the country," I would undertake his defense and aid in according to him the constitutional privilege of a fair and impartial trial before the courts. He was distinct and candid in the statement that he had not a dollar in the world to offer me. Upon me he had no claims, other than those which spring from the bonds of human sympathy and that charity—the "one touch of which makes all the world kin."

In that fierce, internecine strife, which swept the
land like a tornado, dividing families, arraying father
against son and brother against brother, in deadliest
contention, Frank James and I stood in mortal antago-
nism.   It was my fortune to see his flag go down in
desperate defeat, while mine went up in permanent
triumph.   I was victor, he was the vanquished.

Whatever others may say or think, the idea I had
and have of the episode of "the James Brothers" was
that it came as the bitter fruit of that dire strife.   And
when, from the summit of peace on which we stand
to-day, we look back over the trampled fields yet
marked with the red hot ploughshare of war, and recall
the history of civil wars, reciting how slowly nations
recover from the blight—how long it takes the ghastly
wounds in the body politic to heal, I affirm surprise at
the rapidity of our recovery.   And when I recall all
the local bitterness of that day, with its crimination and
recrimination, its reprisals and outrages, peculiar to
neither side in Missouri, with the bad blood it engendered, and to-day behold the magnificent picture of a
civilized state, reposing in peace, exulting in plenty,
and marching on to higher achievements in the arts of
peace and social order, my heart swells with pride and
gratitude to the God of our deliverance.

And when I saw the so-called "James gang"--
the last remnant in the state of unreconciled and unac-
cepted parties to the local predatory struggle, suing
for reconciliation—offering to throw themselves on the
justice of the law and the mercy of the commonwealth,
asking nothing but fair treatment—with but one aspira-

tion and one hope, to devote, if allowed, the remainder of their lives and energies to the duties of husband, father and good citizenship, my whole heart went out in congratulation to the good people of the state.

To the prisoner, his wife and their little boy, I had but one response to make to their personal appeal to me. No man, no creature made in the image of God, could appeal to me for words of justice, for one throb of sympathy, under such conditions, without my heart beating a little warmly for him and his.

As cowardly and mean as the miserable fellows are, who are traducing me for this act of chivalry and grace, I would ask mercy for them, if not justice— should they come to contrition, especially if they had wife and child, with piteous eyes beaming on me, pleading for the life of the man they love.

It was in response to that overture, and to this sentiment, that I consented to defend this man. On my promise to defend him he came from his hiding and handed his pistol to the governor of the state. To keep that promise I am here. What brave man, with any nobility in his soul, will deny the rectitude, the honor of my action ?

I am not here as commissioner, with the judicial ermine around me. I am here as a licensed attorney of this commonwealth, standing on the commission of my manhood, trusting to nothing to rescue this prisoner save the law and the evidence, as I am able to understand and expound them to court and jury.

Gentlemen of the jury, common fame has invested this defendant with unmerited notoriety—giving to his life much of romance. How much of truth and how much of fiction there is in it all you and I know not in this trial. Under the broad shield of the constitution of the state he stands before you in this court room as any other citizen. The bond of your oath is that you know him only as the evidence shows him to be. You are to take him where the evidence finds him, and leave him where it places him.

Public rumor is often a false and a foul thing. It has had Frank James identified with every outrage and bold robbery committed between the mountains of West Virginia and the Ozarks of Arkansas and Missouri within the last six years. During these years rumor has placed him simultaneously in the counties of Clay, Jackson, Lafayette, in this state and elsewhere, wherever daring exploit in outlawry startled the country.

But what does the state's own testimony disclose ? In 1876 he left this state, with all his earthly possessions—a two-horse wagon and his young wife—and went to the state of Tennessee. Everything about that movement indicated what ? To my mind this is impressively significant. The miseries and ghosts of the war hung around his footsteps in Missouri. Weary and heart sick of it all he determined to turn his back upon it, and seek a new home, under an assumed name, in the hope that he might find a new life of peace in humble, honest industry. He had just taken to his bosom and confidence a young, trusting sweet woman. That of itself was highest proof that he was not seeking longer adventure, but that pleasure and happiness which come surest from domestic life and retirement.

I confess myself surprised at the developments of this piece of evidence, touching upon the life and conduct of this man during the years that followed his removal to Tennessee. It strengthens my faith in him. True it is that Jesse James accompanied him from Missouri. But in southeast Missouri they separated, like Abraham and Lot of old, one taking to the right and the other to the left, each pursuing his own course. Frank went to Nashville, not to maraud, not in quest of a new theatre of adventure. He went upon a little farm, and there he toiled, struggled and plead with the generous earth for bread and sustenance. The evidence declares that from early morn of Monday to nightfall on Saturday, week after week, year after year, he delved, drove teams, hauled logs, for one dollar and a half per day; and for nearly five years he was not further from his little home than the nearest trading village or town. Respected and much liked by all his neighbors he ate his bread in peace.

There, too, the first born of happy marriage came to gladden and lend a new charm to that humble home.

As he has said to me, those were the happiest days of his life. His bread was sweet, because it was labor's reward. It was wet with no tears, and cankered by no cares, because it was planted in peace, watered with heaven's dews, and gathered with the hands hardened with honest toil.

There is not on this jury a man who can believe that from the spring of 1876 to the time of the decamp-

ment in the spring of 1881 Frank James was engaged
in any marauding expedition, or any violation of law,
because both the state's testimony and that of the defense establish his constant presence at home and un-
remittent farm labor.

But where, during all those years of peaceful and
honest living by the defendant, was that pink of a witness—Dick Liddil—whom the state has presented as
its chief reliance to convict this man? He himself
admits that in 1879, when there is no pretense that
James was in the state, or in confederation with any
band, he voluntarily tendered his eminent services as
an accomplished thief, cut-purse and cut-throat, to,
what Mr. Wallace is pleased to dub, "the gang."
Where was this? Not in Tennessee, but in Mr. Wallace's own county here in Missouri. Who was that
"gang?" Jesse James, Jim Cummings and Ed Miller.
I do not know that all that has been imputed to them
is true; but if it be true that Dick Liddil was hail
fellow with them, the "crowd" was not suited to run a
prayer meeting or found a moral colony. What was
Dick Liddil doing there in 1879? I asked him if he
was not in the Glendale robbery, he declined to answer
because it would criminate him. Shortly after that he
appeared in Tennessee. He was a bad immigrant.
It was the unhappiest day for Frank James in many
years, when this slimy serpent of evil came crawling
around him. Taking advantage of an acquaintance-
ship relating back to boyhood almost, and of his knowledge of Frank James' incognita, he gained admission
to his fireside and humble hospitality. Frank was in

FRANK JAMES.

From picture taken in 1871.

(His signature.)

Son of the noted bandit. From photo taken 1898, at the age of twenty-two.

JUDGE JOHN F. PHILIPS.
Counsel for defendant.

Counsel for the State.

no condition to "peach" on any of these men. He
could do so only by disclosing his identity, and rendering further flight, with his wife and babe, a necessity.
What was Dick doing? He had found Jesse James,
and was marauding in Kentucky and Tennessee. He
was merely keeping his hand in, by now and then
plucking horses from the racks where the owners had
hitched them, or gently persuading some belated trav-
eler that he could get along best afoot or unburdened
of his cash and watch. He himself, so willing to
swear anything to help Mr. Wallace convict, does not
pretend that Frank James had anything whatever to do
with the Tennessee and Kentucky exploits.

In the progress of this discussion we now come to
the Bill Ryan episode, which seems to be the rallying
point for the state's theory that the defendant was in
combination with the gang. Bill Ryan was hanging
around Nashville with Dick Liddil. Ryan got into
some trouble and was arrested. On his person was
found a large sum of money, and a portable arsenal.
He was jailed; and immediately thereafter Frank
James broke up his home, and he and family disappeared.

Gentlemen of the jury, the best test for understanding the conduct of others is, often, to put yourself
in their places. Surround yourself by the same circumstances which environed Frank James — a man
hunted and outlawed—whose name the public press of
the country had for years associated with that of
Jesse James, Cummings, Ryan and Liddil, to whom
was attributed every daring robbery and outrage from

the north of Kentucky to the valley of the Arkansas river.

When, therefore, Ryan, in a druken debauch, fell into the law's grasp, under circumstances of such dark suspicion, his identity was liable to be discovered, as the sequal proved, and lead to the discovery of the covert of the defendant. The instinct of self preservation is predominant in the average man; and the defendant, with quick apprehension, surmised, that to save himself, Ryan might give up his (James') secret. What was he to do? Ryan's confederates were stampeded; and the dernier resort was forced upon the defendant to break his household idols, turn away from his little home, his wife and boy, and seek safety in a common retreat with those with whom he dared not break just then.

The state's counsel have sought to make capital out of the fact that James retired with the "gang" while he now claims that he wished to rid himself of them. His first care was that of loyalty to his little family. His wife and child he sent, heavy hearted, to her friends in Missouri. Where should or where could he go? Where more likely would the outcast and the homeless man, hunted and watched, turn his eyes than to the door of his nearest kindred? He went with the others to his aunt's—Mrs. Hite. She and her children of all others he had a right to believe had a place of welcome and refuge for him in the hour of extremity. Thither they went. After they left there we have but two witnesses testifying here as to what occurred in Kentucky, where the Hites lived.

Dick Liddil says they agreed to return to Missouri for pillage and plunder. On the other hand Frank James says that Jesse proposed to return to Missouri, and against that proposition he entered his solemn and earnest protest. Why not believe his story in preference to Dick Liddil? Is it not the more rational? It is corroborated by many facts and circumstances in evidence. The defendant says he told his brother they must not go to Missouri, as God knew their dear old mother had already suffered enough on their account. He called up the picture of the sorrow and desolation hitherto wrought in her home, how she had lost her arm by Pinkerton's detectives throwing handgrenades into her room, and also killing her little child and their brother; that their presence in the state would subject her to espionage and additional insult, if not injury and outrage. How natural was this argument and appeal? But Jesse was heady and desperate. On that rock they split.

There is another confirmatory fact, favoring the defendant's story. He sent his wife to her father in Jackson county, Missouri. The family sewing machine was forwarded by express to Page City, Missouri, in care, perhaps, of General Shelby.

Mr. Wallace has discovered a real Trojan horse in this much traveled sewing machine. All that was left to the fugitive, panting, little wife of Frank James was her babe and the family sewing machine. Wallace has run that machine down with the whole detective force of two railroads, and all the express companies, between Kentucky and Kansas. There is nothing

in history or fiction comparable to this discovery of
the efficient prosecuting attorney of Jackson county,
unless it be the cabalistic letters on the curious stone
discovered by Picwick.

I am now satisfied that the extraordinary effort put
forth by Mr. Wallace to run down this sewing machine
was to use this remarkable piece of evidence as a substitute for Dick Liddil's testimony, in the event the
court should exclude Dick as an incompetent witness,
he being a convicted thief.

But to the argument. When Mrs. James reached
Page City she told General Shelby she had come to him
from her husband to request his intercession with the
governor of the state to permit her husband to return to
Missouri, under assurance of the protection of the law.
General Shelby testified that was her mission. So, you
have the absurd, improbable theory of the state, that
while the husband was preparing a raid of brigandage
upon the state he was employing his wife as a diplo-
matic agent to negotiate for his surrender to the chief
magistrate of the state.

Counsel for the state will suggest that that was a
mere ruse—that the defendant was employing his wife
as a decoy duck to throw the officers off the trail. If,
gentlemen of the jury, you are to drink in the suspicious, vindictive spirit of the private, hired counsel in
this case, instead of the spirit of the law, which com-
mands you to judge mercifully—if you are to smother
reason under a load of suspicion, instead of heeding
his Honor's instructions from the bench—to give the
prisoner the benefit of every reasonable doubt—this

trial, under the forms of law, will be a mockery, and I would have no duty to perform here. But, you are a Christian jury in a Christian land, respecting your oaths and obeying yourselves the law; and, therefore, you will judge this man as you would be judged under like circumstances.

Mrs. James' mission to General Shelby was genuine. Shelby's testimony is worthy of all credit. It is but frank in me to admit that the General's deportment on the witness stand was improper, as a matter of propriety. It hurt no one so much as himself, and I know he regrets it. But he spoke truth. His high character needs no defense and no eulogy by me. His name is a household word in Missouri. As splendid in courage as he is big of heart, his home is the model for hospitality. No man however poor or outcast was ever turned from it hungry. Truth and chivalry to him are as modesty to the true woman, and azure to the sky.

He has been denounced in public and in private as a friend of Frank James. Smirking Puritans and lugubrious Pharisees have shrugged their shoulders at the fact of Shelby giving a bed and a glass of water and a pinch of salt to the defendant when he chanced to pass his door; and for extending the hand of assistance and a word of sympathy to Frank James' wandering heart-sick wife. In the midst of so much moral cowardice and starveling charity in this age, I rather admire the quality of heart which prompted Shelby. It was not the promptings of a spirit of disloyalty to law and society, but it was the quick response of a brave and generous heart to that sentiment which makes us humane instead of savage.

11

There are ties betwixt these men which were
formed back in war times, when they stood elbow to
elbow upon "the perilous edge of battle." They had
marched, tented and fought side by side. Who would
dissolve the bonds of fellowship born of such comrade-
ship? It was natural for the defendant, in his extremity, to turn toward such a man as Shelby. He knew
Shelby would give audience and heed to the supplica-
tions of a woman—the wife of an old comrade. The
mistake Shelby made was in not going to the governor,
and attempting to carry out James' wishes. But other
efforts, Shelby states, in that direction had failed. So
he told Mrs. James it was useless to renew the attempt.
Public temper was averse. So with heavy heart the little woman had "the infernal sewing machine" reshipped
to her father at Independence, Missouri; while she
gathered her little boy closer to her bosom, and after a
brief visit to her father, took up her long weary march
to the Pacific slope, trusting to the deliverance of time
and Providence.

There are other facts in evidence confirmatory of
defendant's story, that he broke from the "gang" and
went south. When Jesse James and Dick Liddil
appeared at Mrs. Samuel's—mother of the defendant—
she met them at the door and her first inquiry was:
"Where is Buck (her pet name for Frank)?" Frank
was a delicate boy, and the mother's anxious heart told
her he was dead. She had not heard from him for so
long a time. Both Jesse and Liddil told her he had
gone south. Her solicitude for Frank's welfare and
safety made her press the inquiry, whereat Liddil

assured her that Frank was not with them—he had gone south. If Mrs. Samuels and John Samuels are to be discredited in this statement because of their relationship to the prisoner, what, Gentlemen of the Jury, are you to say to the testimony of Frank Tutt, Crowder, Childs and Shelby, wholly disinterested witnesses, of unimpeachable character? Liddil told them, when he was without any reasonable, or conceivable, motive to lie, both before and after his surrender, that he had not seen Frank James—that he was not in the Winston robbery—that he (Frank) and Jesse had quarreled and separated. Superadded to all this, look at the testimony of the throng of most reputable witnesses from Ray county, who told you what Mrs. Bolton—the State's important witness—over and again declared to them that Frank James was not at the Winston robbery—that he had been trying for years to earn an honest living, and the other parties would follow him up and try to get him into trouble; and he would move away from them to escape the detectives—and that she had not seen him for years, although Jesse, Liddil and others of "the gang" were at her house about the time of this robbery. Now where did she get this story but from Dick Liddil and the rest of the party?

We are next, in historical order, brought to Missouri in the spring of 1881, prior to the Winston robbery. The identification of Frank James, as one of the participants in the alleged homicide of McMillan, depends mainly upon the testimony of Dick Liddil. The learned counsel for the state, who have preceded me in argument, have warned you that I would abuse poor Dick Liddil. If I did not, in this respect, meet their expectation it would be because of the injunction that we ought not to "kick a dead dog." For he is so morally dead that like Lazarus he stinketh in the nostrils of every honest man. If ever there stood a creature in a court of justice as a witness who has justly called down upon him the imprecations and loathings of every manly heart it is this witness. There is nothing—absolutely nothing—in and about the fellow to excite one emotion of pity, sympathy or respect. We are just as the good God has made us. We are endowed with certain instincts and sentiments which we would not resist if we could. The world over the brave and the true despise a traitor and a coward. This man is both: a coward, because to save himself he would, through perjury, destroy his alleged confederate; a traitor he is to friendship, confidence and honor, even among thieves. By his own confession he entered into a common enterprise, and after having shared the common hazard and a common spoil he betrays those with whom he enlisted. He is no youth, corrupted by the defendant. Years before he claims any association with Frank James he was a convicted horse thief, a penitentiary graduate.

For fifty years the British government, from which comes our noble heritage of common law and civil institutions, has suffered no citizen of that realm to be convicted on the uncorroborated testimony of such admitted accomplice in crime. How desperate must be the cause of the state when it resorts to such a witness.

You, gentlemen of the jury, have never met with such a constellation of atrocities in any one man as this fellow represents in his character. He comes, just before this trial, to this state, crawling vampire like, from the jail in Alabama, to drink the life blood of this defendant; to taint the sanctuary of justice with his false breath, instinct with venom, and wreaking with treachery to the offices of friendship and hospitality.

He should never have been permitted to pollute the Bible by taking the "oath on the book." He should have been sworn on the knife—the dagger—the proper symbol of his profession. "A superservicable rogue, coward and pander," he is ready and willing to swear without mercy, stint, limit or conscience, to make sure of his victim.

Did you observe, gentlemen of the jury, while on the witness stand, how he smirked and giggled with evident satisfaction at his smartness, as he detailed the facility with which he snatched other men's horses from hitching posts and stables, as boys pick blackberries in August? By his own confession he is guilty of all that public rumor and indictments have imputed to Frank James. Highway robbery and murder are his pastime.

By the law of this state he is disqualified from exercising the ordinary privileges of citizenship—of suffrage and sitting on juries. The law says, through your state legislature, that this man Liddil is so steeped in crime, so morally tainted, he is unfit almost to be a citizen, disqualified from exercising the functions of official trust, or to handle the ballot, or to sit in the trial

of the rights of property, liberty, or life, between his
fellow men, or the public and a citizen.   There is not
a man on this jury who would this hour consent that
this fellow should sit as a juror between you and your
neighbor to determine the rights of property between you
as to an acorn fed hog or a sheep with scabs and burrs
as ornaments.   Yet the prosecution, on behalf of the
great state of Missouri, are so desperate in their thirst for
the life of Frank James, that, with audacious clamor,
they demand of you to believe this wretch, and take
human life predicated of his credibility.   You will do
no such thing !

Gentlemen of the jury, I witnessed here in this
court house a sight I trust my eyes may never see again
in an American court of justice.   Let me go back a
little.   This witness was confined in jail in Alabama.
Before the last term of this court he was brought to
Missouri to testify against the prisoner at the bar.   He
was bailed, and no doubt offered his freedom, on condition of swearing away the life of Frank James.   He
has been smuggled, hid and concealed from all other
eyes than those of his masters and trainers in Kansas
City.   Like some curious animal brought from Eastern
jungle for exhibition, he has been kept concealed from
the public until the circus opened.   He has been fed
and housed at the court house in Kansas City under the
guardianship of supple officers of that county, exercised
I presume, only between suns.   The day before he was
needed here he was, at the bidding of the prosecution,
put under arrest for some undisclosed offense.   He is
neither jailed nor bailed, but put in charge of a deputy

marshal of that county and brought here as a prisoner, escorted around town, on exhibition, as the master swearer of the age, who was to swear away the life of Frank James as baselessly as the two men of Belial swore away the life of Naboth. No person, outside of the elect, was permitted to come in contact with the creature, as if he were a leper. He and the deputy marshal have been inseparable since coming here. They eat together, sleep together, until they begin to look alike and smell alike. And when the sheriff of this jurisdiction called "Richard Liddil" as a witness, he came into the court house and on this platform, to the witness stand, and by his side came and sat throughout his testimony his *alter ego*—his body guard and shadow—the deputy marshal of Jackson county.

Mr. Wallace was unwilling to trust the man on the witness stand without this physical pressure—without the deputy, with eye of menace gleaming upon the wretch, as if to scream at him: Swear! Swear! You scoundrel, or I will rend you with the talons of the law!

Such are the agencies employed to gratify private ambition to secure a verdict of guilty in this case. It was a spectacle worthy of the worst despotism of the meanest tyranny of ancient times, but a reproach and a shame to a free, Christian Republic, with a written constitution, reposing for its security and glory upon the rights of individual man.

What a galaxy of witnesses—what a cluster of virtues—the state presents to you, gentlemen of the jury, for your justification in taking human life. Circling around Liddil come the Fords and Mrs. Bolton, to swear that Frank James was in the country at the time of the robbery and homicide in question. What a cockatrice's nest that was to hatch out vipers! I dislike to assail a woman under any circumstances. In a land like ours where woman is so universally respected, her very name should at once be "the assurance of her strength and the amulet of her protection:" but my observation has been that a woman, as has been said, is like a stone, the higher elevation from which she falls the deeper she sinks into the mire. When she does fall, like Lucifer, she falls forever.

Mrs. Bolton is a bad woman. Her whole family are wicked and degraded. There is neither virtue nor truth among them. For money or hate they would dare any desperate thing. All their neighbors, the best men in Ray county, come here and testify that these people are unworthy of belief. But if no witness spoke against the general reputation of this household, if their testimony did not destroy itself with palpable contradictions and inconsistencies—the attendant circumstances of the Wood Hite tragedy in the "Bolton Castle" are enough to damn the whole family with ineffaceable infamy and perjury.

Dick Liddil was hibernating in that robber's den. On the fifth day of December, 1881, Wood Hite—cousin of the James boys—arrived at this rendezvous from Kentucky. He was killed in the family dining room before breakfast, the morning of his arrival. Dick Liddil took shelter behind his privilege and declined to tell about it on the witness stand, for the reason that it might incriminate him. Ah, if there had been no innocent blood on his hands, he could have unfolded a plain, unvarnished story, exonerating himself. Mrs. Bolton came upon the stand. She was as close as an oyster. She knew Wood Hite—a man—was slain in her own house on that Sabbath morn when God's bright sun had arisen for his day's journey. She made no out-cry for help—no demand for justice. Like a butchered hog the murdered victim was carried up stairs and covered up in bed, crimson with flowing human blood. During the day she entertained, with hospitable display, her neighbor visitors down stairs, while this horrible corpse was up stairs, breathing no word of the awful tragedy. One false step begets another, and when a witness begins to lie, one lie evolves another. Mrs. Bolton having denied that she saw the murdered man down stairs, says she did not see him up stair, and that she had never since been in the room above, where he lay all that Sabbath day, a ghastly, bloody corpse. She shrunk, I presume, with horror from contact with that domestic morgue.

The woman, doubtless, has some sensibility left; for it is said there is nothing so black it will not burn to something in hell. Every plank in the floor of that room, and rafter in the ceiling, spoke to her of blood and murder, while the moaning winds through the cracks were but the echoes of the dying man's agonies.

But murder will out. From one of her children, whose age exempted him from pleading his privilege, we extracted a part of the truth. After impenetrable darkness had settled down over the world, hiding the damnable deed from other eyes, late at night the

Ford boys stripped from the corpse the pants and coat, which they appropriated to their own use, and wrapping the body, unwashed and all clotted with blood, in a stinking, wornout horse blanket, they carried it out into the woods, and dumped it, uncoffined, without a prayer or a sigh, into a shallow hole, covering it with stones, brush and dirt, and then like ghouls crept back to their den to plan and scheme for hiding this dreadful deed.

Talk of a jury crediting the evidence of such a family; dead to every emotion of human sympathy, insensible to every moral instinct and sentiment which distinguishes man from the savage or the brute, what regard have such creatures—such monsters—for truth or the right?

Now we can begin to discern the governing motive influencing the action of Dick Liddil in turning state's evidence and informer. When he began to reflect upon the possibilities of the discovery of this horrible crime his coward soul quaked. Jesse James was in the country. Would he not, on discovering the murder of his cousin, visit swift and terrible judgment upon the perpetrators? So the conspirators and the assassins fell upon the plan of informers. The state's counsel tell you that Liddil was actuated by a sense of duty in undertaking to deliver over the James boys. Yes, he turned patriot—the last refuge of a scoundrel. It was the ghastly face of Wood Hite, which moved about the murderer's room at night, and dread of the living face of Jesse James, that compelled him to add to his crown of infamies the words: informer and perjurer.

A mysterious bond of interest and sympathy sprung up at once between Liddil and Mrs. Bolton. They became like two roses on one stem—alike in hue and ordor. Mrs. Bolton, dressed in black—appropriate symbol of death and mourning—and thickly veiled— to screen a harlot's mission—went to see the governor of the state, to open up negotiations for Liddil's and her brothers'—the Ford boys—surrender. This terrible butchery of Wood Hite was carefully concealed from the governor.

The surrender proposed was placed on the high ground of weariness with the life the Jameses had led them, and a desire to serve the state by compassing their destruction. Under this assurance indemnity was secured for her brood—Bob and Charley Ford—and her dear Richard. The very bond of this unmixed, unmitigated villain was to destroy this defendant and his brother Jesse. No honor to preserve, no conscience to restrain him, yielding only to the instinct of self-preservation, he is ready to swear anything and everything to serve his master and get the lion—Frank James—out of his trembling footpath. Jesse James soon went down by the assassin bullet of Bob Ford. This knit the Fords and Liddil still closer together. Dick has since been convicted of crime in Alabama; and the men managing and manipulating this prosecution went his bail and brought him here. He is to be freed from that conviction if he can swear Frank James to the death. No witness was ever produced in any court under such a pressure, such motives to swear hard and long. And the question for this jury to first answer, when you retire to consider of your verdict, is, whether you will credit the testimony of such a witness under such circumstances.

If you decide him to be unworthy of belief, that will be the end of this prosecution. The state in putting such a rogue, unshriven, on the witness stand admits that she has not a case without his testimony.

It is useless further to discuss the identification of the defendant in Missouri at the time of the robbery in question dependent upon the testimony of the Ford-Bolton gang. The Bolton children are chips off the old block. They but reflect the teachings of the dragon that bred them. The little girl, about which there is so much gush, was brought here and taken by the old lady Bolton and the prosecuting counsel before James, who was pointed out to her. Why, or how, she recognized him she can not tell. She is to be pitied, and the prosecution should blush.

Touching the indentification of Frank James by the citizens of this county, I beg to say that I do not question the honesty of all of them; but I wish you, gentlemen of the jury, to take this thought with you into your retirement: How unreliable is the judgment, how falible the human mind, in a matter of identity. Much depends upon the accuracy of the eye, the faculty of comparison, the memory—the power of analysis. Nothing which my profession encounters in practice is so uncertain and perplexing as testimony respecting the identity of animals. I have seen twenty and thirty intelligent and respectable witnesses, with positiveness and earnestness, swear to cross purposes as

to the identity of a well known cow or horse, with
clearly defined marks to distinguish them.

In the vegetable world there are no two leaves of clover
alike, yet, how many men can distinguish them? The human vision is as liable to mislead as the human judgment.   The mind, in its operations in psychology,
metaphysics, and perception, is a curious thing.   Its
independent operation is rare.   It is oftener influenced
by the laws of association.   You fix your mind on a
certain object, with the previous suggestion that it is
a certain thing, no matter what its tints and lights,
nine chances out of ten you will conclude it is precisely
what it is represented to be.   Many a child sees the
man in the moon, clearly outlined, because it was told
the man is there.

The whole country was taught to believe that
Frank and Jesse James were inseparable—that where-
ever Jesse was there was Frank.   As it was conceded
that Jesse was in the Winston robbery, Frank's presence, as we lawyers say, went *nem con*.   When Frank
surrendered everybody concluded they had the man
who was engaged in the Winston affair.   Everybody
went to see him, at jail, with that impression deeply
fixed.   So, when the identifying witnesses went to the
jail to see Frank they had no difficulty in pointing him
out, for they were led to his cell.   If Wood Hite had
been in one cell and Frank in the other, there is not
one of these witnesses, unaided, who could have
singled out Frank James; no, not one of them.   The
general description given by the witnesses of Wood
Hite covers James exactly, to the average mind; and

it would require a close personal acquaintance with both to distinguish them.

Take the instance of Potts, the blacksmith, regarded by the State as an important witness. When he first went to the jail he could not say he recognized the prisoner. A second time he saw him, and was not satisfied. After Jesse James was killed and Potts was shown his photograph he exclaimed: "Why, that is the man I saw in my shop!" If Jesse instead Frank were on trial, Potts, and his wife—who swears just as her "hubby" does—would be equally as sure of their man. Old Potts had heard much, in the meantime, of what kind of whiskers the prisoner wore. He had heard talk of "burnsides,"—he called them "sideburns." He put "sideburns" on Frank and Dick Liddil; and if this trial had lasted another week he would have had "sideburns" on the horses. After Potts learned that the horses he shod belonged to the "James gang" he recognized every approaching stranger, on horseback or in wagon, as the same men who were at his shop, and would break out of his shop and cover himself in the impenetrable armor of a weed patch.

So with the other witnesses. They went to the jail for the purpose of identifying the prisoner. They knew Frank was in jail. The process by which they reached the conclusion of identity was simple and natural. The mind was prepared for it. They had a full description of him. They had read it in the newspapers, and talked it over with the diligent prosecution. Does any man on this jury believe, if after two years time, when the whiskers, dress, and whole physical appearance of the man were changed, if any of these witnesses had met, by chance, James in the public road, or in town, they would have recognized him?

Last fall I spoke at a political mass meeting in Kansas City for one hour. The next morning I entered a barber shop, took the chair, and was shaved. The room was small and there were several gentlemen in there. While shaving me the barber and all present discussed my speech—some in praise and some in dispraise. All of them heard the speech, including the man shaving me. I had on the same clothes, yet not one of them recognized me until told of their blunder.

How many of these witnesses would have recognized Dick Liddil had he come to this trial unheralded? Special pains were taken by the drill masters for the prosecution to exhibit him and have him identified. No one can tell how he was dressed on that raid, although they can tell all about Frank James' apparel, because they learned it from Liddil's story. Liddil is as marked a man in appearance as James, or more so. He has a villainous look, with a protruding eye, lying around on his cheek, that no man ought ever to forget.

There has been marked industry and work by the state. Even the kind of toes to James' boots has been described, when the witnesses could not tell anything about the shoes or boots of others of the party. On the witness stand we had a striking illustration of the infirmity and danger of this character of evidence. Mrs. Wolfinberger swore with womanly energy and assurance to the identity of the prisoner. She is a positivist—

never mistaken. She was asked, in test of her accuracy of judgment, if she had ever seen any of the counsel for the prisoner prior to this trial. "O, yes; I saw Governor Johnson here, in this court house, last June." Well, it turns out she was mistaken; she did not see the governor with his smiling, impressive face. She was equallly as positive about having seen the governor as she is of having seen James on the raid.

On such evidence of identity, you, gentlemen of the jury, are asked to take this man's life. Beware!

I must not quit this branch of the evidence without noticing the testimony of old man Soule. This witness is a genius—or rather *sui generis*. He belongs to the Pilgrim Fathers. He came over in the May Flower, beyond a doubt. He is a regular Praise-God-Barebones. In the absence of camp meetings and elections, he is perishing for a hanging. He knows he has the right man. He has brooded so long and intently over the delivery of his testimony on this trial that he actually panted under its burden. He was a regular pent-up Utica. I thought he would burst. He sat one heel on the other of his brogans, threw his head back to the buttons on the back of his coat, and shot up his waist-band where his nose should have been. He started to get out of his clothes, in illustration of an answer to a question put to him by myself, and if the judge had not stopped him he would have been in dishabille before this jury, dancing the "racquette." He saw Frank, "and don't you forget it." He traced the horses which Frank and his companion rode, around to Montgomery's where the party, whoever they were, took

supper that evening.   Clearly therefore the man who is
identified by Soule as Frank James is the same man
who went to Montgomery's and ate supper.   To complete his testimony, therefore, it was reasonable to suppose that the state would introduce the Montgomerys
in corroboration.   The Montgomerys were brought
here on subpoena at the instance of the state, and were
in attendance when the state closed its testimony. Why
did not the state introduce them?   Is the state seeking
conviction, right or wrong?   Does this prosecution represent the dignity and honor of the state, or the ambition of private counsel?

The instrumnentality of the grand jury—the indictment—this investigation and trial—are, under the
theory of the constitution and the law of the land, supposed to be designed solely to develop the truth and at-
tain the ends of public justice.   The prosecuting attorney, in his office, represents the whole body of the
people.   The defendant is equally the object, in contemplation of law, of his protection and vindication.
The public prosecutor who would convict a prison by
withholding part of the testimony violates his oath of
office, and becomes accessory to a great wrong.

But the truth is that this prosecution has long since
passed from the control of the officer designated by
the statute of the state for its management and conduct.
It is under the complete and absolute control of private
prosecutors, who are seeking victory and fame, ambition and revenge have usurped the high province of
justice, and the dignity and peace of the state are

12

bartered away in the greed and struggle of the volunteer and hired aids for cheap glory.

The defense had to put the Montgomerys on the witness stand. Mrs. Montgomery and daughter, who waited on the men at the table that evening, with every favorable opportunity for observation, tell you the prisoner is not the man. And the reasons assigned by them for their conclusion leave no reasonable room for doubt as to the correctness of their judgment.

One other thought in this connection. The striking similarity between Wood Hite and Frank James made it quite plausible for Dick Liddil to substitute Frank for Hite. So much so is this true that if Hite were alive and on trial instead of the prisoner, the same evidence given by Liddil, and that in corroboration, so-called, would apply with equal force to Hite. It must be kept in mind that in order to place Frank James in the Winston robbery the state must show there were five persons in that raid. Four of them are conceded by the State to be Jesse James, Wood Hite, Clarence Hite and Dick Liddil.

Now, only four men were seen together by any witness, outside of Liddil. When separated two were invariably together. To account for the absence of the fifth man Liddil always had him off somewhere on a reconnoitering expedition, to see when the trains would pass the towns or to get provisions. But there came a time when, if there were five men in the party, it was in the power of the state and Liddil to show it by other witnesses. You will remember, gentlemen, that on the day before the robbery and homicide in question Liddil had all the parties on horseback in Daviess county. Jesse, Frank and Clarence Hite were together, Dick and Wood Hite were together,—according to Sir Richard. The party of three are accounted for by other witnesses, who saw the group of three together. But where is the witness who saw the other two at or about that time? Liddil says he and Wood Hite ate dinner together. Where? Who saw you? Mark me here, gentlemen of the jury, on every other day save this Liddil, with wonderful precision, could tell you where he stopped and ate. The name of the family was put on his lips. He could tell you the number of the children in the family—the dress of each—how their hair was combed, and how the nose was kept. He could describe the host and hostess, the character of the house, the stables and out-houses. But on this important day, when he and Wood Hite dined together, and which would have definitely settled the presence of the fifth man on the raid if cor-roborated as to this dining. Richard was not himself, but was all at sea. He could not give the name of the landlord, nor any description of the family, the country, nor anything by which we might catch him in his lie.

The old fox was cornered at last. He and his trainers had not anticipated this crisis. If they had, Liddil would have had this fifth man off alone on some reconnoissance.

We are now brought, in the process of this discus-sion, to the scene of the robbery and homicide. (Here the speaker discussed with elaboration the declarations of law given by the court, especially with reference to

the character of corroborating testimony and circumstances essential to warrant the jury in convicting on
the testimony of an accomplice.)

You, gentlemen of the jury, must not forget in
your deliberations that this corroboration of Liddil
must be as to the *res gestae* that it must be material,
independent, facts showing the actual presence of the
prisoner, not alone somewhere on that raid, but at the
time and place of the homicide.

It must be borne in mind that it is an easy matter
for Dick Liddil to detail, with great particularity, the
events preceding the attack on the train. It is easy for
him to detail the incidents of the raid into Livingston
county, just preceding, and the minutia of the robbery
and what followed, for the simple reason that he was a
participant in and eye witness of it all. But this is not
corroboration in contemplation of the law, as declared
to you in these instructions of the court. Who corroborates Dick Liddil that Frank James was present at the
homicide? This is the all important, material question; and you must never lose sight of this when the
prosecution are talking to you about Liddil being corroborated.

Strike out of this case the testimony of that
scoundrel Liddil and I submit that there is not a scin-
tilla of proof on which an honest, intelligent jury could
base a conclusion that Frank James was present at the
robbery and homicide in question. No one saw him;
no one pretends to have recognized him there. Who
shot the deceased, McMillan, or how the person did it,
no one knows, so far as we can judge from this testi-

mony. Outside of Liddil's testimony, there is not a man on this jury who can place his hand on his heart and say that the prisoner was within ten miles of the tragedy. Under the instructions of the court, and the solemn bond of your recorded oath, you are bound to say there is no corroboration of Liddil as to the actual and required presence of Frank James at the place and time of the homicide. You can not, therefore, convict this man, without disobeying the law, so it seems to me.

You, gentlemen, are courageous and honest enough, I trust, to say so though all hell rise in arms against you. Even were it conceded that Frank James was present at the robbery, the case of the state must fail. Governor Crittenden told you from that witness stand that that Prince of Scoundrels and Liars, Dick Liddil, shortly after his surrender told him that Frank James was not responsible for the killing of McMillan; that on the contrary, that when Frank saw that human life had been taken he upbraided Jesse James for the unnecessary act, reminding him that the distinct understanding was that no blood was to be shed, and that had he (Frank) anticipated this homicide he would have abandoned the expedition. That thereat Jesse replied he had done it in order to bind his band more closely. Crediting this statement of Liddil, it shows that the homicide was not committed in furtherance of the prosecution of a common design or undertaking. Neither was it done from the necessity of the situation in which one of the conspirators suddenly found himself while engaged in the prosecution of the design to rob. It was an act, on the contrary, of pure wantonness, perpetrated by one of the parties wholly aside from the common enterprise, and on his individual responsibility. As such, under the instruction of the court, and upon principles of plain justice, the defendant can not be held responsible for that homicide.

If his Honor on the bench were on trial, you would not hesitate to acquit him on this evidence. Under the law the life of this defendant is as precious as that of the judge, or the chief magistrate of this commonwealth. This is among the chief glories of the Republic; it shields him as it does the most exalted. To sacrifice the life of Frank James at the behest of popular prejudice and clamor is to wound and cut down the spirit of justice, and murder liberty at the alter.

My associates have so clearly shown from the evidence that in fact only four men participated in the attack on the train that I need scarcely add a word to strengthen this part of the defense. The third man who cut the bell rope I am satisfied was the brakeman. Where is he? Why has not the state, backed as it is in this prosecution by the railroad companies, presented him here, or accounted for his absence? He is singularly absent. He was an important witness, as he must have been quite a factor in the transaction. No higher evidence of the desperation and vindictiveness of this prosecution was furnished during this trial than the wanton, cruel and unmanly attack made upon Mr. Brosius. His testimony was pointed. It shows, indisputably and irrefutably, that but two men entered the car. If so the state's theory of the homicide is blasted. Therefore, counsel for the prosecution have sought to destroy the good name and reputation of this young man. How heartless the assault made upon him! He is your fellow countyman—an ornament to the bar and the community. No cloud of dishonor has ever fallen across his pathway.

But for personal ambition, a triumph in this case, counsel, who have known him so long—how pure and manly he is—would relentlessly strike him down, not only before his own people, but before his wife and little ones. Shame, unspeakable shame, on such methods, and such an unchivalrous spirit. Let your verdict be his vindication.

THE ALIBI.

Gentlemen of the jury, the defense might safely have rested its cause where the state left it. But the prisoner had nothing to conceal, pertinent to this issue. It was his wish to take the stand, and lay before you his whole history bearing upon this investigation. Is there either internal or external improbability in his story? When he broke from "the gang" in Kentucky, before their return to Missouri, where and to whom could he more safely and more reasonably and more naturally turn than to his sister's home in Texas? The world was in arms against him. She lived in a remote frontier settlement, where perhaps he might find shelter from the huntsman's pack.

Counsel for the state fancied they had put the defendant in a cul-de-sac when he could not tell all the places and points of his travel to and through Texas

with the same detail, as to hotels, towns and railroads,
when traveling through the south at one time with his
wife and child.   Why is it, they ask, he can not give
the names of houses, etc., in his tour through Texas?
Frank James' ways and methods, Mr. Wallace, were
too deep and strategic for your ken, else you and your
jackal pack would have scented the game, and secured
the prize money before he disappointed them by surrendering to the governor.

The situation and tactics of Frank James, while
traveling with his wife and child, in a densely popu-
lated country, was necessarily, or naturally enough,
quite different from traveling to and through Texas.
What was consummate tact in the one case would have
been mortal stupidity in the other.   In the Atlantic
States he and his wife were utter strangers.   The very
manner of his open travel, with wife and child, at-
tracted no attention.   But in Texas he was alone.   Its
towns and thoroughfares are peopled with Missourians
—with men who marched and camped with him during
the war.   Traveling alone he had no occasion to go to
hotels.   At Denison he trusted alone to a single friend.
From there to his sister's he road, "a solitary horseman."   He asked nobody's name, as he would not
provoke inquiry as to his own.   At his sister's house
he remained in absolute seclusion, for the very obvious
reason, that had he exposed himself to strangers and
"cowboys," it would have excited inquiry as to who he
was, and what he did there.   When he rode out for
exercise he was a "ranger."   When he went to Denison to meet his friend, to hear from his wife, he rode

through the Indian Territory, and accepted the hospitality of the no-talking Indian.

But why don't you give up the name of the friend at Denison, inquire the state's counsel. I'll tell you frankly: It is because Frank James, unlike your pet, Dick Liddil, never betrays a friend or foe. Situated as Frank James was, with the royal posse comitatus of a state after him, with a swarm of detectives and spies scenting his footsteps like sleuth-hounds, stimulated to assassination by large rewards, it was perilous for any citizen to give this hunted man shelter, bread, or to be even the medium of a word of love from his far-away wife. Whatever the world may think of Frank James he is made of that stuff, before he would expose to public obloquy, without his consent, the name of the man who thus succored him, he would march to the dead-fall on the scaffold as calm and intrepid as did the grand marshal of Saxony to his untimely grave.

We had in the progress of this trial a striking illustration of the inviolability of the laws of hospitality and personal confidence. Frank O'Neill, the accomplished correspondent of the Missouri Republican, when asked on the witness stand to give the name of the third person present at the interview had by him with Frank James, just prior to his formal surrender to the Governor, declined to answer, for the reason that to do so would be a breach of confidence, and unnecessarily subject to criticism a friend. It was manly and brave in him to stand firm and keep faith. And the court showed how sacred is the regard for that unwritten law

of friendship, in that he would not enforce a disclos-
ure even in a judicial investigation.

What was a virtue in O'Neill, ought not to be an
incriminating act on the part of Frank James. I honor
the man who would die for a friend rather than the
wretch who would betray even an enemy.

If Frank James was not in Texas, as he testified,
Palmer and wife are perjurers. Had their testimony
been fabricated, Palmer would have had himself a
home all the time James was there ; and Mrs. Palmer
would have had him there on the identical day of the
Winston robbery. But she told her story, let it bear as
it might. Is Mrs. Palmer unworthy of belief because
she is a sister? Is it the unwritten law of a Christian
land that where blood runs thick and sisterly love is
quick, perjury knots and breeds? You, gentlemen of
the jury, beheld her on the witness stand. You looked
into her calm, sweet face, all over which God has
written innocence, purity and truth. Will you brook
its persuasive eloquence and stamp it with perjury, that
Dick Liddil and the hangman may chuckle in their
triumph?

Nor is that all. If that smirking scoundrel, with
a heart all dead to pity, festering with the canker
of multiplied crimes, is to be believed, Nickolson,
John Samuels, Tom Mimms, and old Mrs. Samuels
have each, separately, sworn falsely and corruptly.
But who impeaches them? Public fame speaks here
through no witness against their reputation for truth.
No breach was made in the consistency or reasonable-

ness of their testimony by either a rigid, skillful, or bullying cross-examination.

Mrs. Samuels, it is true, is the prisoner's mother. I know how the unfeeling world and a censorious, sensational press have chided her—even making her the subject of ribald jest. But whatever else she may be to the world, she is to this prisoner a mother. Whatever he may be to the jaundiced public eye, to her he is a son—her boy "Buck." O! How much of divinity and consecration are wrapped up in those two words—mother, child! How the one stirs while it chastens our youth; while the other quickens the pulse and gladdens the heart of old age.

It has been whispered about this temple of justice, and into too-willing ears, that this old mother is unworthy of belief, and ought to have staid at home. The icy heart often tells the mother to let her child go; but the instinct of a mother's heart knows no policy, it employs no strategem and deploys no vidette. Like the intrepid Douglass, who carried with him on the Crusades the heart of Robert Bruce, and flung it into the midst of the foe, where carnage and death rioted, in order to inspire his soldiers to its rescue, the mother will follow her heart—her child—wherever perils most beset him.

Who will banish her from this court room? Who shall set bounds to her devotion, measure, estimate it, or reach down to its fathomless depths, grasp and bind its operations? Rather go tell the earth to cease its revolutions; the sun to cease to warm; and the sea be still.

As "day unto day uttereth speech, and night show-
eth knowledge thereof," this old mother Samuels,
never lifts up in prayer, or moves in her daily round of
domestic duty, her right arm that its missing hand does
not remind her of persecution and suffering endured
because she was a mother. And if, as often as her
children have looked upon that handless arm, they have
felt the beatings of the tiger's heart within them, at
thought of the mercenary vandals who, to slake their
thirst for gold and feed their ravenous maws on prize
money, threw hand grenades into a mother's home,
tearing muscle from muscle and bone from bone, and
murdering her innocent helpless child, is it too much,
in human nature, to say the world ought to forgive them
much!

If Frank James was in the country, at the time of
the robbery and homicide in question, she knew it, as
did her family. They swear he was not; and the mother
was told by Liddil that Frank had gone south. Before
they were placed under the necessity of swearing otherwise, under the compact to destroy the defendant to
save their own necks, Dick Liddil, Mrs. Bolton and
the Ford boys, over and over again, declared that
Frank was not in that raid. Will you believe them then
or now? Dick Liddil told Frank Tutt, Crowder,
Chiles and General Shelby that Frank James was not
here. He then had no conceivable motive to deceive
these men, whereas he now has every motive and incentive that a bad, desperate, cowardly man could have,
to place Frank in the robbery.

DICK LIDDIL.

From photo taken in 1882.

JESSE W. JAMES.

From photograph taken in 1871.

JESSE W. JAMES.

"I hereby certify that the above is the only late photo-
graph of my deceased husband, taken before death." Mrs.
Jesse W. James. [From photo loaned by Howard Huselton,
Kansas City.]

MRS. ZERELDA SAMUELS.

Mother of Frank and Jesse James. [From photograph taken at the Samuels home near Kearney, Missouri, October, 1897, by Howard Huselton, of Kansas City, Missouri.]

The old cabin in which Frank and Jesse James were born. Note the rifle port holes at end near the roof. [From photograph by Howard Huselton, Kansas City.]

Every instinct of humanity, every sentiment of chivalry and justice and mercy plead with you to disbelieve that cringing, crawling recreant, Dick Liddil. A man who lies without oath will lie under oath.

Gentlemen of the jury, exhausted, physically, as I am, in the stifling atmosphere of this crowded room, and weary, to impatience, as you must be, I can not leave this case without saying to you, and to the country, that I had still another incentive in accepting the defense of this man. It was one sentence in the letter asking for my services. Its sentiment touched and entered my soul. It declared that the prisoner had but one object, one hope, which was to devote the remnant of his days to the state as a good citizen, and to earn for his wife and child an honest livelihood.

I had heard of the little woman, spotless as the falling snow, whose youth, like the season it typifies, was "one crowded garland of rich and fragrant blossoms, refreshing every eye with present beauty and filling every heart with promised benefits;" who, spurning the smiles of the world, gave to "the bold rider" her virgin heart, to cleave to him in shadow as in sunshine, in sorrow as in joy. And as I have witnessed how loyally she has kept her vow, how like a good angel she has attended him at rest or wandering, how closer she has drawn the cords of affection about him as the pelting storms of vengeance and hate have pitilessly beaten about the iron doors and grated windows of his prison, I have felt that if I could utter a word that might give to this noble woman the man, unfettered, to whom she so clings, it were an honor more to be coveted than offices and the praises of men.

Before taking my seat, gentlemen, allow me to speak a word of warning and courage. I am mindful of how potential is that which we call public sentiment. Sometimes it is healthful and curative in the body politic. Then again it is morbid and vicious. Sometimes it is honest, just and brave. And then, too often, it is hollow, rotten, ignorant and cowardly. You will be told, doubtless, by the ambitious, volunteer counsel who is to close this case for the state (Mr. Wallace) ostensibly, but who is in quest of fame and popular applause, that the eyes of the country are on you; that the good name of Missouri demands this man's life. For one I am glad of the opportunity to say that I am sick unto disgust over the ceaseless maudlin twaddle about "poor old Missouri." It is the slogan of an unprincipled partisan press. It is the cant of hypocrites and the refrain of demagogues.

I yield to no man in my attachment to Missouri. My people, of my blood, stood by its cradle when it it was born. With rifle they fought back the savage, trampeled down the wild brier and bull knettles, and blazed out the paths that have led to her present splendid civilization. On her generous bosom I was cradled. Her honor and glory are as dear to me as the memory of the sainted father and mother who sleep beneath her sod. I am proud of the state, her peacefulness, her laws, her patriotism. The most lawless and recreant men in the state are the miserable politicians and editors who malign and slander her good name. I do not think it necessary, in order to appease them, or the land agents, or the long haired men and short haired women, who imagine themselves the satellites of higher civilization, to attend the star of empire in its westward flight, that one day out of every seven should be set aside by executive proclamation for the hanging of an old Missourian.

To convict this man because some town politician or public clamor demands it, would not only be cowardice, but judicial murder. The men who cry out for the life of the so-called outlaw, no matter what the proof or the law, are themselves outlaws and demons. No, gentlemen, this court house is the temple of justice. The voice of clamor, the breath of prejudice, must not enter here. You are sworn sentinels on guard at its portals. Do your duty. Stand, and stand forever on your oaths. Remember that after all the true heroes of this world are its moral heroes. The Aztec who can tear out his heart and fling it while still palpitating as an offering to his God, is simply an untaught barbarian. The soldier who can march up to the cannon's mouth, the fireman who can mount his ladder wreathed in flames and go to the rescue of human life, exhibit splendid courage. But often this is mere physical courage. The man who can die for truth, or face the frowning, mad, unappeasible multitude, and stand immovable for the right, is grander and braver than all others.

To uphold the law, and bring offenders to justice, is a most important duty of citizenship. That the higher tribute to the law is when court and jury can rise su-

perior to popular outcry, above the foul air of prejudice and passion, standing calm and serene on the
mountain heights of justice and mercy, declare that
here, in this land, dedicated forever to law and human
freedom, no man shall be convicted on rumor or suspicion, but only on the evidence of lawful witnesses
and according to the law of the land.

Thus spoke our Anglo-Saxon ancestry six hundred
years ago at Runnymede, when the Magna Carta itself
was born.

Freemen of Daviess county, let it not be said of
your verdict that law and personal freedom have, in
their march across the centuries, lost one atom of their
vigor, or virtue, by being transplanted in American
soil. Be brave and manly. If you err, let it be on the
side of mercy. It is Godlike to be merciful; it is hellish
to be revengeful. "I will have mercy and not sacrifice,"
said the Saviour when on earth. Let your verdict be a
loyal response to the evidence and the spirit of the law;
and as true manhood ever wins tribute, when the passion of the day is past, and reason has asserted her do-
minion, you will be honored and crowned.

CLOSING SPEECH FOR THE STATE BY HON. WM. H. WALLACE.

May it please the Court, and you Gentlemen of the Jury.

Appearing in this case as one of the prosecuting attorneys of our state, but in a county foreign to my own, I will not assume to use so holy a word as *duty*, but simply say that it now becomes my *province*, to sum up the evidence for the prosecution, and to the best of my ability explain to you the law as declared by the court. You will be kind enough to accept at my hands the sincere thanks of the people of this great commonwealth for the respectful attention you have given to all the details of so long a trial, and the fortitude with which you have borne the tremendous strain upon your patience and your strength. Our friends upon the other side have consumed over twelve hours in addressing you in behalf of their client; of which no complaint is made—it is right they should. The State has occupied about six hours, and I can only assure you that I will be as brief in the conclusion as the vast task committed to my charge will permit.

It seems to have become the fashion in this cause for gentlemen to explain or apologize for their connection therewith, and some have gone so far as to deal in personal history, and to tell you beneath what banner they drew the shining blade in the unfortunate

13

"war between the states;" and to dwell at length upon their attitude and feelings toward the defendant then
and now.   Raised in a homely way, gentlemen, I am
not much of a hand at explanations and apologies, and
do not feel, in fact, that justice is asking any from me.
All I have to say is, that I am here first, by invitation
from your excellent prosecutor, Mr. Hamilton; and
second, because I feel that an obligation exists between
me and the law-abiding people of my county, that having from the very beginning borne an humble part in
assisting to rid the fair state of the worst band of outlaws that ever cursed a commonwealth, I should remain
true to my course to the end.   As for the war I am
truly thankful that I was too young to have received a
scar either in body—or what is worse and more lasting
—in mind.   I can only say, gentlemen, that with the
wondering eyes of a boy, just in his "teens," I saw
enough to know and appreciate the motive of the counsel for the defendant in going outside of the law and
the evidence to mention the "swords," and "flags,"
and "animosities" "of a cruel war" in a court of justice—enough to know at least the tremendous sympathies and prejudices they would awaken in your
breasts by bringing its horrid scenes afresh to your
memories.   I can only say, that on the border of our
state, where the red lightning of murder played the
fiercest along the western sky and the dogs of war were
turned loose on defenseless women and children, I saw
it all; when torch, and fire, and sword and rapine, and
pillage, and plunder, and robbery, and murder, and
assassination were abroad in the land; when sabred

horsemen shot across the prairies and devouring flames leaped from farm to farm and house to house, until both earth and sky seemed ablaze with living horrors— I saw it all; and like a vast panorama it rolls before me as I speak. I can only say, to quit a subject improperly interjected into this case, that when almost the last vestige of property was swept from our house, a gentleman who wore the same epaulets that Col. Philips wore and fought beneath Col. Philip's "flag" issued a cruel order by which we were denied even the poor privilege of dwelling as paupers under the old family roof ; and with not enough of substance to provide against the storms and hunger of coming winter we turned our backs upon as fair a land as ever greeted the rising sun, to wander as outcasts and refugees in the world—and from that day to this unceasing labor has been my master, and ease, as a friend, buried in my youth. But this I know was the stern fate of war; and if there is to-day in this heart of mine the slightest feeling of hate or prejudice for any man, for anything that then occurred, as God is my judge I do not know it. And I sincerely trust, gentlemen, that wherever you may have been in that dark hour, or whatever may have been your experience, your regard for your oaths will now be such that all attempts to kindle in *your* hearts the hates of other days, will be hurled back by you as insults to your honor, your intelligence, and your conscience. As for me I am truly thankful for such an experience. I look up and thank my God that he led me through fire and flood, adversity and prosperity; for while it may not have made me a better man, it has certainly cast about

me a rough armor, panoplied with which I care but
little for the threats, and shafts, and storms of life. But
enough of an issue buried twenty years ago and whose
skeleton never should have been rattled in a court of
justice.

Some of the attorneys for the defense are loud
and long in their complaints that your worthy prosecutor is assisted in this case. Compare, I pray you,
gentlemen, the number and attainments of the counsel
on either side, and see whether or not there is just
cause for such complaint. Compare the plain men
appearing for the state with the shining orators pleading the defendant's cause. And here you may catch
at the outset a glimpse of their client's innocence, according to his own estimate. Innocence has a voice
more tender and eloquent than that of any earthly
orator, and yet he was unwilling that this voice should
come to your ears through attorneys in ordinary num-
bers and of ordinary ability. He first employs Mr.
Rush, one of the most industrious and accomplished
lawyers at your bar, that all matters of local import—
such as the selection of the jury from the panel, the
suggestion of such matters as would appeal to their
sympathies, and so on—might be skillfully attended to.
He then goes to St. Louis in his search and employs
Mr. Glover, a young man whose opportunities have
been such that he by himself should have been more
than a match for your humble speaker, whose presence
here has been so much criticised and bemoaned; a
young man who has been reared in the very center of
learning and refinement, in the midst of splendid

libraries, and surrounded from childhood up by all the educational facilities that fond and prosperous parents in a great city could afford; a young man whose attainments compare with mine as the star-decker firmament compares with a barren, uncultivated waste lying on the earth beneath. Still the defendant is not satisfied, and he employs General Garner, the grim old lion whose deep voice has been heard reverberating in all the courts up and down the Missouri Valley for thirty years or more, and beneath whose thunders I trembled when he turned upon me, for it is said he has been accustomed for a long time past to eat a young lawyer raw for breakfast whenever his appetite called for so delicate a dish. Still he is not content, and he crosses the river and comes to Independence, and my friend, James H. Slover, a lawyer of large experience, somewhat young in appearance but Nestor-like, brave in battle, cool in judgment, and wise in counsel, is added to his list.

Immaculate innocence still cries out for advocates, and John F. Philips is engaged; a man whose bell-tones have reverberated in the halls of the national congress, and whose reputation as both a civil and criminal lawyer extends throughout the west; a man who—to use Robert Emmet's figure—if all the innocent blood he has caused to go unavenged were collected in some vast reservoir, his lordship might swim in it. Still the defendant wants one more, and Charles P. Johnson, an ex-lieutenant-governor of the state, whose fame as a criminal lawyer is bounded only by the Mississippi on the east and the Rockies on the

west, is besought to come and plead his cause. He
comes, as if looking to higher fields, to make the shining final effort of his life, and show all the world how
with skillful hand he could snatch the greatest of all
criminals as "a brand from the burning;" comes as if
for four short hours to exert his magic power in your
court, and then—laughing at the foolish jury he left
behind, return and enter the gates of his adopted city
like a triumphant Achilles with the poor body of blind
justice, Hector-like, bound by the cords of his eloquence, and dead and dangling at his chariot wheels.
Such, gentlemen, are the giants whom the prisoner
has called forth to fight his battle with the law. I
describe them one by one, that you may know and
understand the tremendous forces that are about you,
least unwittingly you be borne from the path of duty in
the whirlwind of their eloquence and power. All
during the trial you watched them as they grasped at
straws, or placed their mighty forms in line in the vain
attempt to stay back the resistless tide of evidence, as
it came pouring in for the state. You gentlemen, are
the twelve pillars upon whose shoulders, for the present at least, Missouri's temple of justice is made to
rest, and you could not help but notice how these men
in the final argument, like blind Samsons groping in
the dark, reached out to find you, threw their brawny
arms about you, and to secure a firmer hold, thrust
their fingers into every niche and scar left upon you by
the bullets of "a cruel war." Stand firm in your
places as they press against you, lest you and they, the
fair name of our state, and all that is nearest and dear-

est to her people, perish in the ruin that ensues! So much for the attorneys.

Who are the parties to be considered in this most important trial ? To come to an impartial and intelligent verdict it is well to bear them all in memory. The first one that presents himself to an unprejudiced mind is Frank McMillan, but it has been so long since you have heard his name that I almost feel like apologizing for its mention. But it can do no harm—nor good. For two years has his voice been hushed in death ; and even if I so desired, I could not now catch up the faintest echo of his dying shriek and sound it in your ears, pleading for pity from your hearts, or justice at your hands. He was a poor, innocent, insignificant stone mason, who, in the summer of 1881, with the pale blood oozing from his brain, was laid away to rest; and for days have the gifted attorneys of his "gallant" slayer tread above his ashes, with scarcely a whisper of his fameless name. The evidence shows that he, too, had a wife, plain, humble woman, no doubt, dependent upon his daily toil for the food she ate and the raiment she wore. Even now, while I speak with tattered garments and streaming eyes she may sit upon his tomb, trying to fathom that mysterious Providence by which her stay in life lies slumbering in the grave, whilst his murderer sits at his trial "the observed of all observers"—"the most remarkable man of the age." Let her sit there, gentlemen. We have not brought her here as is ofttimes done, in piteous disconsolate widowhood, to crave your sympathy. Let her sit there. Though her heart be as lonely as the grave-yard about her, and her hands as chilly as the rough, rock slab upon which she sits, we do not ask even the poor privilege of bringing her here, to warm for one moment the tips of her fingers at the glow of your hearts.

The second and most prominent party in the case is the defendant himself. His attorneys, as if expecting a response in your breasts, have showered upon him the tenderest touches of pathos, and bestowed the highest encomiums on his life and character—one of them, Mr. Rush, boldly pronouncing him "one of the most remarkable men of the age." For myself, I have simply to say that I neither love, hate, pity, nor admire him. He is simply to be regarded as a full matured man of forty, to whom God has given more than ordinary intelligence, but who has set at naught the laws of his country, willfully and deliberately filled his pockets with the spoils of robbery, and bathed his hands in human blood. "One of the most remarkable men of the age!" In the name of all the Gods who sit on Mount Olympus, in a breath, *remarkable* for what?—charity? benevolence? self-abnegation? profound learning? business enterprise? inventive genius? patriotism? statesmanship? piety—what? I may not answer the question without departing from the record, and I leave it where it was suggested—in the distorted fancy of hard pressed attorneys. For fifteen years, they tell us, he has skillfully evaded the officers, the detectives, the lightning of the telegraph, and all the machinery of modern government; and now that at last he has been overcome, vengeance should be melted into pity, and jurors should bend the knee and acquit him, regardless of law or evidence.

Fifteen years for evasion, gentlemen, means fifteen years for deliberation, reflection, repentance, departure to far-off climes, and that he is placed in his present predicament he has no one to blame but himself. According to the witness O'Neill, he considered long and well, whether it was safest to brave the dangers that beset him in the black night of barbarism, or, taking his chances, with one leap place himself in the full day and blaze of civilization; and if in the undertaking he perishes, as the night-bug perishes when it darts into the glare of the electric light, he has nobody to blame but himself. If after all these years spent without the walls, he suddenly resolves, as if he had done nothing, to pass in and enjoy the sweets of the Eden of civilized life, and the sentry angel who guards the entrance, seeing his garments dyed with blood, strikes him down with the flaming sword of justice as he passes, he has nobody to blame but himself.

A third party, who, though not a party to the record, is touchingly presented to your view by opposing counsel, is the defendant's wife. And while I may run contrary to the wishes of my associates and to the will of the good people of Daviess county—even should I run the risk of losing the case by so doing—I want to say, that I have in this prosecutor's heart of mine the profoundest sympathy for the defendant's wife. Accustomed all the year around to scenes like this, I have never yet seen the time, when a woman similarly situated did not have the tenderest pity of

which I was capable.   I am glad she is here, standing by
her husband in his trial, and I am as willing you should
extend to her your sympathies, as any attorney in the
case.   When the welcome day shall come and I shall
cease to be a public prosecutor, I shall at least have
learned, what I might never have learned, in purer
spheres of life—and that is, that the truest, grandest,
most unchanging thing beneath the stars, is a woman's
love.   Let a man once reign as king in the heart of a
true woman, and she is blind to all his faults, or all his
crimes.   He may pillage, plunder, burn, rob; he may
shed blood until he sits at his trial as a red-plumed
murderer, and justice, and all the world look on and
condemn, but she sees it not, and will ask to sit by him
—and, as I have often known them to, plead with the
jailer to go with him to his cell, to share his bread and
water, and greet as sweetest music the screeching of
his prison doors.   Yes, true to the instincts of a
woman's heart, even Frank James's wife clings to him,
and I am glad she does.   There is one reflection, however, gentlemen, which in these cases, always comes
home to a sworn officer, and I trust has already come
home to you, as sworn jurors, in the discharge of public duty.   I can better illustrate it than describe it.
Husband and wife are gathering flowers on the brink
of an awful precipice.   The husband unmindful of the
law of gravity, carelessly, to complete the comparison
I will say, deliberately, steps beyond the line of safety,
and in an instant is hurling downward.   The wife may
wring her hands and call on nature to stay her law,
she may send after him the warmest, most loving tears,

but they will never catch him ; nature with her law goes
right on, and he is dashed in pieces on the rocks beneath. A little child, just learning to control its body,
is crawling about the floor; it gets hold of a dose of
poison, secreted for another purpose, and swallows it;
in a few moments it is in the throes of death. Loving
father does what he can to save it; devoted sister tries
to arouse it with tenderest kisses on its cheeks; heart
stricken mother implores a God of mercy to change his
law making poison poisonous, and save her child—but
all to no avail; the law of nature goes right on, and
the infant is made a corpse. As in the physical world
God has set in motion certain unchanging laws which
have marched on without exception since the birth of
time, so, and for greater reason, has he promulgated
certain great laws in the moral world, which throughout the ages are to remain eternal, immutable, inviola-
ble. One of these laws, as if to show its immutability,
he wrote with his own finger in enduring marble, in the
words, "Thou shalt not kill," and elsewhere added the
penalty to be inflicted by human agency, "He that
sheddeth man's blood, by man shall his blood be shed."
A legislature representing a Christian civilization has
taken that law and its penalty and embodied it in the
statutes of the state of Missouri, and the court has
declared it to you in these instructions. Frank James,
as will appear when we come to the evidence, has willfully and deliberately broken that law—the law of both
God and man ; and while you may justly pity wife and
child, immutable law should go right on. You can
not on your sacred oaths do otherwise than inflict the

penalty he so richly deserves. So much for the parties
in the case.

Hours are spent, gentlemen, in telling you this is
a railroad prosecution. This, of course, is a direct
appeal to the supposed prejudice of a jury of farmers
against railroad corporations. So far as I am concerned I care nothing about the Rock Island Railroad
Company, and represent it in no way whatever. If I
have a relative or special friend on earth that ever had
an interest in a railroad, or ever saw a railroad bond I
do not know it. I paid my way over this road to your
country, and expect to do the same on my return. A
great ado is made about witnesses having passes. I
proclaim publicly more than was proven—that I requested, obtained, and handed passes to witnesses. A
railroad that would refuse to do as much to obtain witnesses from other states who would not advance their
own expenses, after its conductor had been murdered
at his post and the lives of passengers endangered,
ought to have its charter revoked and its track torn up
by an indignant people. But I say to you that I have
nothing to do with any railroad in this case. If the
Rock Island Railroad had bridged its way across some
vast chasm in your county, deeper than an Ashtabula,
and Frank James had stolen up and burned that bridge,
and all the trains on all its lines, without the loss of
life, had been hurled head-long therein, until the yawn-
ing gulch was filled with hissing engines and crackling
timbers, the railroad might look after its property. I
would not be here to assist. Yes, if all the papers,
records and bonds of all the railroads in the union were

collected here in some great store-house, and, like the
benighted "crank" who burned one of the greatest
temples of antiquity in order to hand his name down
the centuries, Frank James, with lighted torch, should
come hither in the midnight and fire the mighty structure, until the red flames reached through the clouds
and on toward the stars—that would be a stupendous
crime but the railroad might look after their property;
I should not stir one foot out of my county as a volunteer in their behalf. Oh, no, gentlemen of the jury, this
is not a prosecution for the protection of railroad property, and you know it. This is another skillful appeal
to the demon of prejudice, and you know it. With
admirable cunning they would point you to the magnificent cars, take you inside and show you the beautiful
red varnish on the seats and sides, and say, "this is
what this prosecution is meant to protect." But come
with me to the rear end of the "smoker"; behold the
platform and steps and hard by the black soil of free
Missouri, each painted red with the life blood of an
immortal being, every drop of which is more precious
than all the railroads in the word, and let me exclaim to
you, "here is the only issue you are summoned to try."
Did I say *only* issue? No, not the only one. If that
were so, this would be but an ordinary trial for murder.
But precious as is the life of an American citizen, there
is a deeper, grander issue here than that. The suprem-
acy of the laws of Missouri and the strength and
dignity of her courts are at stake. Not only the life
of a human being, but the very life of the law itself is
put in issue in the eyes of the world. For fifteen

years, it is boasted, has Frank James successfully contended with the officers, the exponents of the law; and
now with bold and uplifted front he comes of his own
accord into a court of justice, throws down the gauntlet,
and proposes to grapple with the law itself; and the
question you are to decide is—*which is the stronger in
Missouri, the arm of the bandit or the arm of the
law.*

Let us now look at the instructions, and then at
the evidence. The assertion is ventured that no one of
you has ever attended a trial in one of our courts, in
which the counsel for the defense said so little about
the instructions. They embody the "law" referred to
in the solemn oath you took at the beginning of your
labors. They are the sign-boards set up along the highway of truth to guide you to a righteous verdict. The
first instruction on behalf of the state reads as follows:

"*First.* If the jury believe from the evidence
that the defendant Frank James, in the month of July,
1881, at the county of Daviess, in the state of Missouri,
willfully, deliberately, premeditatedly and of his malice aforethought, shot and killed Frank McMillan, or
if the jury find that any other person then and there
willfully, deliberately, premeditatedly, and of malice
aforethought shot and killed said Frank McMillan, and
that the defendant Frank James was present, then and
there willfully, deliberately, premeditatedly, and of his
malice aforethought aiding, abetting, or counseling
such other person in so shooting and killing Frank Mc-
Millan—then the jury ought to find the defendant guilty
of murder in the first degree."

You will see that this instruction is drawn in the
alternative. If Frank James, with his own hand, in

the manner described, shot and killed McMillan, he is
guilty; or if "any other person" in the manner described shot and killed McMillan, and Frank James
was "present, aiding, abetting, or counseling" such
other so to shoot and kill, then he is equally guilty.
and right here on this instruction there has been a good
deal of technical gimlet-boring, with a small gimlet, by
the defense, in the vain effort to effect some small ap-
erture through which the jury may creep, and let the
defendant out of his predicament. It is contended that
this is a trial for murder, not for robbery, and that in-
asmuch as no eye-witness comes and swears that the
defendant was the particular robber who fired the fatal
shot—even granting he was there—he ought to be acquitted. This is what lawyers call a "glittering tech-
nicality;" a plain, honest man would say the glittering
dagger with which the heart of justice is too often
stabbed in her own courts. Over against this hair-
splitting reasoning let us set a very simple proposition.
Let us stop up these gimlet-holes with the kind of stuff
common sense is made of. Five men rob a train; all
five of them have navy pistols strapped to their persons,
loaded and charged with powder and ball; a man is
killed in that robbery, and the human mind exclaims
instinctively—they are guilty, every last single one
of them. They came prepared to kill. They did kill.
It is murder. By the evidence, in a distant state the
horrible crime was concocted; bent on plunder and
death, they traveled a thousand miles to the scene of
action; each man is loaded with extra rounds of cartridges, and each knows that his companions are simi-

larly equipped; they appear upon the horrid scene
brandishing in their hands the implements of death,
rubbed and burnished till they glisten in the lamp-light;
they shoot at forehead or heart of victim with the unerr-
ing aim of an Indian at a tossed-up coin, and I will tell
you, gentlemen—not to recur to this point again—it was
murder in them all, damned and foul, and you can make
nothing else out of it.

Now you notice this first instruction says if defendant *"willfully, deliberately, premeditatedly,* and of his
malice aforethought shot,'' etc. By these terms you
are to understand that under our law, in all cases where
a deadly weapon—such as a pistol or bowie-knife—is
the means of death, and the killing is not connected
with the commission of some other crime, there are
four elements necessary to constitute murder in the
first degree: first, willfulness; second, deliberation;
third, premeditation; fourth, malice, or malice aforethought. As our law proceeds on that known maxim
of moral philosophy that no act has in itself any moral
quality, but depends entirely upon the mind, or absence
of mind, of the actor, as to whether it is to be considered
with or without moral quality, these terms all apply to
the mind or mental condition of the slayer at the time
the act of killing is committed. *Willfulness* does not
mean *stubborness, doggedness, unreasonableness,* as we
understand it in common parlance. It means that the
killing must come from intention, and not from accident; that there is an intelligence back of the act pur-
posing and intending its commission; to be explicit,
that an intention exists in the brain of the man to do

that which his hands are executing. *Deliberation* is a
wider and more abstruse term than any of the others.
In the language of one of our later decisions—copied
by the court in this case— it means "in a cool state of
the blood; that is, not in sudden passion caused by a
lawful provocation, or some just cause of provocation."
As I take it, deliberation comes from the mental *status*
in which the slayer considers and looks upon the deed
at the time of its commission, and we are to view him
in the light of all the attending circumstances. If at
the time he does the deed his faculties are in their
normal condition, and performing in proper degree their
usual functions (or are distorted alone through his own
fault at the time), and no cause extraneous to himself
destroys the equilibrium, and he weighs and considers
what he is doing, if only for a moment—deliberation
exists, and the killing is murder in the first degree. If,
on the other hand, causes extraneous to himself are at
work, such as a slight blow given to the person or
words used so vile and insulting as to touch to the quick
his pride of feeling, and thereupon that passion common to us all, rages so like a storm in his breast that
the voice of reason crying, "peace, be still," is un-
heeded, and at the instant he kills his adversary, then
the law in its humanity excuses, though it does not
justifiy, and the homicide, in Missouri, is murder in
the second degree, or manslaughter, as the provocation
consisted in words or slight violence. But it is useless
to attempt further explanation of this term, as the
court has prevented any argument as to the existence

14

of deliberation, by the words "and the court instructs
you that in this case there is no evidence tending to show
the existence of any such passion or provocation." It
is easy to understand what is meant by *"premeditation."* Its import is in precise accord with its Latin
derivation, meaning "thought of before." It is the
conclusion of the mind to do the act, antedating the act
(as of course it must) for any length of time, " however short." When the words "I'll kill him" have
been uttered in the mind, *premeditation* exists; and it
makes no difference whether the man is at the time in
cool blood or in passion caused by a just provocation.
Here you are able to distinguish a wide difference between *premeditation* and *deliberation*; the former may
exist in both states—"cool blood" and the "passion"
described; the latter only in a cool state of the blood,
unless, perchance, a man's blood "boils" from his own
viciousness, when the law makes no excuse for him
whatever.

Malice, from *malum*, meaning "badness" in the
abstract, is here used to denote badness in the concrete,
namely, a state of badness, in reference to human law,
existing in the mind of a being responsible to that law.
It does not mean *spite*, or *ill-will*, or *hatred* to any
one as we usually understand it, but refers to a state of
mind—a state of mind, as indicated, out of harmony
with good government and the laws of the land; such a
state of mind as a man is in when he intentionally does
what he knows to be wrong. That I have explained
these terms correctly you can see from the reading of

the second instruction, which is as follows—the court using adverbs where I have used the nouns.

"*Second.* The term "willfully," as used in these instructions means *intentionally*—that is, not accidentally.

"*Deliberately* means done in a cool state of blood, not in sudden passion engendered by a lawful or some just cause of provocation; and the court instructs you that in this case there is no evidence tending to show the existence of any such passion or provocation.

"*Premeditatedly* means thought of beforehand any length of time, however short.

"*Malice* does not mean mere spite or ill-will as understood in ordinary language, but it is here used to denote a condition of mind evidenced by the intentional doing of a wrongful act liable to endanger human life. It signifies such a state of mind or disposition as shows a heart regardless of social duty and fatally bent on mischief.

"*Malice aforethought* means malice with premeditation, as before defined."

The third instruction is given on the second or "robbery" count in the indictment, and is as follows:

"*Third.* If the jury believe from the evidence that defendant Frank James, with Wood Hite and Clarence Hite, or with any of them, and others, at the county of Daviess, in the state of Missouri, in the month of July, 1881, made an assault upon one Charles Murray, and any money of any value then in the custody or under the care or control of said Murray, by force and violence to the person of said Charles Murray, or by putting him, the said Charles Murray, in fear of some immediate injury to his person, did rob, steal and carry away; and if the jury also believe from the evidence that defendant Frank James, in the perpetration of such robbery, with malice aforethought, as

before defined, willfully shot and killed Frank McMillan—then the jury ought to find the defendant guilty
of murder in the first degree."

This instruction needs but little explanation. It is
the instruction in the light of which you are to view the
whole evidence—as to robbery, killing, and all that
transpired. You will perceive that by this you need
not find the existence of either deliberation or premeditation. It is given in accordance with the law as
it now stands in Missouri—that a homicide committed
in the perpetration of a robbery is not necessarily murder
in the first degree. If the killing is purely an accident,
that is, is no part of the plan of the robbery, and not
what the robbers should have known might be a
natural result from the manner of their crime, then it is
still murder, but not murder of the first degree. If,
however, under this instruction, you simply find that
the killing was done in the perpetration of a robbery,
and willfully in malice, then you are bound to say in
your verdict—it was murder in the first degree; and to
my way of thinking, common sense presumes in a robbery like *this* that the perpetrators act willfully and in
malice as to the whole transaction, A train robber,
armed to the teeth, and knowing that death so often
comes as a natural result from this class of crime,
ought to be hung if his pistol explodes in its scabbard
from spontaneous combustion, and kills an innocent
passenger.

The fourth instruction reads as follows:

"*Fourth.* If you find from the evidence that the
defendant, Frank James, at the county of Daviess,

state of Missouri, in the month of July, 1881, shot and
killed Frank McMillan, and that the act was done
neither with the specific intent on the part of
defendant to kill any particular person, nor in the perpetration of a robbery, yet if you further find that
defendant was then and there recklessly, intentionally,
and with malice firing with a deadly weapon, to-wit, a
pistol, into or through certain cars of a railway train,
containing a number of passengers, and those in
charge thereof, and that while thus firing, said Frank
McMillan, being on said train, was shot and killed by
defendant—then you will find defendant guilty of
murder in the second degree.   Or should you find from
the evidence that at the said time and place, said Mc-
Millan was shot and killed by any person or persons
whomsoever, and that such act was done neither with
specific intent on the part of such person or persons to
kill any particular person, nor in the perpetration of a
robbery, yet if you further find that such person or
persons were then and there, recklessly intentionally,
and with malice, firing with a deadly weapon or
weapons, to-wit, a pistol or pistols, into or through
certain cars of a railway train containing a number of
passengers, and those in charge thereof, and while thus
firing said Frank McMillan being on said train, was
shot and killed by such other or others, and that
defendant was present then and there recklessly, intentionally, and with malice, aiding, abetting, assisting,
and counseling such other or others, so to fire into or
through said cars—then you will find defendant guilty
of murder in the second degree.''

This instruction is given out of the abundance of
the humanity of the law, and of the court declaring it.
There is a class of cases of murder in the second degree in
which the malice in the human heart does not assume any
shape with reference to the specific act of killing.   If I

may so express it, when the poisonous soil of malice does
not shoot forth a specific intent to kill the person slain or
to kill any person at all.   These cases occur when the
slayer is recklessly and intentionally engaged in a
wrongful act and one known to be dangerous to human
life, and death is the result.   Here the intent to do the
wrongful act is taken away from the wrongful act, and
by a law of substitution put over against the killing,
and it is murder in the second degree.   As where an
unnatural mother, desiring to get rid of her child, but
not quite heartless enough to destroy it with her own
hands, leaves it in an orchard, and a kite kills it; or
where the artisan, not caring whether he kills or not,
rolls a stone from his wall into a crowded street, and a
passer-by is slain; or where a man recklessly and
intentionally shoots in a crowd, and death ensues—in
all these cases it is murder in the second degree.   So
in this case should you find the killing of McMillan was
not a part or parcel of the robbery or of the regular
plan; that it was a kind of side play; that the act was
not done with specific intent to kill; that defendant
was recklessly firing down the car to frighten the passengers, not caring whether he killed or not, or was
present comforting or aiding others so to do—then it is
murder in the second degree, and you should so find in
your verdict.

"*Fifth.*   The jury are instructed that by the statutes of this state the defendant is a competent witness
in his own behalf, but the fact that he is a witness, in
his own behalf, may be considered by the jury in determining the credibility of his testimony."

You have heard a great deal about the testimony of an accomplice, about the tremendous motive for such an one to commit perjury in his desire to escape the terrors of the law. What about Frank James's testimony? The court tells you he has a right to testify, but you have a right to consider his situation. Is there any motive here for falsehood? His life is at stake, and he sits in the witness chair with the fearful picture of the gallows constantly before his eyes. If ever a man would swear falsely it is then. "But our client is a knightly, chivalric hero, who fears not the king of terrors," I hear them say. This sounds very well in talk or in yellow-back literature, but it is a known fact among officers, gentlemen, that men of the defendant's class do not differ from the ordinary run of humanity, and when their own time finally comes they are usually as timid as anybody. They may put on a bold exterior at their trial, but the heart within is trembling for its fate like an aspen leaf, and ofttimes, when convicted, and the dread hour arrives, they who have waded without a tremor through rivers of blood, shudder and break completely down ere the first ripple of their own cold Lethe has touched their feet.

"*Sixth.* The jury are further instructed that to the jury exclusively belongs the duty of weighing the evidence and determining the credibility of the witnesses. With that the court has absolutely nothing to do. The degree of credit due to a witness should be determined by his character and conduct, by his manner upon the stand, his relation to the controversy and to the parties—his hopes and his fears, his bias and impartiality, the reasonableness or otherwise of the statements he makes—the strength or weakness of his recollection, viewed in the light of all the other testimony, facts, and circumstances in the case."

This instruction is easily understood. Your attention is now called to these words used in this instruction: "The degree of credit due to a witness should be determined by his character and conduct, by his manner on the stand, his relation to the controversy and the parties." "Relation to the controversy and the parties;" you remember the witnesses as to the defendant's *alibi* — brother-in-law, sister, brother, mother — no others.

"*Seventh*. In considering what the defendant has said after the fatal shooting, and previous to the time of his testifying in this case, and with reference to any material matter in issue, the jury must consider it all together. The defendant is entitled to the benefit of what he said for himself, if true, as the state is to anything he said against himself in any conversation proved by the state. What he said against himself in any conversation the law presumes to be true, because against himself; but what he said for himself the jury are not bound to believe, because said in a conversation proved by the state. They may believe or disbelieve it as is shown to be true or false by all the evidence in the case."

The rule of law contained in this instruction is based on the known selfishness of mankind. If a man who has done wrong can say anything in his own favor he is apt to do it—sometimes true, oftener, if his crime is great, it is false. What he knows against himself he is going to keep, unless the heart is so full and a guilty conscience gnaws with a tooth so sharp that he tells in

spite of himself, and then the law presumes it to be true.
If Frank James, just after the Winston robbery, said to
Jesse James, "Why in the world did you kill that man;
if I had thought there was going to be any blood shed
I would never have gone into the affair," it was testimony manufactured in his own favor. Its absurdity, if
nothing else, shows this. Frank James, who knew
Jesse James better than any living man—Jesse James,
whose victims, shot down in robbery, are sleeping
throughout the Mississippi valley — Frank James
"backs" Jesse James in the commission of a robbery,
and when, as usual, a man is murdered, turns around
and says: "If I had thought there was going to be
any blood shed I never would have gone into the
affair." As I have touched this bit of testimony
somewhat out of my regular order, let us finsh it, lest I
worry you with its repetition when I come to the evidence. It has nothing to do with the legitimate evidence in the case, any way, and has simply been lugged
in here in the vain attempt to contradict Dick Liddil by
the governor of the state. You remember the whole
of Governor Crittenden's testimony was, that just after
Liddil's surrender he talked twice with him at Jefferson
City, once when he came with Commissioner Craig, and
once when he came with Sheriff Timberlake; that in
one of these conversations he said to Liddil, "Why was
that innocent man on duty killed? and that Liddil replied that after the robbery was over he heard Frank
say to Jesse, in Missouri, "Why in the world did you
kill that man? if I had thought there was going to be
any blood shed I would have never gone into the

affair." This is all of the governor's testimony. Liddil denies this, and I honestly think the governor has the matter a little mixed in the multitude of details given him by Liddil. But, admitting it is true, it has absolutely nothing to do with this case. "Why was that innocent man on duty killed?" That referred to conductor Westfall. McMillan was not on duty. The whole thing related to Westfall, killed by Jesse James, and not to McMillan, killed by Frank James, and for which he is now being tried. They do but one thing by the governor, and that is to show, indirectly, but unmistakably, by their own witness, that Frank James was in Missouri in 1881, and participated in the Winston robbery; that Liddil told him so before Jesse was killed or Frank had given himself up, or there was any motive on earth presented for Liddil to tell a falsehood, his very life and liberty depending by the contract in such cases upon his telling the truth.

"*Eighth.* The jury are instructed that the testimony of an accomplice in the crime for which the defendant is charged is admissible in evidence, and the degree of credit to be given to the testimony of such accomplice is a matter exclusively for the jury to determine; the jury may convict on the testimony of an accomplice without any corroboration of his statements, but the testimony of such accomplice as to matters material to the issue if not corroborated by facts and circumstances in proof, should be received by the jury with great caution."

This instruction will be read and discussed in connection with the evidence.

"*Ninth.* If the jury entertain a reasonable doubt as to defendant's guilt, they should find him not guilty, but to authorize an acquittal on the ground of doubt alone such doubt must be real and substantial, and not that there is a mere possibility that defendant may be innocent.''

"Well then," some juror exclaims, "if it all depends on a *doubt*, who can be convicted? We have never seen anything, outside of mathematical demonstration, proven with such certainty that every little doubt was swept from the mind. Why have we been kept here for three weeks if that instruction was to be given?" Such is the view that skillful attorneys would have you take of the law in this behalf; but if you will pause just a moment, you will observe the instruction uses something more than simply the word *doubt*. A man by searching may find in some remote corner of his mind a mere *doubt* as to most anything. In fact some of the greatest men of both ancient and modern times have so puzzled themselves with the mysteries surrounding the existence of mind and matter that they lay it down as a cardinal principle in their philosophy, that "We know nothing beyond a doubt." They doubt if they really taste, feel, or see anything; doubt that there is a hereafter; doubt the existence of a God; doubt their own existence. But this is unreasonable; and were others than the eccentric to so reason, all laws and all civilization would soon crumble into dust. You will see the word "doubt," as used in the instruction, is qualified and enlarged in meaning by two adjectives, so that the reading is "Such doubt must be real and substantial." This is done, doubtless, for the express purpose of curbing the play of fancy in a

juror's mind.   What is a "real and substantial" doubt?
It is a doubt founded on law and reality, and not on
fancy; it is a doubt founded on testimony and substance, and not chased down and caught—you know not
where nor how—by a winged imagination.   You are
all farmers, I am told.   One of you is plowing in your
field: a neighbor comes sauntering up to you, and
when you stop he sits down on your plow-beam and
says, "What are you plowing for?"   If it is spring-
time, you say for corn, or oats, as the case may be.
But he says, "How do you know you are going to
raise anything?   I am in doubt this season, and have
put my plow under the shed and turned my horses on
the range."   "Why," you say, "with rarest exceptions, God has always made seed-time and harvest to
come—the rains have descended and the sun has shown
—and with the great bulk of evidence in my favor, I
will plow on and raise my crop."   "Sometimes they
miss," he exclaims—"I doubt it, I doubt it."   This,
gentlemen, is an unreasonable, unsubstantial doubt.
The man went out of the great weight of evidence to get
it.   If you acted similarly, you and yours would starve.
So, in this case, you can easily adopt different rules
from those you are governed by in the ordinary affairs
of life, and shutting your eyes to the great bulk of the
evidence, send out Fancy—fleeter than a swift-winged
Mercury—and she will doubtless bring you back a
doubt.   But this will not do; it must come from the
testimony as a whole, and be real and substantial, **to**
authorize an acquittal.

"*Tenth.* If the jury find the defendant guilty of murder in the first degree, they will simply so state in their verdict, and leave the punishment to be fixed by the court.

"If they find the defendant guilty of murder in the second degree, they will so state in their verdict, and will also assess the punishment at imprisonment in the penitentiary for such term, not less than ten years, as the jury may believe proper under the evidence.

When an instruction like this is read, a juror may say, "There, then, the whole thing rests with me; my God, I don't want to convict anybody; I don't want to deprive any human being of life or liberty—and the whole thing rests right on me." This is what skillful attorneys would have you believe; but it does not all rest on you, any more than it all rests on the grand jury who returned the indictment, or the judge who received it, or the clerk who recorded it, or the prosecuting attorney, who signed it. You are simply a part of the criminal machinery to pass upon the facts. If you find the fact to be that the defendant is guilty, the *law* inflicts the punishment, and is responsible for it, not *you.* The judge pronounces the sentence; but not he, nor the jury, but a wise and just law coming to us from our ancestors, and from God himself to man, carries that sentence into execution. This ends the instructions for the state.

THE EVIDENCE.

Having looked at the law, let us now examine the evidence of the witnesses. In doing this, gentlemen, you will excuse me, and take it as no reflection upon

any one else, when I say that, without skipping about
here and there, seemingly for confusion's sake, I will
give you in substance all of the testimony of all the witnesses, and as nearly as practicable in the precise order
in which it fell from their lips.   To save time I shall
use no notes; in fact, I took none. But I believe I know
the testimony, and can give it to you correctly from
memory by the aid of a list of the witnesses. You will
excuse me too, if I speak plainly as I go along, calling
things by their right names, for I was raised in the same
wild west with these men whose exploits we have been
considering, and I strive to talk as they shot—right to
the mark.

What is the evidence in this most important case?
As the sun is setting in the west, on the fifteenth day
of July, 1881, we see a passenger train rolling slowly
under the vast shedway at the Union Depot in Kansas
City, Missouri, and its engine takes its place by the
side of half a dozen or more of others, each panting
like so many horses ready for the race. To me, gentlemen, there is something sublime about a locomotive
engine; I can look at it and admire it, even if it does
belong to a rich corporation, and I have no interest in
it.   Thank God, in the great realm of vision, we are
equally wealthy.   Rolling rivers, towering mountains,
outstretching plains, bending skies, as well as the splendid specimens of human skill that fret our public
streams and highways, are all in the realm of vision the
property of rich and poor alike.   Yes, what a glorious
structure is a railroad engine, what a giant-like tribute
to man's inventive genius; how like a thing of life with

vast, pulsating heart, it seems "to live, and move, and have its being." When like the queen of commerce it comes gliding along, with gorgeous, resplendent coaches for its train, how the law-abiding soul—with never a dream of stopping it in search of plunder—delights to see it speed on, in magnificent splendor and sublimest power. Many a time, a few years since, while loitering about Kansas City, as young lawyers do, have I stood upon the bluffs and watched the trains as they came in and went out; watched them just at night-fall, when they were all departing for the east; watched them as, hurling down the river bottom, with resounding whistle, rolling smoke, and white, streaming steam, they plunged into the tunnel of the night, and were seen no more.

So the ill-fated Rock Island train departed on July 15, 1881; so it sped on like a meteor through the darkness until it reached the prairies of your own county. What a splendid spectacle is presented by an approaching train on a western prairie in the night-time! I see that train coming up to Winston now, with its beaming headlight, now partly obscured in a cut, now out, trembling along like a rolling, radiant ball of fire. Yes, yes, gentlemen, I see that train speeding across the prairies of your own free Missouri, where the protecting ægis of the law is spread over every head, and we boast that life, liberty, and the pursuit of happiness is guaranteed to every human being within her borders. I hear the rails clicking by the platform; I see the white steam rise; the whistle sounds out on the pure country air, and in a moment the train

is standing at the depot in the town of Winston. Frank
James was there to meet that train, gentlemen. Just
as surely was he there, as that he is here to-day. Just
as surely was he there as that the village was there—as
that Westfall and McMillan were there. Just as surely
was he there, as that the All-seeing Eye was there,
looking down into the foul intention that dwelt in his
heart. Let us look a moment at his surroundings, for
here we may get a glimpse at the superb innocence of
the "remarkable" hero now on trial. It is said that
when a man contemplates doing a wicked deed, if he
will look at some splendid painting or upon some scene
where nature with her brush has eclipsed all human
genius, his vile thoughts may all be taken away. Look
at his surroundings on this fatal night. There stands a
magnificent train, known to him to be laded with
precious immortal beings whose life he is about to
hazard. Perchance the mother is there, returning from
a visit to her children in the west, or the boy going
east to bid farewell to a dying parent. Innocent little
children, unborn when civil war brought the defendant
his much-talked-of "grievance," are there, with tiny
hands against the window glass, and eyes peering out,
asking his pity and protection. The pure, free atmosphere of his native state is about him. The smoke of
the standing engine is towering upward, and as his
eyes follow it they meet the tender light from a myriad
of twinkling stars, each whispering to him with a silver
tongue, pleading with him, as if to woo and win him
from his awful purpose.

But it is all to no avail. Frank McMillan, old man McMillan, his father and the two Penns—all laborers in a stone-quarry hard by—have gotten into the smoking car. Conductor Westfall, little knowing the sad fate impending, waves his lantern for the last time. The bell rings. The train starts. The robbers get aboard. The fiendish work begins. I am going now by the evidence—no fancy. Dick Liddil and Clarence Hite climb upon the tender to take charge of the engineer and firemen. Jesse James, Frank James, and Wood Hite rush into the smoking-car from the front door; one of them—as seen by the witness Maj. McGee, a most intelligent gentleman, and at present United States Marshal—cuts the bell-rope, and doubt- less in doing so gives the signal at the engine which causes the train to stop; but it at once starts up again. "The two tall men," as the witness Penn calls them, come right up to conductor Westfall, at this time en- gaged in putting "tabs" in the hats of Penn and his companions, saying "up, up," or "down, down," the witness, affrighted and thunderstruck with the tragedy of double murder, can not say which. Westfall, see- ing death was lurking, "made some motion thus," as Penn put it; he can not say for what. I believe to de- fend himself, as duty and God bade him do. Just at that instant "the big tall man"—all admit now Jesse James—quick as a tiger for his victim, pulls the cruel trigger, and Westfall goes reeling down the aisle to the rear end of the car; as he goes the firing at him is con- tinued. He opens the door, struggles out, and falls

15

dead from the train; dead in the harness! dead on
duty!

That was a magnificent specimen of oratory with
which Gov. Johnson closed his argument yesterday
evening. He said, you remember, that once in the
city of St. Louis he stood watching a five-story building wrapped in flames. In one of the upper windows
stood a man, with the red flames leaping around him,
and apparently no means of escape whilst his wife below was watching with eager and loving eyes for some
kind hand to snatch him from the devouring fires and
bear him to her arms, till at length a heroic fireman
brought joy to her heart by undertaking and performing
the noble feat. I could not help however, gentlemen,
but think of something real, and directly connected
with this case, as the Governor drew his picture; I
could not help but think of poor Westfall, reeling there
in the railway car, enveloped in the smoke of burning
powder, and wrapped about with the red-hot flashes
from cracking revolvers—he himself being on fire, the
red flames of life bursting through the windows made in
his body with cruel bullets; I could not help but
think of the devoted wife who stood in her door-way
on that fatal night, waiting to give the welcome kiss to
her husband when his "run" was ended and he returned to his home. Alas! she is waiting still.

We are not through with the scene at the train yet.
Westfall has fallen, but the murderous fire still con-
tinues. Now it is contended "it was not intentional,"
"we do not know the particular man who did it," and
so on. It makes no difference, you know from the

evidence Frank James did it; but if you did **not,** **you**
would know that one of the band he belonged to—bent
on robbery and murder—did it, and that is enough.
According to Penn and Major McGee, these men followed Westfall up, and after he had tumbled from the
rear end of the "smoker," they go back again to the
front of the "smoker" and out of the door.   Penn and
Frank McMillan now get up, and in search of a safer
place go to the rear platform of the "smoker," and
take seats on the steps.   "One of the tall men" remains
on the front platform of this "smoker" firing "as
many as six shots straight through the train," crying,
"down, down."   This was doubtless done to keep
the passengers from interfering.   Penn gets up and
looks through the rear door, and one of these shots
hurls the shattered glass against his hand.   Presently
a voice, as if from one in distress, is heard in the
"smoker."   Frank McMillan, sitting on the rear steps,
says, "That's father's voice."   Oh, I think, gentlemen, I know myself how he knew that voice, even in
the din of rattling train and belching pistols. It was the
staid, familiar voice that through all the happy days of
childhood he had heard under the old home-roof; the
voice that many a time had called him up to his work
at break of day—to the country lad, glorious break of
day when rosy-fingered Aurora, sweet dispenser of the
morning dew, came dashing in her fiery chariot across
the eastern hills, and a thousand birds were twittering
greetings to her in the trees.   "That's father's voice!"
and he bounded to the door, and death met him as he
he came.   The whizzing ball of the idle, roving as-

sassin meets the sweated brow of hard-working Frank
McMillan, he falls dead from the train, and the soil of
free Missouri drinks up his honest blood. "Oh, he
is but a poor laborer," I hear them say; "what is his
life when measured with the precious existence of a
daring, chivalric hero? Gentlemen, when the Almighty
God of the universe came into the world, and took
upon himself the form of a man, he paid such a compli-
ment to the dignity of labor that he became himse'f a
carpenter, and for years there stood upon His brow, as
upon poor McMillan's, the sweat of honest toil.
Much has been said to induce you to think this is a
prosecution backed by corporations in the interest of
capital; but I tell you it was not *capital*, it was *labor*
that was foully murdered when Frank James's ball
went crashing through the brain of the humble stonemason at Winston.

Thus ended the killing at the robbery. I have
scarcely mentioned those whose hearts were made to
bleed the most. Hours have been spent here in pa-
thetic rhetoric about the defendant's wife, his child,
his mother, his sister, and all thought to be near and
dear to him. The wives and children of *our* sleeping
dead have been left in the background. This is no
place for such issues. I could not depict the anguish
of the widow whose heart is withered with the purple
blast of murder, nor the wail of the orphan, that, for
aught we know, may cry for bread; and I would not
if I could. In cases like this the anguish of the dying
and the dead is far less than that of the beloved living left
behind, and I could only feeby imitate the example of

a painter of ancient times, of whom I have somewhere
read. Agamemnon, a noble chieftain of the Grecian
forces, was at last captured, together with his family,
by his enemies. They studied long how they might
contrive to torture him the most. At last discovering
that he had an only daughter, a girl of extreme beauty,
whom he seemed to love far better than he loved himself, they brought her forth and put her to death by
slow torture, compelling the brave old warior to look
upon the fearful scene. A great painter came to the
frightful scene to put it on canvas, especially the
horror that sat on the father's countenance, and to
hand, with his picture, his name and his genius down
the ages. He drew the crowd, torturers and all, just
as they stood; he painted the suffering girl with the
flush of death on her cheek, with matchless perfection;
but when he came to the father, standing in grim,
silent agony, his genius failed him, and he simply drew
a veil over the face, in confession of his inability to
depict the horror that sat within. So all I can do in
this case is to place Mrs. Westfall here to my right,
clad in mourning, with a thick black veil hiding the
saddened face; and Mrs. McMillan here to my left,
similarly attired; and the little children hiding their
faces in the folds of their mothers' dresses—and let me
say, *these*, Colonel Philips, are the trophies of *your*
kind of chivalry.

By the Court. Gentlemen, this is a court of
justice. Mr. Sheriff, you must stop this applause.

Sheriff. Gentlemen, all this noise must be
stopped; I say all this noise must be stopped right
now; you are in court.

By the Court. Now I want to say to this intelligent audience that this applause must not be repeated. If so, the sheriff will clear the room. Proceed, Mr. Wallace.

Mr. Wallace. Gentlemen of the jury, laying aside everything that savors of feeling, what is the plain, unvarnished evidence before you? What are the *dry facts*, to which, without the least appeal to passion, I now promise to confine my remarks. Who committed this double, dastardly, diabolical murder? If Frank James was at Winston, away with your knighthood, away with exclaiming "who fired this shot," or "who that;" away with technicalities, for justice cries out with a thousand voices, "If he was there he is guilty." If he, who publicly trod the streets of Nashville for four years, was in Texas in his sister's "cellar," or "upstairs," so that not even a neighboring cow-boy might see him, he is innocent. If present he is bound to be guilty of murder in the first or second degree ; and the whole case turns on the question—*was he at Winston or was he in Texas?*

The testimony is absolutely overwhelming that there were five men in that robbery, and that this defendant is the fifth man. It was confessed from the outset that Jesse James, Dick Liddil, and the two Hites, were in this robbery, and for four days they proceeded here on the confession that there was a fifth man there ; and you saw them vainly striving to show this fifth man was Jim Cummings, and not this defendant. Right in the midst of the trial, for sheer necessity, the "four-men theory"—an insult to your intelli-

gence—was concocted; and the case has been argued
to you, by those who did not argue mostly from "flags"
and "swords," on that hypothesis. Let us examine
the "four-men" dodge. A moment's analysis of the
testimony shows its absurdity. The evidence is four-
fold that there were five men: First, the five horses
ridden are unmistakably described; second, five men
are unmistakably described; third, five men were seen
about sundown near the scene of the robbery; fourth,
five men are seen and counted at the robbery. First
as to the horses,—

No. 1, big bay gelding, heavy mane and tail,
about sixteen hands high, described by a number of
the witnesses who saw these men. No man who had
been on a farm two months could mistake him for any
of the other four. This horse Jesse James rode; John
Samuels, his brother, owned him, and tells you Jesse
was riding him that summer.

No. 2, a little bay horse (gelding), stolen by
Frank James and Liddil, in Ray county, and described
exactly by a number of local witnesses. This was
Wood Hite's horse.

No. 3, a sorrel gelding, about fifteen and a half
hands high, ordinary mane and tale, collar-marks, no
blaze in face, described by a number of local witnesses.
This was the Lamartine Hudspeth's horse, ridden by
Dick Liddil.

No. 4, a tall sorrel, stolen from the witness Matthews, most noticeable of all, blaze face, light mane
and tail, white hind feet, sixteen hands high, described
by a number of local witnesses. This was Clarence
Hite's horse.

No. 5, a little, light-bay mare, stolen by Frank James and Liddil in Ray county, described by a number of local witnesses; shod by Potts, who identifies her in Timberlake's hands, at Liberty, and she is returned to her owner in Ray county. This horse was ridden by Frank James to Winston.

Here are five horses traced by local witnesses to and from this robbery, all totally unlike. Any man on this jury hunting stolen horses could trace them, by description, through the country: First, big bay gelding; second, little bay gelding; third, ordinary sorrel gelding, no blazed face; fourth, big sorrel gelding, blazed face, light-colored mane and tail, and white hind feet; fifth, little light-bay mare. Who rode the fifth horse?—a myth? a Will-o'-the-wisp? while Frank James was in his sister's cellar?

2d. Five men are unmistakably described by the witnesses,—

No. 1. Tall man, heavy, erect, high cheek-bones and broad across face, darkish whiskers all over his face, dark hair, good talker; described in the same way by Mrs. Hite, the Brays, Wolfinbergers, and others. This was Jesse James.

No. 2. Man about thirty, average height, stoop-shoulders, light-complexioned, inclined to heavy build, not much whiskers, very slouchy, said but little; thus described by Mrs. Hite and a number of your local witnesses. This was Wood Hite.

No. 3. Man about thirty, dark-complexioned, with dark hair, dark whiskers, short and all over face, average build and weight. This you can see yourselves was Dick Liddil.

No. 4. Tall, slender, light-complexioned fellow of about twenty, front teeth bad and prominent, little fuzzy whiskers; thus described by Mrs. Hite and a number of local witnessess. This was Clarence Hite.

No. 5. Tall, slender man from thirty-five to forty, light-complexioned, wore lightish "burnside whiskers," intelligent, good talker, neat in dress; described in the same way by the Tennessee witnesses, and local witnesses to some of whom he talked about Ingersoll and "spouted" Shakespeare. This was the "remarkable" man on trial.

3d. Just before the robbery five men were seen near the scene of the robbery,—

Ezra Soule, near sundown, comes upon two of them in the woods. One of them, he testifies, positively was Frank James, and the other he describes as "a tall young fellow, fuzz on his face, big bad teeth"— Clarence Hite, beyond question. Just about this time, at early supper, two men are at Mrs. Montgomery's, close by. The family are here, and described them: "One a tall, heavy-set, independent fellow, whiskers tolerably long all over his face, darkish, ate with his hat on"—Jesse James; "the other ordinary size, ordinary looking, light-complexion, did no talking"— Wood Hite beyond question; "both rode bay horses." Bad-tooth Clarence, with his blazed-face sorrel, was not there, gentlemen, nor was slender, polite, "burnsides" Frank. No witness yet brings in "ordinary-sized." Dick Liddill, dark complexion, short whiskers all over his face; but Mrs. Kindig and her daughter are put on the stand, and testify that such a

man ate dinner at their house on the day of the robbery, by himself, being on horseback; and they swear
positively that Dick Liddil, whom they see at this trial,
is the man.   Here, then, are the five men seen in the
neighborhood just before the robbery.   Everything
hangs together in this case.   Watch as I proceed, and
see if it does not.   The eternal consistency of truth is
seen at every step from Nashville to Winston.

4th.   Five men are seen at the robbery,—

My friend, Mr. Slover, may fly around in his argument like a feather in a whirlwind, trying to account
for the fifth man by making an omnipresent being out
of Clarence Hite, and placing him on the engine, in the
"smoker," on the ground, or in the express-car, all at
the same instant; but with fair men it will not do.   If,
like a wonder-worker, he can deceive you with such
legerdemain as that—I am charging nothing improper,
let a defending lawyer ply his skill—we may as well
give up the case.   Mr. John M. Glover, you remember, went through the same sleight-of-hand performance
by a totally different method.   With him, *Wood* Hite
was the everywhere present robber, that by the magic
wave of Mr. Glover's wand would flit unseen, from
car to car, like the mystic egg, from hat to hat.   Now,
the five men robbed this train is as clear, from the evidence, as the shining sun.   The train stopped three
times; first, within twenty yards of the depot; second,
three or four hundred yards from town; last, a mile or
more from town.   Bear in mind, both men are killed
between the first and second stops, while the train is in
motion.   Maj. McGee says: "Three men entered the

smoking-car. I am positive." "One at once cut the bell-rope." Penn is positive, also, that *three* men entered. As the train is moving, after the first stop, the firing commences—all the men being in the car by the positive testimony of three witnesses. The engineer testifies that just as he was starting up after the first stop (three robbers being in the "smoker,") "two men came over the tender, with revolvers, into the cab." Two and three make five. The engineer is futher positive "that these two men were both of them all the time on the engine from the time they first came until he left the engine," just as the robbery was ending. The point at which he left the engine was beyond where both dead men had been found on the ground. Thus he swears that two men were on the engine during the identical time the three men were in the "smoker." Again, by the testimony of the baggage-man and express messenger, both being in the same car, no man passed through the baggage-car, and they knew nothing of the robbery until the robbers appeared at the side door of their car, on the ground, which was at the second stop, and after the killing. How, then, could Clarence Hite get from the engine and back into the "smoker" to be counted as one of the three, the train being rapidly in motion, without passing through the express-car? If he did, how did he catch up and get back on the engine again? for the engineer says, as the engine halted at this second stop, these two were still there, and made him go on; in fact, he says, had been there all the time, right by him. Again, just while two men are ordering the engineer

to go ahead, three men are at the express-car door, **two**
get in, the express messenger says, one stays by the
baggage-man (pulled out on the ground), as the train
moves off again, as the baggage-man says; and still
the two, according to the engineer, are on his engine,
and are there when he leaves it, some distance beyond.
It is too plain, gentlemen, for further argument.   To
make you believe there were only four men on that
train is to make you believe you can not count five.

How have the defense acted on this point ?   Have
they made an honest defense from the outset, treating
you as honest and intelligent men on oath ?   I say they
have not.   Knowing the evidence showed five men in
this robbery, they deliberately tried for four days before you to put Jim Cummings in as the fifth man. Did
they not do this ? 1881 is the year of this crime; and,
you remember, during the first part of the trial, when
old man Ford, by a *lapsus linguae*, said he saw Jim
Cummings in the fall of 1881, how they rolled it as a
sweet morsel under their tongues, and what a fight was
made against letting the old man correct his mistake by
saying he meant 1880. You remember, when John
Samuels was put on the stand, that he was asked:
"Please give the names of all the men at your mother's
in the summer of 1881 ?" and he answered, "Jesse
James, Dick Liddil, Wood Hite, Clarence Hite, and
after the Winston robbery, Charlie Ford."   "Were
these all; please name them over again ?" and he
named them precisely as at first.   Then came the suggestive question. "Did you see Jim Cummings in the
summer of 1881 ?"   Answer; "Yes, sir; he was

there with the others several times." Mrs. Samuels
was put on the stand, and she was asked to give the
names; and she did it just as John did, exactly.
"Please repeat them all?"—and she gave the same
names again, leaving out Cummings. And then the
suggestive question was asked, and answered as John
had answered it. A direct, persistent attempt to put Cummings in this robbery; and then
they would have argued, "Cummings was the man all
these good witnesses took to be Frank James." But
their plans are suddenly thwarted. Frank O'Neill,
the correspondent of the St. Louis *Republican*, who
had a long interview with the defendant just before his
"surrender," testifies that in that interview the defendant described Cummings as an illiterate, indolent fellow,
and mocked his long drawl in talking, which I had
O'Neill to reproduce: "There—now—that—d—d——
Frank James—has—gone—and told—on me," etc.
The defense could go no further. To claim this ignorant drawler and the smooth repeater of Shakespeare
and adroit discourser on Ingersoll were one and the
same person was too absurd, even for this case; and
right in the midst of the river they change horses, and
the question is asked. "Was not Wood Hite very
much like his cousin Frank?" and they all answer
"very much." Is this the way to make a sincere *bona
fide* defense? I blame not my professional brothers,
but venture that in the history of criminal trials never
was an honest jury so grossly trifled with. General
Garner is one of those ponderous bodies, which, when
well under headway, it takes time to stop; and so thor-

oughly had he gotten started on the Jim Cummings
theory that he clung to it for sometime in his speech,
but finally came around all right.

But let us go deeper into the evidence.   The guilt
of the defendant becomes more apparent as we examine
the motives and plans leading up to the crime. In Nashville, Tennessee, in March, 1881, four men are dwelling together under the same roof.   They are seemingly
quiet citizens, but in reality are a band of outlaws, each
passing under an *alias*.   Frank James has been about
Nashville for more than three years, has a wife and one
child; and is known as B. J. Woodson; Jesse James
is better known than his brother, has a wife and two
children, and passes as J. D. Howard. Dick Liddil is
living with them, known as Mr. Smith.   Bill Ryan is
also there, known as Tom Hill.   These facts you have
learned from the testimony of W. L. Earthman, back-
tax collector at Nashville; James Moffat, depot-master
at the Louisville and Nashville depot; Messrs, Horn,
Sloan, and others.   "Much obliged to you for this evidence," say our friends on the other side,"it shows our
client wanted to lead an upright life, and was living as
an industrious citizen in Tennessee.   Yes, I reply, and
it shows as much for Jesse James, whom you, yourselves, have held up as a monster in crime.   It shows
that Dick Liddil and Bill Ryan, so far as outward ap-
pearances went, led quiet and honorable lives in Nashville, Tennessee.

A   curious incident caused this band to flee from
Nashville. Bill Ryan, on March 26, 1881, mounted
on a splendid steed, as you remember by Earthman's

testimony, was traveling north, and when at a country store, some eight miles from Nashville, became intoxicated, flourished his pistols, said his name was Tom Hill, and that he was a desperado and an outlaw, and tried to kill Earthman, who was then a justice of the peace. He was arrested on the spot—having besides his arms, a buckskin sacque next to his person, containing about $1,300 in gold—and was lodged in jail at Nashville, charged with assault with intent to kill. An evening paper contained a description of the man arrested, and the remainder of the gang made their flight the ensuing night. Frank James mounts a horse, stolen, though not by him, from Mr. Duvall, of Ray county, Missouri, and since recovered by the owner, as he told you, in Nelson county, Kentucky. Jesse and Dick steal horse flesh on the commons of Nashville; and when this is exhausted, two more are stolen as the three pass their rapid retreat to old man Hite's, the uncle of the Jameses, who lived some fifty miles north of Nashville, in Logan county, Kentucky, Frank James tells you from the stand—Mrs. Hite and her father were here, and he could not deny it—that he made this trip, but he was not a member of the gang, and did not want to go along. Oh, no! did not want to go; but the fact is, that with the four points of the compass and the wide world all about him, he did go. He wanted to go, gentlemen, and at every jump of his steed he cried out to the others as did Ruth to Naomi, "Entreat me not to leave thee, or to return from following after thee, for whither thou goest I will go, and where thou

lodgest I will lodge." On the twenty-seventh day of
March, about sun-up, Mrs. Sarah Hite and her father,
Mr. Norris, say these men came to old man Hite's. The
recently stolen horses had been turned loose, and Jesse,
Frank, and Dick came, one riding, two walking, two
having guns, all having pistols. They stay a few days
and go away; and in about two weeks come back
again, four in the gang, Wood Hite being now with
them as they prowl around. In a day or so they go to
Nelson county, Kentucky, and are at Hall's, Hoskins'
and other places. This is proven by the defendant's
admission on the stand. This is the county from
which, by the record evidence of the express companies
and otherwise, it is shown these two guns were shipped,
in May, 1881, to John Ford, at Richmond, Missouri.

Now, then, we come to the removal of all the gang,
and the families of those married, to Missouri.
Here, it is contended, all came but Frank. This
is, because he is the one on trial. If Liddill were on
trial, all would have come but him: if Jesse James, all
but him. There is plenty of positive proof that Frank
James came; but aside from this, the attending circumstances all show it. To begin with all the band to
which he belonged, Jesse James, Dick Liddil, Wood
Hite, and Clarence Hite, it is admitted, came. This
is the gang as just recruited in Kentucky, and to which,
by the testimony of Mrs. Hite and her father, Frank
James more truly belonged than did the Hite boys.
Shall the oldest and shrewdest man in the gang remain
behind when boys like Clarence Hite came along?
Shall fledglings be brought on a daring flight in search

of prey, and one of the parent birds be left at home. All came in April and May, 1881 "except" the man on trial. Even Jesse James's wife with little children came, and took up her residence in Kansas City, Missouri, as shown you by the testimony of Thomas Mimms, her brother. Frank James's wife herself comes; and as it now turns out, comes first of all, early in April, 1881. It was hard in the outset to show by testimony independent of the gang that she came; but when we traced by the railroad records a sewing machine to Page City, in Lafayette county, Missouri, and from thence to her father's, at Independence, Missouri, the truth had to come, and Thomas Mimms tells you on the stand that he met her at the St. James Hotel, in Kansas City, and took her to her father's. The claim that she came to have General Shelby intercede for her husband with the Governor—long before the Winston and Blue Cut robberies, long before the reward of $10,000 was offered, long before the Governor and local officers were working in unison, and in dead, hard earnest to rid the state of shame and outlawry—is a subterfuge, and too preposterous to be believed by intelligent men.

But positive proof that he came is abundant. It is just as clearly shown by disinterested witnesses that Frank James was at the home of the Fords in Ray county, Missouri, in May and in the summer and fall of 1881, as that he was at Mrs. Hite's in the early spring. I only mention one witness now, the one they did not attempt even to impeach, and whose testimony, all attorneys for the defense have striven to get away

16

from as quickly as possible. This is the mod-
est, intelligent, truthful, little Ida Bolton, of thirteen summers, and as nice a child in manner
and deportment before you as the daughter of any
man who hears my voice. She is placed upon the
stand by the state. She utters not a word, except in
simple answer to questions asked. Leaving out the
questions she testifies: "I know Mr. James over there;
they called him Hall at our house—at Uncle Charley
Ford's where I was in 1881. I knew him well; he
came to our house in May, 1881, and was there several
times that summer; he was upstairs a good deal and
read. I know him and picked him out by myself from
amongst all the men, when I came into court. He was
at our house that summer with Jesse James, Dick
Liddil, Clarence and Wood Hite. I know all of them.
Frank James, Clarence Hite, and Charlie Ford left our
house for Kentucky, they said, in October, I think,
1881;" and a rigid cross-examination never caused her
to waver in the simplicity of her truthfulness. Every
man said—that is the truth. The defendant and his
attorneys may storm and deny, but they can never get
away from it. We read in the Scriptures of a little
maid who lived within, or close by, a worse house for
murder than that of the Fords—the house of Pontius
Pilate, or of the high-priest, I forget which. When
the time for the crucifixion was drawing nigh, and all
were deserting, Peter, the bold disciple, said he would
stand by the Savior, to the last; but as he was warm-
ing himself by the fire, this little maid, who had probably
ably seen him but once before, came along and said,

"Thou also wast with Jesus of Nazareth," and he denied it; and the maid saw him again, and he said the
same, and again he denied it and began to curse and
swear. But it was the truth, despite his denial and
profanity. So in this case the defendant may deny,
and swear, and rave; but I tell you the little maid saw
him, and with honest men he can never get away from
her testimony. I say nothing now of testimony to the
same effect by Thomas Ford, Cap Ford, Martha Bolton, and Willie Bolton.

Having traced defendant by disinterested testimony, circumstantial and positive, from Nashville to
Kentucky, and thence to the Ford farm in Ray county,
Missouri, let us come to your own county. Here we
find from this and an adjoining county twelve witnesses
who testify to you that he was here. They are all as
honest, honorable, and intelligent citizens as can be
found anywhere. They say he was here in your vicinity
about two weeks before, and on the day of the Winston robbery. They conversed with him, he ate at
their tables, and they know him. Three of them, the
Bray family, say they believe him to be the man, and
the remaining nine swear to him without a doubt.
One of them, Ezra Soule, swears positively that he saw
Frank James just before sundown on the evening of the
robbery, and within half a mile of the place. "Yes,"
it is said, "but that is just where the case falls to the
ground; you prove Frank James to be there in the
woods, but you can get him no further; you fall a half
mile short in making your case." Gentlemen, were
you put in the jury-box as fools, as sticks, or as men

endowed by Almighty God with noble reasoning
powers? Jurors, I tell you, you are expected and required to use the common logic of the human mind,
and when a conclusion follows with mathematical certainty by comparing one state of facts with another, it
is your duty to adopt that conclusion. Otherwise there
could be no enforcements of the law in criminal cases.

Five men placed with undeniable certainty in the
woods there, and Frank James one of the five!
Five men at the robbery, just as certainly as the light is
coming in at these windows! Four of them admitted
to be Jesse, Liddil, and the two Hites—and then say,
the fifth one *may have been* some other than the defendant? What became of Frank James when they
left the woods for the train? Did he by omnipotent
aid ascend Elijah-like into the skies, and some honest
farmer come and act his part? and when the deed was
done, did the Almighty let him down again into his
saddle, and the honest farmer go home to his couch?
Oh, no, gentlemen, he was there; and every one of
you know it. The conclusion is logical, unavoidable,
irresistible.

You will perceive, gentlemen, that I have arrived
at this point in my argument without the mention of
Dick Liddil's name as a witness, and without relying
upon his testimony for any conclusion whatever. I
have done so at a disadvantage to myself, for my custom is to strive to push all the testimony along together, but I deemed it best in order to refute the
oft-repeated assertion that "everything depended on
Liddil," by demonstrating the defendant's presence at

Winston without Liddil's evidence. But by the law of the land, Liddil is a competent witness; and I now propose hurriedly to discuss his testimony, bringing it along with the testimony of the other witnesses, but not in such manner, I trust as to weary you.

Dick Liddil was a member of a band of train-robbers, known as "The James Gang." This nobody denies. If he had not been, he could not have rendered the state the vast benefit that he has. When men are about to commit a crime they do not sound a trumpet before them. They do their work in secret and in darkness. Neither when they are forming bands for plunder or death, do they select conscientious, honest citizens. A man contemplating murder would not say, "come along, Mr. Gilreath, or Mr. Nance, and join me in my fiendish task." Their work is done when honest, law-abiding men are asleep, and "beasts creep forth." For this reason, when the state would break up a band of criminals, it must depend upon the assistance of one of their peers in crime to do it. Hence it is a custom, as old as the law, to pick out from a desperate band one of their own number, and, use him as a guide to hunt the others down. No honest, law-abiding man objects to this. When men go about where this is done, crying "perfidy," "traitor," "treason," you can put them down as the enemies of good government, or so steeped in prejudice that they know not what they do. Liddil, the least depraved man in the most secret, desperate band, perhaps the world ever saw, has thus been used; and the state has chosen, also to call him as a witness in this case.

Mountains of abuse have been heaped upon him; the English language has been ransacked for terms of villification.   Once, forsooth, and after he got to be a trainrobber, too, he was a splendid fellow; splendid enough to be the boon companion of so pure and great a man as Frank James.   You remember that the defendant himself testified that Liddil, passing under an *alias*, was his guest, ate at his table, and slept under his roof.   Liddil was one of the heroes then, of whom we have heard so much.   But suddenly he makes a change.   He leaves the shades of crime and comes out into the sunlight of law and order; and all at once, strange to say, he is transformed into a "viper," a "villain," a "scoundrel," a "demon" or such "execrable shape" as his old tutor's counsel can give him. But let the attorneys for the defense go on with their abuse; it is a part of their business.   I shall not retort by calling the defendant a "viper," a "perjurer," a "demon" and the like.   Even the way in which Liddil comes into court is dwelt upon.   To appeal to your prejudices by intimating that the United States, Frank James's enemy, in 1863, was trying to convict him, Col. Philips says Liddil came guarded by a "United States marshal;" when the fact is, he came with Capt. Maurice Langhorne, deputy marshal of Jackson county, Missouri.

Col. Philips.   I did not say anything about a United States marshal.

Mr. Wallace.   Possibly it was a slip of the tongue, but I insist that you *did*, and so did one of your colleagues; and it was followed up by you by denunci-

ation of Langhorne, who never opened his mouth as a
witness, simply coming here in the performance of an
official duty. It will surprise you, gentlemen, to know
that Capt. Langhorne, who has thus been introduced
to you, was for four years an officer with Gen. Shelby,
the much-lauded witness for the defense. Thank
Heaven, too, gentlemen, I can say for Capt. Langhorne, that he found out long ago that the war was
over, and he is in favor of prosecuting and punishing
train-robbers and murderers, no matter who they are,
or where they were in days gone by.

It is said Dick Liddil surrendered, and bargained
with the governor of the state, and Craig and Timberlake, to convict Fank James, guilty or innocent, in order
to obtain immunity for himself. I deny that. There
is no proof about it, and I have a right, in answer, to
emphatically and *positively deny* it. The only contract with Liddil was that always made with those turning state's evidence, as we call it, namely, that he
should tell the whole truth and nothing but the truth;
and if he told a falsehood he did it at his peril, and the
contract was ended. To say that these gentlemen would
coolly bargain with a man to swear away the life or liberty of a fellow-being, guilty or innocent, is simply
monstrous. The governor, their own witness, was on
the stand; why not ask him about the contract? They
did not dare to. Timberlake was on the stand; why not
ask him? They did not dare to. Craig was here, sub-
pœnaed by them; why not put him on the stand and
ask him? Why let him go home?

Col. Philips. There is no evidence that Craig was here, and I do not think it proper to bring it before the jury.

The Court. I understood at the commencement of Mr. Wallace's argument that all exceptions would be taken in writing. I do not know Mr. Craig, and can not say as to his being present.

Mr. Wallace. The records of the court will show that a subpœna *duces tecum* was issued by the defense for Henry H. Craig, and that he bring with him the written confession of Dick Liddil, made just after his surrender. In obedience to that subpœna, Capt. Craig sat for a long time within this bar. I know him, saw him, and talked with him. What a magnificent opportunity to contradict Dick Liddil—to show by his confession in writing he had sworn falsely. Instead of groundless declamation about the falsehoods Liddil has concocted since his surrender, how much better it would have been to ask the Governor, Craig, and Timberlake, about his conduct and truthfulness. Why not ask them if in any instance he had ever misled the officers, or told a single falsehood?

It is urged that Liddil has been contradicted by impeaching witnesses, but the effort to contradict him was a downright failure. They declaim mostly on the testimony of Gen. Joe Shelby, who says that in the fall of 1881 he met in Lafayette county, Missouri, Jesse James, Dick Liddil, Wood Hite, and Jim Cummings, on horseback, going south; and that he there learned from them that Frank had not been in Missouri for a long time, and of course was not at Winston. I will

be charitable enough to say, that had Gen. Shelby been
fully at himself, it is trusted he would not have so testified.   I blame some of the attorneys more than I do
him.   You remember that during his cross-examination
one of them twice arose and said, "the witness is in no
condition to testify," and asked that he be excused for
the present; but they had deliberately put him on the
stand, and despite the storming of the witness at me—
for which I care not a fig—I was determined they should
not put a lot of questions, all written out by them, at
him, insist until he answered them just as written, and
then dismiss him from the stand.   I am not here to
accuse a man situated as Gen. Shelby was, with false
swearing—let gentlemen from the other side—

Col. Philips.   Mr. Wallace, do you mean to say
that I, as an attorney, would write out a false question
and put it to a witness?

Mr. Wallace.   The gentleman is getting excited.
Not even the hint of the court to keep quiet is enough
to curb his fiery spirit.   I will be charitable enough
with you, Col. Philips, to say that your client bade you
write these questions.   You know that I am telling the
truth—that these questions were all written out, and
that you had a contention with the witness before he
would answer them at all.   But Gen. Shelby is bound
to be mistaken as to seeing these men thus, in the fall
of 1881.   The other evidence overwhelmingly shows
it.   He puts Cummings with them, when by the remod-
eled defense Cummings was not with the gang at that
time at all.   Besides, it is shown by Mrs. Hite that
Jesse James, instead of associating with Cummings

after February, 1881, was hunting him to kill him on
sight.   It is further shown beyond question that the
gang, after the Winston robbery, adopted the plan of
walking as safer, and had no horses. Besides this, Tom
Mimms says that Jesse James remained in Kansas City
until late in the fall of 1881; he saw him continually;
and when he left —he found afterward he went to St.
Joseph—that he never went south that fall at all. Mrs.
Samuels, too, swears that Jesse never went south for
any purpose in the fall of 1881. But it is useless to say
more.   The contradicting testimony of Tutt, Joe B.
Chiles, and the marshal of Lexington, granting it true,
is simply what you might expect from any man constantly importuned by hundreds of curious inquirers.
Brosius can make the robbers on the cars "fifteen feet
high and three feet through, with pistols having muzzles as big as your hat"—all in a joke; yet Liddil,
besieged to answer by a thousand persons, can not put
a man off but it must be construed into a contradiction.

Let us now examine Liddil's testimony, not him,
but his *testimony*.   If any one of you is prejudiced
against him—and I see no reason why you should be,
for you have certainly seen no more candid, straightforward witness—look at his testimony, not at Liddil.
Scrutinize his testimony, and let it stand or fall on its
merits.   If the judge of this court should hand me a
glass of water, and Liddil should also hand me one, if
I felt squeamish as to whether the contents of the two
were equally pure, I would proceed to examine the
water, mainly, at least, and not the man. But your
mind suggests "you could analyze this by chemical

formula and apparatus and see whether or not it contained poison.'' So you can, with equal certainty analyze the testimony of Liddil in this case. The formula is contained in the eighth instruction, to which I said, when on that branch, I would call your attention in discussing the evidence. By this, if you are in doubt after listening to the bare statement of an accomplice, upon which alone you may convict, then you call to your aid your formula; and the test is *corroboration* or *no corroboration*. If corroborated by other truthful witnesses, you are bound to believe his testimony. Let us, then, standing here in the great laboratory of the law, make a chemical analysis of Liddil's testimony, and see if every time the test of corroboration is applied to the glass of water he has handed you, it does not bubble and sparkle with the truth. And at the outset I say to my friends on the other side, find me a case in your practice, find me a case in the books, find me a case in the history of trials, where an accomplice has been so wonderfully corroborated as this man Liddil.

Liddil says that for some time before coming to Missouri they all lived in or near Nashville, Tennesee; that Frank James went by the name of B. J. Woodson, Jesse James as J. D. Howard, Bill Ryan as Tom Hill, and himself as plain Mr. Smith; and he is corroborated as to every word by Earthman, Moffit, Horne, and Sloan. He says that on March 25, 1881, Ryan was arrested, and gives particulars; and Earthman corroborates him in full. He says they all lived in Nashville in March, 1881, at 814 Fatherland street, and disappeared about April 1, 1881; and John Trimble, Jr.,

who rented "B. J. Woodson" the house, and James B.
May who purchased the same, came, with books and
dates, and corroborated him in detail. He tells you
that he, Jesse, and Frank, on Ryan's arrest, fled to old
man Hite's, in Kentucky; and Mrs. Hite and her
father, Mr. Norris, corroborate in every sentence he
utters. He says they then went to Nelson county, Kentucky, and shipped guns from Adairsville, in that
county, to Missouri—what a fine chance to contradict
him, if untrue, by the express books; but N. G. Bishop,
at Lexington, Missouri, and the agent at Richmond,
Missouri, show you by their books that a box came, just
as Liddil says, to the first and thence to the latter town,
directed to J. T. Ford. He testifies that the families of
Jameses then came to Missouri, giving dates and surrounding circumstances, and he is corroborated by other
witnesses; that he, Jesse, Frank, and the two Hites
came to Missouri; and all is admitted, except as to
Frank, and here he is corroborated in a dozen ways;
that Frank James' wife came to Shelby's with a sewing
machine, thence to Kansas City, and thence to her
father's; and Geo. Hall, of Page City, Dan. Bullard,
agent of the Mo. P. R. R., at Independence, Missouri,
and Thos. Mimms corroborated him at every step, with
dates and records.   He says that Frank James and the
others of the gang were frequently at the Ford farm, in
Ray county, Missouri, in the spring, summer, and fall
of 1881; and old man Ford, up to the time he clashed
with the matchless James, as good a man as Ray
county had, Cap. Ford, Martha Bolton, Willie Bolton,
and Ida Bolton come on the stand and testify that

Frank James was there, and corroborate him in a score of details.   But just here I am tempted to pause a moment.

The Fords are abused and defamed by the hour by defendant's counsel.   Once they were most respectable citizens of Ray county, entertainers of chivalric knights; but now their house is called a ''robber's roost,'' where guests are murdered and buried in the night ''unshrouded and uncoffined.''   As if you were friends sitting weeping on the tomb of Jesse James, the question was put to the Fords as occasion presented ''are you the father,'' or ''the sister,'' or ''the brother'' ''of Bob and Charlie Ford who assassinated Jesse James?''   If the house of the Fords was a most disreputable place, who did as much to make it such as Frank and Jesse James?''   If it was a robber's roost, with devouring vultures sitting on the limbs, what were Frank and Jesse James when they congregated there with the younger birds?   By whose counsel, example or encouragement, were all the young members of this band induced to join it, and to give themselves over to lives of shame and bloodshed?   Who but Jesse James induced Dick Liddil to leave the vocation of a farm hand in The Six Mile, in my own county, to be a bandit and a train-robber?   Who but Jesse James took Bill Ryan from his little home, there on the Blue?   Who made of him an outlaw and a desperado, until he fills a felon's cell, and his widowed mother an untimely grave?   Frank and Jesse James.   Who led Wood Hite along the slimy way of vice until he perishes from his own viciousness, and is tumbled into the ground

without a tear, and without a shroud? Frank and
Jesse James. Who took the green, "gangling" boy,
Clarence Hite, from his home in old Kentucky, rushed
him along the path of robbery and murder, until he
fills a convict's cell, and a convict's grave? Frank
and Jesse James. Who taught the Ford boys to kill
for money? Jesse James. I am not here as a defender
of the Ford boys. I have nothing but condemnation
for their method and their motive in slaying the bandit
king. But neither he, nor his admirers, can be heard
to complain. He fell at the hands of his pupils, and
according to his own methods. As the old eagle to
teach her young to brave the winds in search of prey,
bears them upon her wings from off the craggy cliff,
and trains them above some serging vortex in the sea,
so did Jesse James hold the Ford boys above the black
vortex of crime, and train them for robbery and assassination. Well might the poet say of his fall, as he
did of the eagle, struck down in his flight for prey,
by the aid of a feather dropped from his own wing,—

> "So the struck eagle stretched upon the plain,
>   No more through rolling clouds to soar again,
>   Viewed his own feather on the fatal dart,
>   And winged the shaft that quivered in his heart.
>
> "Keen were his pangs, but keener far to feel,
>   He nursed the pinion that impelled the steel,
>   And the same plumage that had warmed his nest
>   Drank the last life drop from his bleeding breast."

Farewell, Jesse James, prince of robbers! Missouri
cries a long, a glad farewell! Cruelest horseman that
ever wore a spur or held a reign, seeming oftner like

Death himself on his pale horse charging through the land, than feeling man, farewell! farewell! Foulest blot that ever marred the bright escutcheon of a glorious state, farewell! farewell! Yes, thou bloody star of murder, hanging for years like a thing of horror in our very zenith, frightening science and civilization from our borders—I condemned the manner of thy taking off, yet I could but join the general acclaim, when, seized with the shock of death, we saw thee reel in thy orbit, and then plunge forever into old chaos and eternal night.

But while I talk thus of Jesse James, I will deal more justly and tenderly with his memory than has his brother now on trial, and those of his kindred who have come as witnesses to screen him from his crime. I will not desecrate a dead man's memory and heap additional infamy upon his widow, and children after his voice is hushed in death. Missouri's sunshine and showers will kindly nourish such flowers as the widow of Jesse James may plant upon his grave, and so will I. Let it remain for brother and kindred to go thither and scald their lives out by pouring upon them the hot blood of McMillan, shed by Frank James at Winston.

Possibly I have followed my defending brothers in their far-fetched attemps at sympathy or prejudice farther than I should have done. Let us return and take up Liddil's evidence at the house of the Fords. He says the defendant was frequently there in 1881, and all the Ford family say the same. Frank James made these people his associates; they are at least as good as he; they are his peers, and let him stand by their testimony.

We have now come to the preparation proper for the robbery. I will omit the procuring of horses, in which Liddil is corroborated in every item. He says, with the Samuels' homestead and the Fords' as head-quarters, they made three trips in search of a train to rob. The first trip to Chillicothe I will omit. The details are given by him, but the defense fails to con tradict him at any step. The other two trips were both made to your own county, one about two weeks before the robbery and the last when it was perpe-trated. The corroboration of these two trips is won-derful. You can actually trace the band through and back again without his testimony.

Take the first trip: Liddil says he and Frank got breakfast at a house in your county—which he so minutely described that you know it is Mrs. Frank's, and Mrs. Frank corroborates him; that he and Frank James then went a few miles to a blacksmith shop to have Clarence Hite's horse shod, and Jonas Potts cor-roborates him—picks Liddil out here on the street dur-ing the trial, and identifies the defendant; that they then started back, staying all night at Wolfenbarger's, describes the house, barn, family, tells of Jesse being sick here, helping to load wood, etc., etc., and Wolfen-barger identifies both him and Frank James, and cor-roborates him in every detail; that they then passed on to a place and got dinner, and Jesse was taken to town in a buggy, describing surroundings to you, family and everything, and the Brays come and corroborate him in

full. This was the first trip. I have not given half
the minutiæ; you remember them; he was contradicted
in nothing. Look at the trip when the crime was committed. He says they rode from Mrs. Samuels', starting at the usual time, good dark, and rode about all
night—five of them on five horses. He describes these
horses, and your best citizens come and describe them
just as he does. He says that on the day after starting, as they came they separated, Frank and Clarence
turning off slightly to one side, and the balance to the
other, and minister Machette—just in the right neighborhood—picks out Frank as being at his house with a
tall young fellow for dinner just at this time; that they
came and camped at night in the woods, just about a
mile from Gallatin, so describing two houses close by
that any citizen could go at once to the place; that on
this trip Frank and Clarence went to the same blacksmith shop to get Frank's little bay mare shod, and
Jonas Potts, Mrs. Potts (his wife), Wash Whitman
and 'Squire Mallory corroborate him, and identify the
defendant; that when they broke camp in the woods,
near Gallatin, on the morning of the day of the robbery, they separated, Jesse and Wood going together,
Frank and Clarence together, and he (Liddil) by himself; and thus, taking different routes, they went from
here to the appointed place of meeting in the woods,
close to the scene of the crime; and in making this
trip, about nine miles, all loiteringly, he got his dinner
at a little house, describing it "where they had a blind
girl," and Mrs. Kindig and her daughter say this was

17

their house, and corroborate him in all details, and say
they picked him out since the trial in crowded Gallatin
as the man; and sure enough, we find them thus separated, for Ezra Soule says he saw Frank at this place
of meeting in the woods, and describes Clarence as
with him; and Mrs. Montgomery and her daughter put
Jesse and Wood, by accurate description of them and
their horses, bays, at their house for supper. He says
they then went from this place in the woods and committed the robbery, and tells all the details as to the
manner of its being done; and those on the train corroborate him in every particular.

   After the robbery he says they went to the Fords'
and Mrs. Samuels', and tells as to the turning loose of
the horses; and in all he is corroborated, for they are
found and the owners get them back. He says they
stayed on this side of the river for some weeks, and
then bought a wagon from Mrs. Samuels, hitched his
horse and Charlie Ford's pony to it—Charlie joining
the gang, as is conceded, after the Winston robbery—
and crossed the river at Kansas City, one of them having on women's clothes as they went over the bridge;
and separating in Jackson county, the wagon was left
at J. W. McCraw's, in the Six Mile, and his horse
returned to Lamartine Hudspeth, from whom he purchased it—and the Samuels family corroborate him as
to everything except that the living James was along,
and McCraw as to the balance. He is finally fully
corroborated as to the time and manner in which
Frank James left Ray county for Kentucky, in October,
1881, by Ida Bolton and the balance of the family, and

by Mr. Hughes, a banker at Richmond, who says he
believes Frank James to be the man he saw taking the
train at this time.   While listening to gentlemen for
the defense, I counted fifty-six material instances in
which Liddil is corroborated, and I could have extended
it to a hundred or more.   With all these details, he is
not contradicted in a single instance.   It is only contended he is in *two places*.   One when Liddil, in
describing a house close to Gallatin, said he "thought
it was a two-story white house;" and witnesses are
actually put on the stand to show it was "a story-and-
a-half white house."   What a miserable effort to break
a man down, who is describing scores of places he
never saw before nor since.   The other contradiction
is only attempted by one attorney, Mr. Slover.   He
says Liddil says there were five men at Bray's, and the
Brays say four.   But even Mr. Slover's associates, and
every reporter in this trial, will bear me out that Liddil
said Wood Hite had gone back on the train, and that
Jesse, Frank, Clarence, and himself were at Bray's.

   This is Liddil's testimony.   He was cross-examined for hours without ever varying from his testimony in chief, in a single instance.   In the very nature
of things it is bound to be true.   No man could manu-
facture such a story, carrying it along with hundreds of
details over a distance of sixteen hundred miles, without contradicting himself; much less, have scores of
witnesses come in and corroborate him at every point.
No man could put an innocent person in an expedition like this, on different horses, at dozens of places,
sometimes alone. sometimes with all the band, some-

times with one other, on trains, in houses, with families,
in the woods, under all the varying vicissitudes, covering five months of time and a distance of sixteen hundred miles,—and then be rushed through a searching
cross-examination for half a day without an error. He
could as easily perform a miracle. The state has
simply taken Liddil's statement and drawn it together
link by link, and then invincibly forged each link to its
fellow, by corroborating testimony, until we have an
unbroken and unbreakable chain stretching from Nashville to Winston. We sometimes follow the streamlet
making its way feebly but unbroken down the moun-
tain-side, but after a little another streamlet meets it,
then another and another, until at length, a resistless
torrent, it sweeps on to the plain beneath. So the evidence, taken as a whole, gathers and strengthens in this
case. So ultimately, like a torrent, it sweeps along,
bearing upon its surging crest all the "banners" and
"flags," prejudices and technicalities with which the defense have striven to resist its flow.

The strongest, yet far shortest, part of the evidence
is yet to be examined. This is the testimony of twelve
conscientious, intelligent witnesses, who identified
Frank James as one of a band seen in this section about
the time of the robbery of this train. Most of them,
without any assistance, have picked Liddil out from
the crowd of strangers on the street here since the trial,
and identify him as easily as they do Frank James,
though not a peculiar man in appearance, as is the defendant. Neither the reputation nor intelligence of
these witnesses can be attacked, for they are all splendid

citizens. Something must be done; and wandering as far from the testimony as Neptune wanders from the Sun, each lawyer for the defense makes a witness out of himself, and cites numerous instances of mistaken identity from the books, and other instances which they assure you they know about themselves, until they would reason you into the conclusion that there is no such thing as identification. To listen to them, you could not swear to one another a year hence. Having been housed up here for two weeks, you will fail to identify persons living along the road to town as you return; and will not know beyond a doubt your wives and children when you reach your homes. Such a doctrine as they have sought to instill into your minds is simply monstrous. It is contrary to all human conduct and experience. We act upon the law of faith in what other men see, every day of our lives. All history is founded on what others saw, and bear witness to. The Christian world to-day, containing teeming millions of human beings, in considering the fate of the immortal soul—the profoundest topic presented to the mind of man—is resting its faith upon a simple question of identification. The religion recognized by the laws of this nation, and which required you to take an oath to our God at the outset, hangs upon the testimony of twelve plain witnesses as to the miracles and identity of a risen Savior. Paul, the greatest of these witnesses, and one of the most logical and towering intellects the world has seen, based all his hopes for eternity on a single sight of the risen Lord.

The testimony of our twelve witnesses **is as** follows: The first three witnesses are William Bray, his wife, Mrs. Bray, and their son, R. E. Bray, well appearing, intelligent people, living, as you remember, where the four came for dinner, and Jesse James was taken to town sick.   They all describe Frank James with his "burnsides," and testify that, to the best of their knowledge and belief, the defendant is the man.   You remember Earthman, of Nashville, says Frank wore long, full, lightish whiskers in Nashville; and Liddil and all the Ford family say he had pretty long "burnsides" this summer, having shaved the chin.

4. The fourth witness was Jonas Potts, the blacksmith, who had two good opportunities to see Frank James; and he identifies him and testifies positively that he is the man.   He picked Liddil out in a crowd, and singled out the little bay mare in a livery stable in Liberty and recognized her shoes as his workmanship; why can he not as well be absolutely correct in identifying Frank James, confessedly one of the most unusual men in appearance in the country.

5.   Mrs. Jonas Potts saw Frank and Clarence at her table at breakfast—says Frank called the young fellow with him "Clarence;" and she tells you she has no doubt about this being the man.

6.   'Squire Mallory is one of your oldest and most intelligent citizens.   No man can breathe aught against him.   He tells you he realizes a man is on trial for his life, but he saw this defendant at Potts'

shop just before the robbery, and is so positive of it he has no hesitancy in swearing to it.

7. Wash Whitman shows by his appearance and demeanor that he is a most excellent and sensible citizen. You know I am not saying more for any of these witnesses than they deserve. You could not select better persons in your thriving county if given your own time for the task. Whitman says he was at Potts' shop at the same time 'Squire Mallory was, and to use his own words, says: "I am as confident as I am of anything this is one of the men I saw there. If I had any doubt about it, gentlemen, I would not say so." Whitman was a most sturdy, honest-looking fellow; and the defense as good as said, "That's the God's truth," by not venturing to ask a single question in cross-examination.

8. Mrs. James Frank, you remember, is the lady at whose house two men got breakfast before going to Potts'. She says positively Frank James is one of the men. All of these witnesses, you remember, also describe the defendant in the same way as to demeanor, clothing as far as they can recall, and say he had lightish "burnsides," or, as some termed it "side-burns."

9 and 10. Frank Wolfenbarger and his sister, Mrs. Charlotte Lindsey, are wide-awake, industrious, well-educated young people. They testify that defendant stayed all night at their house at the time Liddil says they did, and they have no question as to his identity. Each of them identified the defendant positively the first look they ever got at him.

11. Ezra Soule is a somewhat peculiar old
gentleman, perhaps, as the defense claims, but his
curious, inquiring turn makes him all the better witness. He says he was hunting blackberries in the
woods and ran across Frank James; took him and his
partner to be horse-thieves, and talked with, and
watched them especially on this account, and testifies
that this beyond question is one of the men.

12. Rev. Mr. Machette, a minister of the Christian church, is a gentleman of considerable culture and
extraordinary memory. He notices minutæ like a
woman. He tells you that a few days before the
Winston robbery two horsemen were at his house for
dinner. He charged nothing, but they paid anyhow.
He says that he is so sure that Frank James is one of
the men, that had he charged for that dinner and met
the defendant yesterday in the road, he would have
presented his bill without hesitation; that there can be
no doubt about his being the man. After relating
both on direct and cross-examination, what occurred
while the horses were being fed, when the call was
made for dry feed (for a long ride, etc.), he says they
went into the house, and Frank James, noticing he had
a library, began to talk books. In an effort to find
out something about his mysterious visitors, Machette
asked questions as to their acquaintance with towns
lying south of him, and was puzzled with skillful
evasions. Once, in answer to a question about who
he knew at a small town, the defendant said: "What
do you think of Bob Ingersol?" Finally the defendant, he said, got to Shakespeare, and after passing

encomiums on this great genius, arose and recited
extracts from his plays (the slouchy Sphinx, *alias*
Wood Hite, *alias* "Old Grimes," no doubt). A man,
gentleman, may change the exterior of his person, but
he can not change the complexion of the mind within.
This is a most remarkable mental characteristic for a
western bandit. To say that it is nothing uncommon
for a train-robber to go through the land spouting
Shakespeare is preposterous. There is no getting
away from the identification furnished by Mr. Machette. It "makes assurance doubly sure." Dr.
William E. Black, one of your best citizens, testifies
that since Frank James has been in jail, he had a long
conversation with him, in which he talked much of
Shakespeare, and of his plays, naming, I think, Mac-
beth, Richard III, Hamlet, and others; and passing his
opinion on Barrett and others, whom he said he had had
the pleasure of seeing. The nail was driven through
by the other witnesses, but the testimony of Machette
and Black, taken together, rivet forever the identity of
this defendant. This completes the evidence for the
state—abundant, conclusive, irresistible.

What is the defense? To meet such overwhelming
proof on behalf of the state, an unprejudiced mind
would naturally say it ought to be honest, genuine,
complete. What is it? Any honest defense, known
to the charge of murder—self-defense, insanity, an
alibi? They are actually ashamed to name it. Col.
Philip says, "I don't know what you would call it."
Mr. Glover's definition would do credit to some of
our modern scientists: "It is an *alibi* whose strength

consists in its weakness.'' The fact is, gentlemen, it
is an attempted *alibi*; but to sensible men so trans-
parent a dodge that they are ashamed of it. The
attempt is to show that Frank James was in Texas,
and not at Winston, in the state of Missouri, on the
fifteenth day of July, 1881. Every witness brought to
show this is a member of the family; Mrs. Samuels,
the mother of defendant, John Samuels, his brother,
Mrs. Palmer, a sister, and Palmer and Nicholson,
brothers-in-law, and defendant himself, are the witnesses. Mrs. Samuels is a mother testifying for her
son. She says he was not at her house in 1881. I am
not going to abuse her. Her testimony is contradicted
by near a score of absolutely disinterested witnesses.
She is bound to have known Jesse and his band were
robbers and plunderers, and yet she willingly fed them
all; and readily said on the stand: ''Yes, Mr. Wallace,
I furnished them a dress when they went off in the
wagon; I did this so you officers over there could not
catch them.'' Would she not shield Frank from the
law as quick as she would Jesse—now the scape-goat
of all the sins, it would seem, of both. Take her
testimony, gentlemen, together with Col. Philip's
eulogy, and give it the weight you know it deserves.
Mrs. Palmer is a sister testifying for her brother on
trial for his life. I am going to leave her, too, without any abuse, or criticism even. No sadder sight is
ever seen in life than a woman put on the stand as she
was. You know that Frank James was not at her
house in the summer of 1881, as she says. I will say
this for her: she seemed to appreciate her terrible

situation on the stand, and to feel relieved when the awful task was ended.

I can not say as much for her husband, Allen Palmer, of Clay county, Texas. He travels a thousand miles to utter a single sentence: "I worked for a railroad in the summer of 1881, and when I came home in August, Frank James was there." This is all; and his mouth is closed as with the grip of death. He is one of those *alibi* witnesses seen quite often in our courts, who bobs up and swears to one single fact, and then falls back forever into the oblivion of forgetfulness. He knows it was 1881 when Frank was there, because he, Palmer, "worked for a railroad." "On what part of the road, Mr. Palmer?" "Can't remember." "For what contractor?" "Can't remember." "For what boss?" "Can't remember." "Give name of any men working with you or near you that summer?" "Can't remember." "Was your name on the pay rolls of the company?" "Can't remember." Of course not; we might examine the rolls. "Who did you board with?" "Can't remember." "Give the name of any man who paid you any money, or who saw you there?" "Can't remember." No man who heard him was fool enough to believe a word he said. What a contrast between Liddil and Palmer—between open truth and skulking error.

John Samuels defendant's half-brother deserves scarcely a mention. Every attorney for the defense stamps his testimony as false. For twelve hours they have exclaimed, at the top of their voices, that the band beyond question was composed of only four men, Jesse

James, Dick Liddil, Wood and Clarence Hite—and
turn their backs in scorn on John Samuels who named
these four, and also Jim Cummings. His evidence does
but one thing, and that is to show the impossibility of
Liddil's putting an innocent man in the gang and trac-
ing him through such multiplied and changing vicissitudes; for you remember when Samuels was put on the
stand, doubtless for the express purpose of putting
Cummings in the band, he left him out twice in naming
the gang, and then only put him in in answer to a most
leading question; and Mrs. Samuels the very first time
she tried it made exactly the same mistake.

For Thompson Brosius, who testifies he was on
the train and thinks Frank James is not one of the robbers, a man has nothing but astonishment and sympathy. He has been visiting James in jail until, in pursuance of a maudlin sympathy, he has possibly brought
himself to think he is not the man. The truth is, like
Major McGee and every other witness on the train, he
knows nothing about who it was. Ten or twelve of
the best citizens in Gallatin come before you and impeach Brosius in a most terific manner. To some he
said he was so scared that ''The men looked fifteen feet
high, and their pistols four feet long, with muzzles as
big as your hat,'' and ''he would not know them if he
saw them.'' Those in search of an accurate description
went to him, and he said he could actually give none;
and to add to his pitiable plight as a witness, his own
brother-in-law and partner takes the stand, and says
Brosius went to see defendant since his being placed in
jail, and came back and said he ''could not say whether

James was one of the men on the train or not—could tell nothing about it.''

The only witness for the defense whose evidence is worthy of consideration is the defendant himself. And what a failure he made. You never saw a poor wretch caught in the very act of theft who did not go on the stand and tell a more reasonable story. To those unaccustomed to such things he recited his story on direct examination with some plausibility. He admits he went into Kentucky, but there he was constrained to leave the boys, after imploring them in the name of his mother, and all that was holy, not to come into Missouri. This was, you remember, in the spring of 1881. He then went, he says, to Louisville, thence to Memphis, thence to Denison, Texas, and thence to his sister's, in Clay county, Texas. In this last section he remained most quietly until September 9, 1881, when he left and went to Kentucky and met his wife, thence into Virginia and North Carolina. The cross-examination comes. To understand this entire evidence you must reflect that when he said he went to Texas, no effort was being put forth to capture the band, and that the pursuit commenced in terrible earnest after the Winston robbery of July 15, 1881. The latter part of his testimony as to going into Kentucky, Virginia, and north Carolina, was doubtless true; and knowing he would delight to corroborate himself, I first went over this ground with him —all subsequent to the robbery and when the band were falling one by one in the hot pursuit. He gives the towns he visited in Kentucky, gives exact dates, describes hotels, and gives *aliases* under which he registered. No man could ask more. He goes into Virginia, and does the same in a number of instances and does as well in North Carolina. He then comes back into Virginia, and at Lynchburg, where he says they lived, he describes their house, from whom rented, where they bought groceries, and gives names of citizens who saw them. This was splendid. All at once, however, we change, and he is asked now to go over his trip to Texas, *covering the time of the robbery*, and give details as on his trips through Kentucky, Virginia, and North Carolina; and alas! our light goes out, and we at once sit down with him and Allen Palmer in eternal oblivion. Not a single hotel can he name or describe from Louisville to Clay county, Texas. Not a single place where he registered from April to October, 1881. He finally mentions just one man he saw during this whole time, at Denison, Texas, and he absolutely refuses to give his name. A man with scores of details, on a trip in the fall of 1881 and winter of 1882, when no crime for which he is charged is committed, can not get outside of his own fancy to give a corroborating straw as to his whereabouts in the summer of 1881, when this train robbery and murder was going on in Missouri.

It is idle to talk about such testimony. Frank James was at Winston, engaged in robbery and murder. Every man on this jury knows it. God and his angles know it.

We have now, gentlemen, examined the law and the evidence. One would suppose that in a court of justice, where remarks must be confined to the law and the evidence, my task was ended. Yet I should fall far short of my duty to the state of Missouri, if I sat down without noticing some extraneous appeals that have been ingeniously made to you for the acquittal of this man, and upon which some of the attorneys laid far more stress than upon the law or the evidence.

First the appeal is made that Frank James ought to be acquitted because he "surrendered." When ordinary men place themselves in the hands of the officers—as they frequently do, and are often convicted, too—we say, "he gave himself up;" but when Frank James places himself in the hands of the officers, his attorneys continually talk to you about it as if they announced the close of some great war, in the "surrender" of the last chieftain—but let the term be used for what it is worth. Col. Philips says that because he came in and surrendered he ought not to be prosecuted.

Col. Philips. I said no such thing.

Mr. Wallace. You said it in substance a dozen times. Your speech was full of wails about the "persistency" and "revenge" "of this persecution," after the defendant has "surrendered." You want him prosecuted right easy, then; *right easy*, which is worse. A milk-and-cider prosecution is worse than none. The term "surrendered" was used hundreds of times by opposing counsel during the twelve hours consumed by them in argument, oftener than any other except the word "Chivalry." "Surrendered!" Frank James "surrendered!" When did he "surrender," gentle-

men,—when, I ask? When, as the last one of the
band, he was left helpless and alone, and the messen-
gers of the law were hot upon his track; when Jesse
James "slept the sleep that knows no waking;" when
Bill Ryan's pistols had been taken from him and he
was held in the iron grasp of the law; when Jim Cummings had fled forever from the deathly vengeance of
Jesse James; when Wood Hite, awfully shrouded,
slumbered in his awful tomb, and the green grass of
Kentucky was springing upon the grave of Clarence;
when Dick Liddil and Charlie Ford had come in, and
the officers, fully informed, were pressing swift upon
his heels; when a ten-thousand-dollar reward, like a
vengeful Nemesis, hovered about him by day, and
stood like a horrid spectre beside his couch by night.
And now, having fled from the terrors that beset his
path, and given himself up, we must all join in one
general acclaim, and he must be acquitted because he
"surrendered." Now, that the storm of the people's
wrath has blown so hotly across the crimson sea of
murder upon which he launched his boat in 1881, and
the lightning played so fiercely, and the waves dashed
so high, that like an affrighted, tempest-tossed pirate,
he has rowed his way hither to the shores of civilization, we all forsooth should meet him on the beach,
and with waving handkerchiefs and loud hurrahs conduct him, like a returning Cæsar, in triumph through
the land; charming ladies should flock about him as if
to kiss his hands, and make their lips the redder and
their cheeks the rosier; counsel should only speak of
him with becoming reverence; the judge upon the

bench should twist the law to suit his case, and jurors in supplicant homage should bend their oaths and issue a pardon to him without leaving the box. In the name of justice, gentlemen, I beseech you to stand by your oaths! You have no right to pardon this defendant, for the pardoning power, under our system of government, is lodged elsewhere than in the jury-box. Such appeals as counsel have made to you might in the earlier times, have been made with propriety to a Greek or Roman jury, for they could lawfully pardon one on trial; but what was proper performance of duty with them, might be perjury in an American jury.

Again, you are most cunningly urged to acquit because the defendant was a soldier in the "lost cause." Your sympathies and prejudices are continually appealed to in this behalf. In the opening statement for the defense, before they had even introduced their evidence, the counsel boldly told you, that you, yourselves, would remember some man, naming him, an ex-confederate, who at the close of the war returned from the army to your county here—as his client fain would have returned to his county—and was shot down like a dog. He even went away from your county, and named some returning confederate soldier who was similarly shot down on the streets of Lexington, Missouri. Governor Johnson once, or more, referred to the defendant as having been a "gallant soldier;" and any number of times you heard from them the expression, "a soldier with Gen. Shelby." But the climax was reached when Col. Philips, in speaking of

18

the surrender of the defendant, said that when he saw
that Frank James had handed his pistols to the Governor of Missouri, he was surprised that the whole
matter was closed up so quickly; was astonished that
in twenty short years all the "bitter animosities of civil
strife were ended;" in plain English, gentlemen, that
the surrender of Frank James is to be taken as the end
of the "lost cause"—that the "lost cause" wound up
in pillage, plunder, train-robbery and murder. Gentlemen, when he said that, I thought I heard Rob't E.
Lee, Stonewall Jackson, Sterling Price, and all the
gallant host of southern chiefs who slumber by them,
roll over in their graves and murmur "no," "no,"
"no." Yea, I thought I saw every confederate grave-
yard throughout the south, yawn in an instant, and
each and every sleeping soldier come forth in battle
garb from his narrow home, and all shout out in clarion
voices "no!" "no!" "no!" And even as they went
back, like receding ghosts, I still heard them shouting,
"no!" "no!" "no!"

Col. Philips talks to you about the confederate
flag, or, as he puts it, "Frank James' flag;" "my flag
went up; Frank James' flag went down," and so on.
Why unfurl the old confederate banner here? We
hear the drums beating; we hear the hoofs of horses
prancing; we see the sabers gleaming; we see the old
banner floating in the sky, and beneath it we behold,
dashing into shot and shell of battle, as honest, gallant,
and conscientious a host as ever fought and bled
on glory field; and when at last—repulsed, rid-
dled, conquered—they lost the day, we see them lay

down their arms, and with tearful eyes, nearly twenty years ago, fold the tattered old banner and lay it away forever to rest, and each soldier depart for his home with the language of their poet laureate on his lips,—

> "Furl that banner, for 'tis weary,
> Round its staff 'tis drooping dreary;
> Furl it, fold it, let it rest."

But it remained for one of Frank James' counsel, near a score of years thereafter, to unfurl that banner before a jury in a court of justice, and to ask them to heap insult, upon it and upon all who bore it, by besmirching it with the fresh blood of McMillan and Westfall, and rolling up and hiding beneath its honest folds the paltry plunder obtained by hellish robbery and fiendish assassination at Winston. Will you acquit the defendant and do it? God forbid.

Col. Philips. No such statements as you have been repeating were made direct, or indirect.

Mr. Wallace. I took your language down, and appeal to every man who heard you, to say if I am not correct. You are interrupting for the sake of interruption. You had four hours yourself and now you are growing all through my speech. You are like an old setting hen—cross both off and on the nest.

Again, it is adroitly urged that the defendant ought not to be held strictly accountable for this crime, because, if done by him, it was done in just revenge. Possibly some juror says, "there is something in that, too;" we will see. Gov. Johnson, you remember, said, "possibly the defendant could not live here and lead a quiet life after the war." I give his words in

substance. All through the speeches for the defense
this idea was evolved in divers ways, namely, that the
acts of depredation committed in Missouri since the
war were done in pursuance of a just revenge, or such a
revenge as would naturally cling to the human heart.
The hardships of the defendant and the "bad treatment" of the family of Mrs. Samuels, could have been
held up in glowing colors by Col. Philips and others
for no other purpose. Of course they do not admit nor
do I insinuate, that the defendant had anything to do
with these acts. But by whomsoever committed, I
deny that revenge had anything to do with it. Money,
money, money has been the ruling motive every time.
As so much has been said about this, go back in memory over every daring bank-robbery and train-robbery
committed, from the Alleghanies to the Rockies, since
1866, and see if former friend and foe have not both
suffered; and see if for every drop of human blood
that has been shed, there has not been a corresponding
shining dollar in the murderer's pocket. Oh, no,
gentlemen, this is all a pretext. *Money*, not revenge
is the demon that has wrought this woe.

Lastly, and chiefly, you are urged to acquit on the
broad ground of chivalry. Here the pyrotechnics of
the orators played in reddest splendor, and such ex-
pressions as "no man with a spark of chivalry in his
bosom," and a hundred kindred others, fell about you
in greatest profusion. The man of chivalry, with his
deeds of daring, was dressed up in shining, fiery apparel, and held up in glory to your enraptured view.
Gentlemen, every man extols a noble, unselfish, daring

deed; every man admires genuine bravery; and I believe I can go in admiration along the line of chivalry as far as any man alive. Bring forth your soldier, stern, cruel, and powerful as an ancient, giant warrior; give him shield and helmet and two-edged sword, and in time of war lead him forth to battle, and let him deal death and slaughter right and left, till the air is full of moans and his track is thick with dead and dying, and before I have thought I have followed him with admiration at every step. In time of war equip your horsemen; give him torch and glittering blade, and let him dash into the land of the enemy, spreading fire and desolation along his way, and plunge into the ranks of the foe until blood flows up to the bridle-bit; and when he is done, while I have condemned his horrid work, I have applauded his valor at every bound of his steed. We have all found within us a disposition to dwell in admiration on deeds of blood and daring, as when we hastily left the page of history, where we found recorded the bloodless wonders of the Holy Land—where olive branches grew, and shepherds watching their flocks by night heard angels chanting in the skies "peace on earth, good-will to men;" and turned to dote on the blurred and bloody page of Rome, the military academy of the world, and ofttimes its human slaughter house; to follow the victorious eagle soaring above the crushed-out lives and liberties of nations; to stand with the noisy rabble and watch the triumphs of Roman generals returning from gory conquest; or sit and gaze on the dread arena where man and beast, or man and man, struggled in deadly combat to amuse

the cruel crowd.   But there is a length to which we
can never go—a boundary line lying between bloodshed
in war, or from necessity, on the one hand, and bloodshed for money on the other, which the human heart in
all its admiration for chivalry will never cross.   Seven-
teen years have rolled away since the last alarum of
war was sounded; a great nation is intently engaged in
honest toil, and the whole land, from one end to the
other, is wrapped in the sweet embrace of peace.   A
pioneer axman, with the sweat dropping from his
brow, is felling his tree in a western forest; and an
idler, armed to the teeth, steals upon him, shoots him
down and rifles his pockets for money.   Or, as in the
case now on trial, a noble train is steaming across a
western prairie; it is a summer's night, and the hush of
peace is bounded only by the silent stars above and the
voiceless dewdrops on the earth beneath; a band of
outlaws comes sneaking forth from the woods, attack
the train, shoot down unarmed, unsuspecting men, all
for a few miserable dollars in money—and before I am
through the human heart and brain are exclaiming,
"There is no chivalry there! that is murder—cold,
cowardly, foul as hell!"   Call such work bravery if
you will till the tongue is tied, but there is no bravery,
no chivalry about it!   There is no chivalry that goes
beyond the rule laid down by that immortal poet whom
Frank James seems to have read so much, and whose
injunctions he should have heeded—

> "I dare do all that may become a man;
> Who dares do more is none."

Gentleman of the jury, I have taxed your patience long enough and will close. However much you may sympathize with the defendant or his family, the evidence for the state is absolutely conclusive, and must sweep from your minds every doubt as to his guilt of this crime. I have striven to perform the task assigned me as best I could; you know your duty far better than I do. Some of you are young—in the spring-time of manhood, with the flowers of hope all budding about you, and looking to the future with bright and glorious anticipations. It is a matter of importance to you that your lives be spent in a land where life and property are protected. Some of you are in middle age; upon your farms and in the midst of your substance and your families, and surrounded by all those sacred and tender interests suggested by wife, children, home, fireside. It is a matter of vast importance to you that law and order may prevail, and that robbery and murder come not to you or yours, when sleeping beneath your roof or traveling upon our public highways. One or two of you, I see, are growing old, and the silver locks upon your temples, like whited plumes on the slow-moving hearse, remind you that your narrow home is not far away; yours is the solemn duty of handing down intact to your children and children's children, those laws and liberties intrusted to you by those who went before. All of you, as citizens, and now as public servants, are intensely interested in the peace and prosperity of a glorious state. The eyes of the world are upon you, and the sacred honor of Missouri is intrusted to your charge.

Col. Philips tells you that he "loves the state of Missouri; loves her institutions; loves her people; loves her honor." Had not one older than myself, with all propriety, used the word "love," I do not know that I would have arrogated to myself so much of patriotism as to employ so strong a term; but now that the example has been set, I trust that I, who have been reared from boyhood on Missouri soil, may follow along and say that I, too, love my grand and glorious state; love her forests and rolling prairies; love her hills and flowing streams; love her free air and black old soil, yielding quick to the touch of man in abundant grain, fruit or flower; and most of all do I love her hospitable, big-hearted people, in whose midst even prowling robbers, as in this case—unknown except to a few, as such, thank Heaven!—may find, if they choose, abundant food and shelter without a farthing's pay. What a magnificent state!—with her hundreds of thousands of happy, prosperous, intelligent, law-abiding inhabitants, and resources enough within her own boundaries, if tested, to supply their every want; with thousands of miles of railroads built largely with money received from the toil of her own sons, for the welcomed incoming and onward march of progress and civilization; with towering, cultured cities springing up on her borders, and fretted within with churches, colleges, and innumerable schoolhouses. While all this is true, I must also agree with Col. Philips that Missouri has been maligned, slandered, villified, as has no other state in the union. It is a proud fact that good laws are as firmly and impartially executed here

as in any state in America, but common candor forces
the admission that while the bad stories heralded abroad
have been exaggerated a thousand fold, they are not totally without foundation. A few desperate men *have*
perpetrated on Missouri's soil as daring robbery and
bloody murder as the world ever saw, and thus heaped
odium on the people of the whole state. For you
know by the evidence that the town of Winston in this
state, was the scene of such a horror on July 15, 1881.

You now have it in your power, on overwhelming
testimony, to proclaim to justice and the world our
people's disapprobation of this horrible crime. Alas!
if with Frank James' guilt as clear as noonday, you
should—from sympathy or prejudice—find as these gentlemen are beseeching you to find, what eternal stigma
would you bring upon yourselves and your state.
Gentlemen, hear me when I say it, let the court hear
me, for after all that has been said, it is my duty to
proclaim it in deliberate reply—and would that I had a
voice so loud and shrill that it might resound in the
remotest corners of your minds, and Heaven's most
distant bounds might hear it—I say that a verdict of not
guilty, on this overwhelming testimony, would bring
greater shame upon the state than all the robberies,
small and great, committed within her borders since
1866. It were far better for us, that this defendant had
never given himself up to the officers, and had never
been tried.

Col. Philips talked much about popular clamor,
whose mighty storm he seemed so much to regret and
fear, and he implored your bravery to stand against it.

So, no matter who the defendant is, or was, or who his friends may be, *we* ask and implore you to stand bravely by your duty and your oaths given to your country and your God.

Gentlemen, my task is ended. May the "God who ruleth in the armies of Heaven, and doeth his pleasure amongst all the inhabitants of the earth;" "who holdeth the hearts of all men in his hands, and turneth them as the rivers of water are turned;" may the "God of the widow and the fatherless"—of McMillan's wife and child—come into your hearts, and guide you to a righteous verdict in this case. I thank you for your kind attention. [Applause—suppressed by the court.]

Mr. Wallace closed his argument at 12:30 P. M. whereupon the jury retired and court adjourned until 4 P. M., at which time the jury promptly returned the following verdict:

"State of Missouri v. Frank James—murder: We, the jury in the above entitled cause, find the defendant not guilty as charged in the indictment. (Signed.)   WM. T. RICHARDSON, Foreman."

DICK LIDDIL'S CONFESSION.

My name is James Andrew Liddil. I was born on September 15, 1852, in Jackson county, Missouri. My father's name is James M. Liddil, and he lives in Vernon county, Missouri. I have known Jesse W. James since the year 1872 or 1873. I met him at Bob Hudspeth's, who lives about ten miles east of Independence, Missouri. I was working there at the time. Jesse came with Ben Morrow, whose father lives one and a half miles from Bob Hudspeth's. I think Ben Morrow was making his home at Bob Hudspeth's at this time. Within a few days after this I met Frank James, at Hudspeth's house. They were both outlaws at this time, and were on the "dodge," though they did not appear to be very apprehensive. I lived at Bob Hudspeth's for nine years, off and on, beginning in 1871 or 1872. During the first four or five years I saw Jesse and Frank James a great many times at Hudspeth's. He entertained them as friends, not through fear. During these four or five years I have seen them very often at Silas Hudspeth's, Bob's brother. He also entertained them as friends. They never told me, nor did I hear them tell any one that they were train robbers up to this date. Both the Hudspeths knew all this time, as I did myself and people generally, that they were dodging the officers.

283

I never knew them to stay longer than one or two nights during these years. Clell Miller, Cole and Jim Younger, Tom McDaniels, use to frequent some of the above named houses. They were dodging the officers, too, at this time. The first time I saw Jesse James was after the Northfield Bank robbery at Ben Morrow's, in Jackson county. I met Ben and he told me Jesse was to be at his house that evening, and had said he wanted to see me. About 2 o'clock I went to Ben's, and found Jesse in the yard getting some water out of a barrel. We had a little chat, and went out to where his horse was tied in the woods. He said he was broke, and wanted to make a raise, and wanted me to help him. I agreed. This was on Sunday. We separated then and went to meet at Ben Morrow's, next Wednesday evening. We met, according to appointment, and he told me he wanted to rob the C. & A., or Missouri Pacific train. He said that he had two other men besides himself. He said that he had come up from General Jo Shelby's, in Lafayette county, where he had been since seeing me on the preceding Sunday. We then went up to Jim Hulse's, getting there about 1 o'clock at night. We found Ed Miller there. Hulse entertained us as friends. We all three left the next night. I had no arms at that time. Jesse had a pair of Colt's 45 calibre, and Ed Miller had a breech-loading shot gun, a pair of Smith & Wesson's 44 calibre, and an old-fashioned navy pistol. We then went from there to old Thomas Eddington's, not to the house, but hitched our horses out in the woods. Next morning I went up to get some food for us. I told them for whom I wanted it. After eating breakfast, Ed Miller started over to Clay county for "father Grimes," (Wood Hite), nd a man by the name of Smith, who lives about five or six miles from Kearney, and about three or four miles from Mrs. Samuels. He was a single man, I learned Ed Miller was gone two days, and returned with Grimes and Smith. The former he got at Mrs. Samuels, his aunt's. During this time Jesse was hiding at Ben Morrow's, and I was at old man Eddington's Upon Miller's return I told him to hide out in the brush and I would go after Jesse, which I did. When Jesse and I returned, Smith had run off and left. He was afraid he would be killed. He thought Jesse was going to do it. After he left, we disbanded,—Grimes and Jesse going over to Mr. Ford's, near Richmond, Ray county, and Miller to see what had become of Smith. I stayed at Lamartine Hudspeth's.

About three days after this Jesse and Grimes came back, and we three went back to Jim Hulse s. A little after this Ed Miller came up there also. He said Smith had gone home and was playing off crazy, and had lost his pistol, hat, etc. The next morning I came up to Independence, took the train for Kansas City, and bought me a pair of Smith & Wesson pistols, forty-four calibre, from Blitz the pawnbroker in the Times Building. I went back to the train, mounted my horse and road to Independence, road down towards Dick Tolley's, and met Jesse and Ed Miller on the road. We went off by the creek in the woods, where we found Grimes and Bill Ryan. We talked the matter over, and determined to rob the C. & A. train at Glendale. We then broke up that night. Miller and I went to Tucker Basham's house,—I don't know where the others went, but we were all to meet at the schoolhouse, several miles from Glendale. I did not know at that time who Basham was, and we did not know his real name until after he was arrested. They called him "Arkansaw." The next evening, about sun down, Miller and I started for the schoolhouse, and "Arkansaw" was to follow. The schoolhouse is about one mile from Basham's house. We met at the schoolhouse, and all went to Glendale together We arrived there between six and seven o'clock on October 8, 1879, and hitched our horses about thirty yards due south of the station. Basham, Ryan and myself captured Joe Molt's store, and about fifteen or twenty men who were in it; and Jesse James, Ed Miller and Wood Hite captured the depot. Jesse, who was the leader, then sent word to us to bring our prisoners over to the depot, which was done—and we put them all in the depot and guarded them. I think Jesse tore the telegraph apparatus to pieces. Basham thought it was a sewing machine, and wanted him to stop,—as destroying it would do no good. A little east of the depot, obstructions were placed upon the track to stop the train in case flagging failed. When the eastern bound train came in sight we made the operator signal the train to stop it. The train stopped. Our plan was this: I was to capture the engineer and fireman, Bill Ryan was to uncouple the express car from the train, so that we could after backing the train

run the engine forward again and leave the passenger
coaches all to themselves. Basham and Hite were to
keep the passengers on the train, while Jesse and Ed
Miller robbed the express car. The cars had a patent
coupling, so that Ryan could not unfasten them; so he
helped Basham and Hite keep the passengers in. We
carried our respective parts with the above exception.
Fifteen or twenty shots were fired in all—most of them
in the air, and a few of them at a man with a lantern
at the rear part of the trian. Jesse said he fired three
times at this man. Ed Miller got a sledge hammer
out of the engine and struck the door of the express
car several times before the express messenger would
open it. They went in, and I think the messenger
tried to get out and James struck him with his pistol.
After the car was robbed, we were all standing on the
depot platform together, when some one fired a shot
from the train which went through the drawers and
pants of Wood Hite, on the outside, between the ankle
and knee of the right leg. Jesse remarked, "they are
firing on us and we had better leave." We then went
to our horses, carrying our plunder in a common meal
sack. We mounted and rode about six or seven miles
south, .c a little old log cabin, uninhabited, where we
dismounted. Ed Miller carried the plunder Here
we divided the plunder equally, each getting about
$1,025. There were a great many bonds etc, and
these were all destroyed. We left there all together,
and retraced our steps several miles. When we began
to break up, Ryan and Basham going home. We
took Hite into the Kansas City road, about half way be-

tween Independence and the bridge over the big Blue, and left him. He went to Kansas City, I think, to Charlie McBride's. I did not know what Grime's right name was until the next spring, when I learned it was Robert Woodson Hite, and that he lived near Adairsville, in Logan county, Kentucky. Jesse, Ed and myself rode down into the "Six Mile" country, after the robbery, and I left them in a thick woods, about three fourths of a mile from Bob Hudspeth's, and went on to Lamartine Hudspeth's. Lamartine lives about two miles from Bob's. From Thursday to Saturday, I carried them food.

Saturday night, the time the big raid was made, Jesse and Ed Miller left about 10 o'clock in the direction of Kansas City; and Jesse afterward said that some time during the next day, (Sunday) they saw members of the raiding party returning to Kansas City. For two or three weeks after this I continued to stay in "Six Mile," and then left for Ft. Scott, where I hauled coal for about four months. A few days after going toward Kansas City, Ed went to George B. Hite's, near Adairville, Kentucky, and Jesse went to Nashville, Tennesse, where his wife was then living. Frank James and his wife were also living here at this time. After leaving Ft. Scott, I went to Carthage, Missouri, where I teamed it for about two months— having two teams. Sam Strickland, colored, was with me nearly all of this time. From there I came to Jackson county, and stopped at McCraws, where I learned that officers had been looking for me ever since I left Jackson county. I sent McCraw down to Carthage after Mattie Collins, Strickland and m' teams, and they drove them up. I dodged around from one place to another, staying at Lamartine Hudspeth's, principally. The same day that they returned from Carthage with the teams, Ed Lee, now deputy marshal under Murphy, and then constable of Osage township, got after me at Lake City, and we had a run of about two and a half miles. I was riding a horse of Bob Hudspeth's, which I had down to Lake City for the purpose of running a race. I had ridden him two heats, before the chase began. I was unarmed at the time. Lee fired two shots at me; but I rode hard straight to Hudspeth's, put the horse in the stable, struck out on foot, and next day went to Ben Morrow's. who knew I was dodging the officers, and bought a horse from him in a trade. I gave him for it one of my wagon horses and a set of harness, all valued at $125. I then rode to Jasper county, Missouri, where I stopped at the house of a man named Johnnie Lohr, a German, for whom I worked by the month. I stayed there about a month. While at Ft. Scott and Carthage I went by my right name, but at Lohr's I went by the name of James Anderson. I came back on horseback to Jackson county, and went to the widow Broughton's, who lives near the Hudspeths. I stayed there about one day, and went from there to Mrs. Samuels, near Kearney in Clay county, Missouri. I went to see Ed Miller, as Johnnie Samuels had come over and told me he was there. I crossed the river at Blue Mills. Upon arriving, I made myself known to Mrs. Samuels. I

19

had been there but a few minutes when Jesse James
came in He had been there several days. While I
was there, I sold him one of my horses, a set of harness and a wagon for $125. He never paid me, how-
ever until he robbed the paymaster at Mussel Shoals,
Alabama. We stayed about two days at Mrs. Samuels,
and then he and I went over to Mrs. Bolton's. about
one and one half miles east of Richmond. This is the
same place where Sheriff Timberlake and Commissioner Craig made the raid, in the early part of January, 1882. We found there Charlie Ford, "Cap"
Ford, Mrs. Bolton and the children. They knew
Jesse, but did not know me. We stayed there a day
and night, and left for Bill Ryan's, in Jackson county,
crossing at Blue Mills. We found Bill Ryan at home,
and left next night, taking him with us. We crossed
through the state to Cape Girardeau, where we crossed
the Missouri river and went directly to young George
Hite's, in Logan county, Kentucky. He was living at
the house of his father, George B. Hite, where Jeff
Hite was afterward arrested.

    We were on the road about three weeks, and I did
not see any friends en route We found Grimes there,
and learned for the first time his real name—Robert
Woodson Hite. Jeff (Clarence) Hite was there also.
We stayed there a couple of days, and leaving Bill
Ryan there Jesse and I went to Nashville, Tennessee.
From there we went to Jesse's house, which was about
three miles from Nashville, on the Hyatt Ferry Pike,
and a quarter of a mile from the Cumberland river.
Jesse was going under the name of J. D Howard, and

he pretended to be a sporting man. His wife, son and daughter were living there as was Frank James, his wife and their little son. Frank was going by the name of B. J. Woodson. His little son, who was then about three years old, was named Robert. Jesse's son was seven years old, and named Tim; and his daughter was three years old and named Mary. Frank's wife was named Fannie, and Jesse's wife was called Josie. Frank was engaged at the time in hauling saw-logs. We all went up to Nashville very frequently, and made no attempt at concealment, apprehending no special danger. After remaining there about two weeks, Jesse and myself went back to Hite's, where we had left Bill Ryan. Young Joe Hite knew we were dodging the officers; but he entertained us as friends, and not because he was intimidated. During the day we kept hid in the woods, and at night we slept in the house. Old man, George B. Hite, brought food to us in the woods oftener than anybody else. Clarence and Wood Hite brought it when their father did not. Bill Ryan was going under the name of Thomas Hill. The last time we arrived in the night and left the same night, taking Bill Ryan with us. We started to rob the Mammoth Cave stage. It rained so hard, however, that we gave up the idea after getting within one mile and a half of the place, and we came back to Hite's again. We stayed in the woods that night, and next morning I left for Jesse's place, near Nashville, leaving Bill Ryan and Jesse, who said they would knock around the country and see what they could rob. In about ten days Jesse came home and told me that he and Bill Ryan had robbed the Mammoth Cave stages. This was, I think, in the latter part of August, 1880, or September 7. The stages were robbed within an hour of each other. A lawyer by the name of R. H. Roundtree, of Lebanon, Kentucky lost a handsome gold watch. Jesse got the watch and the key to it. On the key was inscribed the name of "J. Proctor Knott and Mr. Roundtree." Jesse has the watch yet. Miss Lizzie Roundtree lost a fine diamond ring, which Jesse James' wife has had made smaller for her finger, and she wears it now.

Jesse also got from her another plain gold ring which he gave to Nellie Hite, sister of Clarence Hite. Bill Ryan got one silver watch and a small gold chain. Jesse got another silver watch which he gave me. This watch I traded to Frank James for a gold watch and chain, I giving a good horse to boot. This gold watch and chain I gave to Mattie. They got about $30 in cash which was divided equally between Ryan and Jesse. Bill Ryan afterward pawned the silver watch he got in this robbery to Dick Talley for a saddle. These silver watches, I learn from book accounts, belonged, one to W. G. Welsh, Pittsburg, and the other don't know to whom. When Jesse James come home after this robbery, he left Bill Ryan up at Hites again. After remaining about a week Jesse and Frank left for Hites in order to get Bill Ryan; and all three to go up into Kentucky to rob a store about sixty miles from Adairsville. Jesse road horse-back and I went on the train to Springfield and walked out to Hites. The following night, Clarence (Jeff) Hite and I went up to Adairsville for

the purpose of borrowing somebodys horse for an in-
definite length of time. We found it hitched to Dr.
Hendricks hitching post in front of his office. I held
Clarence's horse while he got down and unhitched the
animal. It belonged to young Simmons, whom I afterward learned was visiting the Doctors daughter. This
mare was a jet-black one, with four white feet—was a
fine one. We went back to Hites, and same night
Ryan, Jesse and I started for the store—were two days
getting there. Tuesday morning the fifteenth day of
September, 1880, I left Jesse and Ryan in the woods,
and went to John Davey's store, can't recall the name of
the town. It was some railroad station where they were
mining coal, to reconnoiter. Came back in a short
time and reported, and then went down together. I
was to guard the door and not let any one out, and
Ryan and Jesse were to rob the safe. We carried out
the programme, but only got $4.23, and a gold watch
and chain from Davey. The watch I pawned with a
friend in Jackson county, Missouri, and can get it any
time. Ryan got the chain; don't know what he did
with it. This took place between 9 and 10 o'clock,
A. M. We left and went across the county on a bee
line for Hite's. Got there the following night. We
told old man George B. Hite, Clarence Hite and Wood
Hite where we had been and what we had done. None
of them made any objections to our staying around them.
The horse that we got in Adairsville was put in a stall
at a camp meeting ground close to Adairsville for the
purpose of letting the owner find her—which was done.
In a day or two Clarence Hite took Bill Ryan to Nash-

ville in a buggy and left on a train for Jackson county, Missouri; we intending to follow soon. Jesse and I stayed at Hite's for a few days and rode down to his, (Jesse's) house near Nashville—remaining there about two week's attending the races at Nashville and then went to Atlanta, Georgia, to attend the races. When they were over, came back to Nashville, stayed three or four days, and then Jesse and I took the train for St. Louis; from there to Richmond, Ray county. Before leaving, Jesse took his family to Nashville where they stopped at a boarding house. Just after Ryan had left for Kentucky, and while Jesse and I were still at Hite's, we concluded to go down and rob the Gallatin stage. On the way down overtook two young men and attempted to rob them and had a shooting scrape. One man saw me drawing my pistol, when he drew his first and shot at Jesse, who was a little ahead of him. The other man started to draw his when I shot him through the right leg. He then turned and galloped off. The other one and Jesse exchanged a few shots, when Jesse took to the woods. My horse had run about fifty yards when I turned and the young man and I were closing in, he fired his last shot and turned and galloped off. Jesse fired two shots at him from the woods, and four shots before running to the woods. I shot three times. We didn't get any money this time. We went back to Hite's and from there to Nashville as I have before stated. After Jesse and I had reached Richmond, we went out to Mrs. Boltons. Met Jim Cummings there; remained a day and night, and went up in Clay county, to Mrs. Sam-

uel's. We were preparing for anohter strike. Put up
at the house and locked our horses in the stable; stayed
there two days and nights, when I left and rode to
Bob Hedspeths crossing at Missouri City; stayed all
night and went from there to Bill Ryan's. Went to
tell Bill not to go away, as Jesse and Cummings would
be over in a few days. Found him at home. Stayed
until Jesse and Cummings came over—they rode over
and crossed the river at Leavenworth (bridge). We
then all started back to Nashville on horse back,
having given up the idea to make a raid. Down on
Iron Mountain road I took the train and the other
boys led my horse. Got to Nashville about December,
1, 1880.

Before starting back to Tennessee this time Jim
Cummings and I took a horse a piece from a man by
the name of Duvall who lives five or six miles from
Richmond, Missouri. Charlie Ford told us where they
were. These were the horses Jesse and Jim Cummings
rode over to Bill Ryan's. Jesse and Bill Ryan took
horses from men near Independence. After getting to
Nashville I traded my horse to Frank James for the
watch, as I have stated. Jim Cummings sold his
through a man who stays at H. H. H. Hammer & Co.
livery stable. Bill Ryan sold his at same place and
Jesse sold his at Maysville, Kentucky, to some one.
Cummings went by the name of Wilson. Just after
getting back Jesse rented a house over in east Nashville
(Edgefield) and took his family and Ryan and Cummings to live with him. I stayed out at Frank's until
just before the Mussel Shoals robbery. Frank moved

to Edgefield, near to where Jesse was living, and I
went with him.   During this time—about three months
—Jesse, Cummings and Ryan made frequent trips
about the county—up to Donny Pences' and other
places.   While living at Edgefield Jesse tried to get us
to agree to have Cummings killed.   I would not agree
to this and Cummings left and we, fearing that he
would inform on us, scattered.   I went to Hite's.
Jesse's family moved over to Frank's house and Frank,
Jesse and Bill Ryan left for Alabama, where they
robbed the United States paymaster, Smith, at Mussells
Shoals.   They got $5,200, about, and a pistol.   This
robbery took place about ten days after we left
Edgefield.   I did not know anything about it until after
Bill Ryan's capture.   After the robbery the three came
straight back to Nashville and Jesse came on up to
Hite's after me and then rode back to Nashville.   Clar-
ence drove me to Springfield and went down to Nashville on train with me.

*   *   *   *   *   *   *   *   *

Jesse and I stayed in Nelson county about a week
longer and then rode to Louisville, Jesse riding a sorrel
horse he had stolen from a man in Nashville and had
left with Donny Pence.   This horse was stolen before
Ryan's capture a little while and I rode the one I had
gotten from near Adairsville.   This was a brown.   We
left these horses at a livery stable near the center of the
city, fronting east, I think, and told the proprietor to
keep them until we called.   Have never called yet.
When I arrived next morning at Mrs. Samuels'
Jesse was absent.   Frank and Wood were there and

Clarence did not arrive until late in the evening. The first thing Frank wanted was for me to go with him up in Platte county and get horses for him and Wood. We went and were gone four or five days but did not find any good horses and did not get any. When we got back Jesse had arrived. We all stayed in the house. Our horses—that is Jesse's and mine, were kept in the stable. In three or four days Wood and I took the evening train at Kearney; went to Liberty and got two horses saddled and hitched to a rack near the Athens House; rode them back to Mrs. Samuels'. She knew we were going to Liberty after the horses. The horses that we got in Liberty were turned loose near Richmond, Missouri, by Frank and Wood, Frank keeping one of the saddles, and the other, not being much account, was thrown away. He and Wood stole two other horses near that point and rode them up to the old lady's. Frank still was not satisfied with his mount so he and Wood took another tour way up in Platte county but did not get a horse. When they got back Frank and I started out after a couple of horses. We went down to Mrs. Bolton's and next night stayed on Elk Horn, between Kearney and Richmond; got a dark bay horse from a man by name of Frazier, and a mare from a man who lives about a a mile further toward Richmond and about ten miles from that place; turned the other two horses loose and rode the new ones back to Mrs. Samuels'. All five of us were then there. About the next night Jesse, Clarence and I went over to a man's by the name of Mathews who lives about one mile from Kearney and got his sorrel horse with bald face and white legs. That night we all stayed out in the woods near the old lady's with our horses and the following night we all started out in the direction of Winston for the purpose of robbing a train.

*　*　*　*　*　*　*　*　*

We dismounted at the public spring at Independence and sent back the horses by the boy named Andy, (Andy Ryan). All came according to agreement to meet the other boys at the wagon bridge south of Independence, about one and one fourth miles down the Chicago & Alton railroad. When we reached it we found Jesse, Frank, Charlie and Wood. Our object in meeting was to perfect arrangements for robbing another train. We went up and examined the Missouri Pacific railroad that night and stayed in the woods about one mile from Blue Tank. We prowled around here for several days and finally concluded to rob the Missouri Pacific railway train eastern bound. This was Friday night—Frank and Jesse about sundown, unknown to us, went out, ostensibly for the purpose of hunting railway ties with which to obstruct the track, and while absent fastened a piece of iron on a rail for the purpose of ditching the train. This plan did not suit the balance of us but as the train was almost due not much was said. The train came along and ran right over the iron and passed along safely. The next night we went to take the Chicago & Alton about three miles west of Glendale but we were very tired and gave up this idea. The train came along and it was guarded by men whom all plainly saw standing on the platform. We then came up near Independence and disbanded. Wood and I went to Mrs. Bolton's, crossing in a skiff near Lexington, the other four came back to Kansas City. We stayed down there about two weeks or more when Jesse sent us word by Charlie Ford to meet him right away at same place as our first meeting near Independence. Charlie had been going backward and forward between Richmond and Kansas City.

* * * * * * * * * *

Charlie went back on train and Wood and I went to appointed place crossing at Napoleon after being at the rendezvous.

* * * * * * * * * *

While staying at Mrs. Bolton's during this time Charlie Ford and I robbed the stage that runs between Excelsior Springs and Vibbard. There was in it a merchant from Vibbard named Gant and the driver. Charlie made them stand and I made them deliver. We got about $13 from the merchant and about $17 from the driver. Charlie had on a mask but I had none. This took place between sundown and dark. We went back to Mrs. Bolton's from there. About a week after this Charlie and Bob Ford, Wood Hite and myself robbed the stage going from the short line depot and Lexington. It was down in Ray county, Missouri, All were masked. It occurred about dark. A mover first came along and found us hid and wanted to know what it meant; we explained the situation to him by capturing him and taking $20 of his hard earnings. In about five minutes the stage came along. There were

eight passengers I think in it, two of them women.
Bob and Wood made them stand and Charlie and I
robbed them. We made the men get out. Did not
molest the women. We got about $200 in money,
"one gold watch and chain," "one nickel plated watch
and gold chain," one silver watch, no chain" and one
pocket knife. Wood Hite got one of the watches (the
silver) which he afterward sold to me and I gave it to
Bob Ford and he has it yet. Bob got the nickel plated
watch and chain. Wood afterward won or bought it
from him and he gave it to "Cap" who has it now.
The gold watch and chain fell to my lot. I gave it to
Ida Bolton. She has it yet. Hite got the knife and
lost it. We went back to Mrs. Bolton's after the robbery. Found Charlie Ford and afterward Frank
came and we went down to within about one mile of old
man Ralston's where we met Jesse and Clarence.

We then went down to Chicago & Alton road
about a half mile south of Doc Reeds. Stayed there all
night and next day. The following night we went up
to within two or three hundred yards of old man
Ralstons, where we met Frank who had left us for the
purpose of getting provisions. He had a basket full,
suppose he got it at his father-in-law, Ralston. We
went from there the same night to about three miles of
Glendale. Laid in the brush all next day, I went
down to the section house and got some bread and raw
meat. That night we robbed the Chicago & Alton
Western bound train. It was the night of Wednesday
the seventh of September, 1881. This was called the
Blue Cut Robbery. Our programme was this: Wood

and Charlie Ford were to stop the train by swinging a red light, this was an ordinary lantern with a red piece of flannel tied around it. We had piled rocks upon the track so as to obstruct it. After the train had stopped, Charlie and Wood were to capture the engineer and fireman and then rob the express car. Jesse and Frank were on one side of the track upon the bank and Frank and myself were on the other side, besides our pistols, I had a breech loading shot gun, and Frank had a Winchester rifle, Jesse had a breech loading shot gun, and Clarence had a Winchester rifle. The train came along in due time and was stopped by the lantern and the fireman and engineer captured. The fireman was made to take his sledge-hammer and attempt to beat down the door to the express car. After several blows the messenger opened it. Wood and Charlie went in and robbed the safe, Charlie struck the messenger several times with his pistol and made him open the safe. Very little was found in the safe and Jesse suggested robbing the passengers. Charlie and Wood commenced at front of the train. Wood carrying the bag and Charlie making the passengers disgorge. Clarence stood at door on platform. Jesse and I at one time were on the rear car This was after the passengers had been robbed, Frank got on one of the forward coaches. Just after the train stopped some one started down the track with a lantern. We fired a number of shots after him, but when told he was going to flag the freight train we stopped shooting. There was no one participating in this robbery except we six. There was no one in sight when we stopped the train besides ourselves. Before the train started again we all had started toward Independence. About half a mile or more we stopped in a woods and divided the booty. This consisted of a "breast pin and set of earrings, five watches, two with and three without chains I think ; two rings, one a plain gold ring and one with a set in it, and some money. Everything in the jewelry line was put up and sold to the highest bidder, except these two rings Jesse kept one of these and I kept the other. The prices bid were turned into the common fund as so much cash and then this fund was divided equally between the six. All got about $160 apiece—as near as I can now remember. Jesse got one of the watches, a nickel plated watch. Wood Hite got a gold watch belonging to the messenger. Charlie Ford got two—a gold and a silver one. Don't know what disposition he made of them. Clarence got a silver one. Jesse said he throwed his ring away and I gave mine to Mrs. Bolton. After the division Wood and I started to Blue Mills Ferry with the intention of going to Mrs. Bolton's and the other four started to Kansas City. Wood and I came near running into some officers at Blue Mills Ferry, but we dodged out into the woods. There we separated, Wood went down to cross the river near Sibley and went to Mrs. Bolton's and I went down to Ben Morrows. Got there in the morning after staying out in the brush near by till night.

I told him about the robbery, told him I was in it. I also told him that Frank, Jesse, Wood Hite and Clarence, and a man by the name of Johnson from

Texas was in it. I did not wish to tell on Charlie
Ford is the reason I gave him this alias. Took breakfast with Morrow, and stayed around, then hid in the
woods and stable two days and two nights. Morrow
knew where I was all the time and furnished me food—
all that I got. He brought me a couple of bottles of
whiskey, also. When I left he told me where I could
get a skiff to cross the river. I did not go there, however, but went to Sibley and crossed over in a skiff that
I cut loose from the bank and used. After crossing
I went to Mrs. Bolton's. After being there a couple
of weeks Charlie Ford brought us word from Jesse that
he wanted us to go to Kentucky, and rob the Louisville
and Nashville road. Wood and I then took the train
at Richmond and sent word to Jesse we would meet
him at old man Hites near Adairsville, Kentucky. We
arrived at Mr. Hites and after being there about four
days, Wood and I had a shooting scrape and I took the
train and came back to Mrs. Bolton's, Ray county,
Missouri. Had been back only two or three nights
when Clarence, Frank and Charlie Ford came in.
They stayed a day and night and started for Kentucky,
wanting me to go with them. I declined to do so.
Remained there two or three weeks, and then Bob
Ford and I crossed over at Missouri City into Jackson
county. We went to McGraws and stayed about a
week. He was out with a threshing machine while I
was there. Did not see him but once while there. We
then went to Mrs. Bolton's, crossing below Sibley in a
skiff. Arrived there Saturday night, December 3,
1881. Next morning I came down to breakfast, and

Wood Hite who had come from Kentucky three or four days before was there, and Bob Ford came down a few minutes afterward. When he first came in he spoke to me, and I told him I did not want him to speak to me as he had accused me of stealing $100 at the divide in the Blue Cut robbery. Told him he lied; said he could prove it by Mrs. Bolton, and I wanted him to prove it. He then denied ever saying anything of the kind. I told him he did, and we both commenced drawing our pistols. We fired about the same time. He shot me through the right leg between the knee and hip and I shot him through the right arm. He fired four times at me and I five times at him, and then snapped another barrel at him. I drew my other pistol when he commenced falling. Bob Ford fired one shot at him. Did not know this until afterward when he exhibited the empty chamber. The wound that killed Hite was through the head. It struck him about two inches above the right eye and came out in front and a little above the left ear. Bob claimed that his shot was the fatal one. Hite lived fifteen or twenty minutes but did not speak. We carried him upstairs, and that night of December 4th "Cap" and Bob dug a grave in the woods about a half mile from the house and buried him. My leg was too sore to help. Did not use a coffin. I never had a physician dress my wound or give it any attention until after I surrendered. On the night of Thursday, the twenty-ninth of December, Jesse and Charlie Ford came down to Mrs. Bolton's, where I had been since being wounded and tried to get me to go with them. They claimed to have come from

Nebraska. I declined to go. I mistrusted Jesse wanted to kill me and so left. This was on Saturday night, December 31, 1881. Jesse and Charlie left the next night for the old lady's I was told. This was the last time I ever saw him, and I never have seen Charlie Ford since. After the raid on Mrs. Bolton's house early in January, 1882, I concluded to surrender. Negotiations to that effect were made, and on the night of January 24, 1882, by directions of Gov. Thos. T. Crittenden I surrendered to James R. Timberlake, sheriff of Clay county, Missouri. Dick Liddil is a nickname for me.

J. A. Liddil

Subscribed and sworn to before me this twenty-ninth day of March, 1882.

HENRY H. CRAIG,
Police Commissioner, Kansas City, Mo.

20

CLARENCE HITE'S CONFESSION.

Made a short time before his death, in the Warden's office of the state penitentiary at Jefferson City, Missouri, in the presence of Gov. T. T. Crittenden, H. H. Craig and Sheriff Timberlake.

HIS FIRST CONNECTION WITH THE GANG.

I met Jesse and Frank James about ten years ago, just after the war. They came to our house and staid two or three months. My first act of lawlessness was at Winston, Missouri. I came to Missouri the first of May, 1884. I was with Jesse's wife. We came from Nelson county, Kentucky. She was staying at Donny Pence's. He was sheriff of the county. She had been staying there about one month. Jesse and Frank were in Nelson county at the time. Frank was at Aleck Sears', and Jesse and Dick Liddil were at Bob Hall's. Jesse staid at Pence's several nights while I was there. Before I got there (Donny Pence's) they staid at Dock Hoskin's. The latter lived about twelve miles from Pence's. Hall lived about one and a half miles from Pence's. Myself, Jesse's wife and her two children came on to Kansas City. We left Pence's the last of April (1881). Put up at the Pacific house, Louisville. She was registered as Mrs. Jackson, or Wilson, and

306

two children, Bowling Green, Kentucky. I registered as C. Browler, Bowling Green, Kentucky. When we reached Kansas City we stopped at Charlie McBride's, on seventeenth street, between Oak and McGee. Got there Saturday night. Monday I went over to Mrs. Samuels' and she came over to see Jesse's wife. I staid over there about one week, when Jesse and Liddil came. They staid there off and on till the last of July, 1881. The Winston robbery was on July 15, 1881. Frank arrived at Mrs. Samuels' one week after Jesse and Dick Liddil did. No one came with Frank. He remained there until the robbery.

When the robbery was planned at Mrs. Samuels', there were present Jesse James, Frank James, Dick Liddil, my brother, Robert Woodson Hite, and myself. We five were the only ones engaged in the robbery. I do not know where my brother is now. I last saw him in 'ast November, at home. His name is Robert Woodson Hite. He left home without saying where he was going.

We robbed the train about one month after the robbery was planned. We went there once before to do it, but all got wringing wet, and Jesse caught the toothache out in the woods, and his face swelled up so he could hardly see, and we gave it up for the time being, and he (Jesse) got a man who lived one half mile from the Hannibal & St. Joseph Railroad to take him to Hamilton in a buggy. He had a large flock of sheep, and his house was a long way from the fence. Jesse took the train at Hamilton and came on to Kansas City. Frank helped him in the buggy. To Ham-

ilton was about three miles. As you go east the man
lived on the right-hand side. Jesse told me he paid
the man $1.50 to haul him to town. When the party
first left Mrs. Samuels', Jesse, Frank, Dick Liddil and
my brother rode down to Ray county to Mrs. Bolton's,
and I came on to Kansas City to get some newspapers
and cartridges. I got them and went down to Ray
county to Mrs. Bolton's. I got there one night and
left there next morning for Richmond, Missouri, and
then left for Plattsburg, Missouri. Frank, Jesse, Dick
and my brother went on horse-back to Gallatin. I
went to Plattsburg to get a bill changed. I then took
the Rock Island train for Gallatin. We all then went
out in the woods and had a talk. They got on their
horses and rode to Kidder and I got on the train and
went there. I went on the train because I had no
horse. When the party was at Mrs. Boltons' her three
children and Charles Ford, Captain Ford, Robert
Ford, and another Ford, a great big fellow, were
there. Neither the Ford boys nor Dr. Samuels or his
wife or their son knew what was brewing when the
party was at Gallatin, they stayed out in the woods.
After Jesse was put on the cars I rode his horse and
Frank and Dick led my brother's. We went down
near Mirable, and went from thence to Mrs. Samuels'
and Dick and Frank went from there to Mrs. Bolton's.
My brother got on the train and went to Mrs. Samuels'.

A week or so afterward Jesse wrote to John Samuels to bring his horse over to Kansas City. He
(Samuels) did so the following Sunday. He received
the letter the preceding Saturday. Jesse and his wife

were keeping house in Kansas City. I went over to Kansas City on the fourth of July, 1881 (on Monday after Samuels took the horse over). Jesse rode over to Mrs. Samuels on the night of July 4, and John Samuels and myself came back that night. Jesse said he crossed on the ferry boat at Kansas City. He said he came by some newspaper office and read the Garfield bulletins. (The details of a watch presentation omitted by Mr. Craig.) He said he gave ———— a watch. A few days after Jesse arrived at Mrs. Samuels', Frank and Dick came up from Ray county. They got there Wednesday night. We all remained there about one week. Frank and Dick went back to Mrs. Bolton's before going to Winston.

The gang came back again to Mrs. Samuels' before going to Winston. It is about thirty-five or forty miles from Mrs. Samuels' to Winston. When we started to Winston we left on the Sunday night before the robbery, about 8 o'clock. We went above Platt-burg, about six miles, the first night. A few miles from Mrs. Samuels' we met a man riding a whitish horse, whom Jesse said he knew, named Pence.

We arrived at the point above Plattsburg at daylight. We laid down in the woods and went to sleep. We slept till about sunrise. We then crossed the Rock Island road and went close to a little town, and Dick and myself went in and bought some candy and stuff. Dick had a shoe put on his horse. This was on Monday morning. The rest went on outside of town and stopped. We went through the edge of Cameron and Frank, my brother and myself went up to an oat field, pulled down some shocks and laid down, while Jesse and Dick went into town and bought some sausage, etc., and looked at the Rock Island train. We three slept until daylight. Jesse and Dick came and waked us up about 11 o'clock, and they went past us down into the woods.

We then went on close to Cameron and staid in the woods till late in the evening and then went on up to Winston. Frank and myself went on through to Winston, and the rest came on afterward. We all went down in some woods below Winston, and that night (Tuesday) Frank and myself went back to Winston and got something to eat. We went back then to where the rest were and slept till morning. Frank and myself then went above Winston, about five miles northeast, and had our horses shod. We all then went up near Cameron, intending to rob the train there, but there were too many people got on, and we went back in the woods, and slept all night (thirteenth). Got up before sunrise (fourteenth). We went to Gallatin. That night we intended to rob the train at Gallatin, but we hitched our horses too far away, and the train passed. Friday morning we got up about 9 o'clock. Frank and myself went together; Jesse and my brother went together, and Dick by himself. We went to Winston. Thursday night we stayed about one and a half miles from Gallatin. We got to Winston about sundown. Went into town after hitching our horses three quarters of a mile out in the woods east of Winston. Horses were hitched on the south side of the road. The horse I was riding Jesse and Dick got from some one near Kearney. They stole it on Sunday night. Jesse was riding a bay horse belonging to John Samuels. Frank was riding a little bay mare belonging to a man in Ray county. Dick Liddil was riding a chestnut sorrel horse that he bought of Lamartine Hudspeth and sold back again. My brother was riding a bay horse about nine years old that Frank and Dick got near Vibbard, in Ray county.

We were at Winston when the train came along. Jesse was our captain, our relations were as follows: Frank James, Jesse James and my brother got on the smoking-car, and Dick and myself got on the front platform of the express car. The understanding was that Dick and myself, as soon as Jesse or Frank should pull the bell rope, were to climb over the coal and pull down on the engineer and fireman and make them obey orders. As soon as they rang the bell, which was before we reached the bridge we climbed over the coal and made them stop the train. The understanding was that we were to stop the train anyway before reaching the bridge. Jesse, Frank and Wood were to go in and rob the car. At the first stoppage Frank ran around to the side, seized the baggageman by the leg and pulled him out of the car. They then commenced firing into the car and the express man opened the door. They went in and robbed the car. All this took about half an hour. We got $126 and some cents apiece. Jesse said the conductor started to draw his pistol and he (Jesse) told him if he drew it he would kill him. He did not desist, and was shot. Jesse did not know the conductor. There is no truth in the story that Jesse killed him because he supposed he (the conductor) had carried Pinkerton's detectives out to his mother's (Mrs. Samuels) house.   The stonemason was shot accidentally.

We were about a quarter of a mile from the horses after robbing the train.   We then went to our horses. I cut mine loose, leaving a part of the hitch-strap.   We went across the Hannibal and St. Joseph road between Kidder and Hamilton, beyond Ninable, to Crooked river.   Rode all night.   Stopped in a little woods after pulling down a fence and going through a field.   I went to sleep; so did Frank.   This was about daylight.   We staid about an hour, then went across fields till we reached Crooked river (Saturday).   Jesse and Frank said they knew the country.   We went down the river five or six miles and stopped on a bluff; Dick and I bought some bread of a woman.   This was about 10 or 11 o'clock.   Saturday morning the sixteenth, about half an hour before sunset, Jesse, Frank and myself went west in the direction or Lawson.   Met a man named Skidmore in the road, and going on took supper at a woman's house.   We went then to Lawson.   Just before reaching there we met several men in the road; said "Good evening" to each other.   Went through Lawson to about three miles of Mrs. Samuels'; laid down and slept till morning.   Next morning went to within three or four hundred yards above the house. Staid there about a week.   While there Will Nicholson and Mrs. Samuels furnished us supplies.   We would go near the house and Johnny Samuels would bring us food when near their respective houses.   Mrs. Samuels came out one night with Nicholson.   We divided the plunder the next Monday after the robbery in the little woods I have spoken of. We discussed whether we would rob the passengers, and decided not to. Jesse said he was sorry he had killed the conductor, but when he learned that he had brought the train to Mrs. Samuels (the time the explosion occurred which shattered Mrs. Samuels' arm) he said he was glad of it. We got the papers regularly. Nicholson and John Samuels brought them to us. After breaking camp we went to Mrs. Bolton's in Ray county.

Wood and Dick did not go to Mrs. Samuels'. They went direct from Mrs. Bolton's to Crooked river. We staid at Mrs. Bolton's about three days, and all five of us went back then to Mrs. Samuels'. We stopped in the woods north of the house about three hundred yards. Nicholson and young Samuels still brought us food. Dr. and Mrs. Samuels came out to see us. When at Mrs. Bolton's we staid in the house in day time and in the woods at night. (This is a custom.) One night at Bolton's Dick staid at the house, got scared at some people riding over the bridge and ran out of the house leaving his clothes and pistols. When we left Mrs. Samuels' we bought a wagon of her for $25 and a set of gear from Nicholson for $18, and drove Dick's horse and that of Chas. Ford. He (Chas. Ford) had come up from Ray county.

LIVING IN KANSAS CITY.

We then separated and Charlie went to McGraw's and got his horse and he, Dick and Wood went over to Mrs. Bolton's. Jesse and myself went to Kansas City,

and Frank went to Ralston's. I staid at Jesse's house
two weeks. He staid there all the time. He walked
out at night and I would go down town at night.
Jesse's house was east of the fair grounds. It was a
white one-story house. Don't know the street. It was
some "avenue." Think it was about the middle of
the block. It was in the edge of town. One house
was about thirty feet from it. He was going by the
name of J. T. Jackson. In about two weeks after I
got there he moved to a house near the Woodland
school house. This was on the north side of the street.
He went by the same name there. The night before we
moved to the second house Frank came to the first
house. A grocer, who has a store just across from a
butcher shop, forty or fifty yards from the school house,
east of the fair grounds, hauled the furniture. The
furniture was new and his wife bought it when she came
from Kentucky and while she stayed at McBride's.
Then she went to Colorado Springs, where she boarded
at a hotel. She had her two children with her. After
returning she went to keeping house. The little boy
in Kansas City was called Charlie. Before she moved
to Kansas City she called him Tim. While at the first
house they bought groceries of the man that moved
them to the same, and their meat from the butcher just
across the street from the grocery. These parties delivered the goods. While at house number two they
bought meat and groceries from a grocer and butcher
near Forest avenue, on the north side of Ninth and east
of Forest. These parties delivered the goods also.
There was no insurance on household goods. The

furniture was poor—not very fine. He (Jesse) called his wife Mary. When Frank came he also went up to the new house and staid three weeks. Jesse and myself were also there. Jesse's wife did not visit the neighbors. After remaining in the new house a week Jesse wrote to Charlie to come over to where they separated near Independence, which he did in a few days. He was then met near Independence by Jesse and Frank.

THE BLUE CUT ROBBERY.

The object of this meeting was to plan another robbery. Charlie then went back home and got Dick and my brother, and we were all to meet at the same place three or four nights afterward, which we did. Six of us went there to rob the Chicago & Alton train. That night we came down between Kansas City and Independence and staid in the woods. We intended to rob the Chicago & Alton train the next night—the western bound train, I mean. We would have robbed the eastern-bound train, but there were two of them, and we did not know which of them had the most money. Jesse was our leader here also. The arrangement was as follows: We were to blockade the track with rock and stop the train if possible by waving a lantern with a piece of red flannel around it. Jesse and myself were to take the north side of the train. We were to keep the people from coming out by firing, etc. Frank and Dick were to take the south side of the train, and Wood and Charlie were to flag the train, take out the engineer, make him break open the express car door, and then they, Charlie and Wood, were to rob it. This arrangement was carried out on the night selected next night.

When the Chicago & Alton train stopped at Blue Cut, Charlie and Wood made the engineer get his hammer and knock on the express car door (side door), the side Jesse and myself were on. After knocking several times the express messenger opened the door and jumped out and sat down on the bank. Charlie and Wood then went in, but they couldn't find the messenger, they supposing that the man who jumped out was the baggage man. One of them (Charlie and Wood) called out to Jesse that they could not find the messenger. Jesse then said: "There he sits on the bank with the engineer and fireman. Kill him if he does not get in and open the safe."

The messenger said: "I am not the messenger."

Charlie and Wood then covered him with their pistols and said: "Get in or we'll kill you."

The engineer said: "You had better get in. They have found you out."

He then got up and went in, opened the safe and I think they made him put the contents in the bag. We had a bag for the plunder. They then accused him of hiding part of the contents, and Charlie hit him over the head with his pistol once or twice and fired it off for the purpose of scaring him. He was scared. They made a further search and found the messenger's pocketbook, containing about $60 (a $50 and a $10 or two $5's), and his watch and chain.

This watch and chain Wood kept, and afterward pawned it in Louisville, where it afterward found its way into the keeping of Detective Blight, of Louisville, after this manner: Wood, when he was arrested for killing the new negro, left the pawn ticket on the mantlepiece up stairs at home, from which place Silas Norris, my father's present father-in-law, who was then living with us, stole it and gave it to George Hunter, of Bardstown, Kentucky, who in turn gave it to Blight. My father afterward went to Louisville for the watch, got it, and Blight presented the ticket about ten minutes afterward. He saw my father, told him it was a stolen watch, then father gave it up. Wood shot the negro on the fence for calling him a horse-thief, etc. He did not know my brother heard him, and begged hard for his life.

After Charlie and Wood came out of the car they told Jesse they did not have any money. Jesse then said: "We had bettor rob the passengers." They then started through the train, beginning at the smoker and going to the rear. Wood carried the bag (a common meal sack). Charlie went in front with a pistol in each hand and made the passengers deliver up their valuables and put them in the sack. I stood at the front door of each car as Charlie and Wood went through to prevent their being shot in the back. When we reached the chair car Frank got on. He did not go through the car, however. Everybody was badly scared. As we were coming back through the sleeper Charlie found a bottle of wine and took a drink. We also got some cake out of a basket. We got five

watches, including the expressman's. Wood took the
one which I have spoken of. Charlie Ford got two,
one a fine gold one and chain (English make) and a
silver one. I got a silver one and Jesse got the conductor's, a nickel, open-faced, stem-winder. We settled the division of jewelry as follows: Each article
was sold to the highest bidder, and this bid was put in
as so much cash and then the cash divided equally.
Frank in this way got a set of Mexican jewelry. To
go back a little. After we got through searching the
passengers, Jesse came into the sleeper from the rear,
and told the porter if he didn't hunt up all the money
that was hid he'd kill him. The porter said he hadn't
hid any, that they had gotten it all. Jesse then went
to the first seat, turned it up and got about $60 and a
gold watch. He then went to a brakeman and told
him the same thing. The brakeman said "I gave you
50 cents—all I had." Jesse then gave him $1 or $1.50,
saying: "This is principal and interest on your
money."

We then released the prisoners, and waited until
they had removed the obstructions, shook hands with
the engineer and fireman, and the train moved on. We
all then went north of the road, about half a mile, in a
big bottom and divided the proceeds as I have said.
Each man's share was estimated to be worth about
$140.

Jesse in this robbery had a pair of pistols, a 45
Colt and a 44 Smith & Wesson, and a breach-loading
shotgun of smaller calibre than No. 10. He had a
cartridge belt for his buckshot cartridges. He had

about thirty of these cartridges. This belt had a supporting strap over the shoulders. Had also two cartridge belts for pistols. Frank had a pair of 44 Remingtons and a Winchester rifle and two cartridge belts. The same cartridges fit both pistols and rifle. Dick had a breech-loading shotgun, which two convicts escaping from the penitentiary took from a guard and traded to Bill Ryan for two suits of clothes, who in turn traded it to Dick Liddil for a horse. Dick also had a pair of Colt's of 45-caliber and two cartridge belts. He carried his gun cartridges in his pocket. Charlie had one 44 Remington and 44 Smith & Wesson and two belts. Wood had one 44 Remington, a Winchester and two belts. I had two pistols, one 44 Smith & Wesson and one 45 Colt's and two belts. Before we got there (Blue Cut) I swapped my arms for Wood's.

After dividing, Jesse, Charlie, Frank and myself went through the fields, passed through the edge of Independence, struck the Missouri Pacific track near Independence and walked down it four or five miles, left it and crossed the Chicago and Alton track, and crossed the Blue at the bridge on Independence avenue, and continued on the road to Kansas City. All of us went to Jesse's house. We were just in the edge of the city when the heavy rain came up. Dick and Wood tried to cross at Blue Mills, but found officers guarding it. They went up the river, separated, and Wood crossed somewhere and went to Mrs. Bolton's. Dick went to one of the Hudspeths'. He also staid one night at the house of some one who was mother to the girl that went to Oregon with the man that murdered some one [the wife of Bud Thomas, hanged in Oregon]. In a few days he crossed the river at Lexington and went to Mrs. Bolton's. Charlie, next day after the robbing, took the train at Kansas City and went home to Ray county. Frank and myself staid in the house for two or three weeks. Frank and his wife and child, who had within the last two or three days returned from California, where they had been visiting their brother, young Sam Ralston, then went over to Mrs. Samuels' in a buggy hired of some liverymen in Kansas City. Charlie, in a day or two, drove the buggy and horse back. He stayed at Jesse's a day or two and then went back to Mrs. Samuels'. He stayed there a day or two and then came back to Kansas City. Then he went home to Ray county. Frank drove over to his mother's Sunday evening, and I left for the same place on the train next evening; walked out from Kearney. I staid there four days. Frank and I then rode down to Mrs. Bolton's. I rode Charlie's horse and Frank rode John Samuels'. We staid there two days, having arrived Friday night and leaving Sunday night. Took the Wabash train at Richmond and Lexington junction for Danville, Illinois, and from thence to Indianapolis, Indiana. Frank, Charlie and myself were together. Charlie and Frank went to Cincinnati, Ohio, and I went home. Have been there ever since till arrested. Don't know what became of Frank's wife. Frank said he was going to Covington or Cincinnati and rent a house and Charlie and myself were to stay with him.

AFTER THE LAST ROBBERY.

About the middle of October, 1881, Frank wrote me a letter, mailed at Samuels' depot, Nelson county, Kentucky, and dated there, which read about as follows:

"I will be at your house on (some stated date).

Respectfully,   Joe."

This letter was addressed to Clarence B. Hite, Adairsville, Kentucky, and meant: "Meet me at Doney Pence's or Mr. Sears', Nelson county Kentucky."

I replied that I was sick and could not come. I wrote in this way in order to have an excuse for not going. I directed this letter to "Joe," and signed my name. "Joe" inclosed it in an envelope, and mailed it, without explanation, to Dony Pence, Samuels' depot, Kentucky. Pence would understand what to do with the letter. A few days afterwards Frank wrote me another letter expressing regrets at my illness. This was the last I ever heard from him (Frank) or his wife, directly or indirectly. Have never heard from Charley since this last letter was written. I have never seen Jesse nor his wife since the day I left Kansas City for Mrs. Samuels', as I have above stated.

When I left he (Jesse) walked with me west on Ninth street to a little church on the northeast corner of Ninth street and Lydia avenue, Kansas City. We shook hands and parted. I have heard from him, however, since. About two months after I left Kentucky

21

and about one week before Johnnie Samuels was shot
Jesse wrote me a letter.   It was postmarked Kearney,
Missouri, but I think was written in Kansas City.   The
envelope inclosing this letter was directed to Miss Nannie Mimms, Adairsville, Kentucky.   He said in substance that I had better leave home; Dick was in with
the detectives and they would soon take me away.   He
wanted me to come to him, and said I could go either
to Tom Mimms', of Kansas City, or to his mother's
and find out where he was.   This letter began "Dear
Jeff," and was signed John Samuels.   I answered this
letter in three or four days, and directed it to Tom
Mimms, Kansas City, and on the inside I wrote in substance, after giving date and my address, that I could
not leave home, that I did not consider myself in danger, etc.; to write again in about two weeks if he did
not hear from me.   I signed myself "Clarence Browler"
(my first two names) and commenced it with "Dear
Tom," and at the top wrote "Please deliver."   Mimms
would understand by this that the letter was for Jesee
James.   This was the last I ever heard of him, directly
or indirectly.   I received this last letter during Christmas.   I omitted to state that I received another letter
from Jesse about one month prior to this one above described.   It was mailed at Kearney, Missouri, and addressed to Miss Nannie Mimms, Adairsville, Kentucky.
It began "Dear Jeff," and was signed "John Samuels."
It stated, in substance, that he was getting lonesome
and wanted me to come out and live with him.   He
asked me all about Wood's scrape with the negro, and
all about the family.   He told me to address my ans-

wer to John Samuels and he would deliver it. I answered this, also, and addressed the envelope to "John Samuels, Kearney, Missouri," and signed my name "Clarence Browder." I told him, in substance, that my business was of such a nature that I could not leave home very well; that I was in business, and that if I left I might not be able to get back into it again, that I could not come. I am perfectly familiar with Jesse's and Frank's handwriting and also their mode of communicating with their friends, and the foregoing are samples. When letters are written to any members of thd gang in Clay county, Missouri, the envelopes are addressed to "John Samuels, Kearney, Missouri," and he delivers them. When written to any of them in Jackson county, Missouri, they are addressed to "Tom Mimms, Kansas City, Missouri." When written to any member in Logan county, Kentucky, they are addressed to "Miss Nannie Mimms, Adairsville, Kentucky." When written to any of them in Nelson county, Kentucky, they are addressed to Donny Pence, Samuels' depot.

These parties are all firm friends of the fraternity, harbor and give them information.

To resume; my brother and Dick left Mrs. Bolton's in Ray county, Missouri, about two week before I left Missouri for Kentucky and came to my father's house. Wood and Dick had a shooting scrape about one week after they arrived and Dick left, leaving his baggage and cartridge belt. He came back to Mrs. Bolton's in Ray county in just a few days before Frank, Charlie and myself left for Kentucky. I have never

seen nor heard from him since. Wood, about one
month after reaching home, shot the negro, and about
ten days afterward was arrested, made his escape and
left, saying we would never see him again, Since the
Blue cut robbery Jesse nor Frank have not been at our
house.

*   *   *   *   *   *   *   *   *

Jesse killed Ed Miller. He killed him in Jack-
son or Lafayette counties last spring was a year ago.
They were in a fuss about stopping to get some to-
bacco, and after riding for some distance, Ed shot at
Jesse and shot a hole through his hat and then Jesse
turned and shot him off his horse. The young fellows
now in jail charged with being in the Blue Cut robbery,
I have never seen. They were not in the robbery.
The watch I got out of the Blue Cut robbery is at home.
Just before I was arrested I hid it between the bed ticks.
The fine gold watch Charlie got he traded to Dick
Liddil. The silver watch he left at home when he
went east with us. Frank gave the jewlery to his wife
that he got out of the Blue Cut robbery. No jewelry
came out of the Winston robbery. Jesse, Dick and
Bill Ryan all told me that last spring a year ago they
met four officers in Jackson county and rode by with
drawn pistols. Not a word was spoken.

Jesse said last summer if he only knew on what
train Governor Crittenden was he would take him off
and hold him for a ransom—thought he could get about
$25,000.   CLARENCE B. HITE.

HISTORICAL SKETCH OF "JAMES GANG."

For several years prior to the civil war, there existed a border warfare between what was known as the Kansas Jayhawkers and the Missouri Bushwackers. This trouble was principally along the state line just south of Kansas City. The Jayhawkers were first organized for the purpose of capturing negro slaves in Missouri and taking them into Kansas; the Missouri forces were organized to meet the raids these men were making and the fight soon became very bitter. The Kansas men eventually begun to rob and plunder and the Missouri men quickly took to retaliatory measures.

It was the custom in those days for freighters to haul goods from Independence, Westport, and other western Missouri towns, by ox wagons, to Fort Kearney, Denver, Santa Fe, and other points in the west. A man named George Quantrell and his brother were engaged as freighters across the plains. They were attacked by this Kansas band of free-booters. George Quantrell's brother was killed, and he himself left for dead.

For the purpose of revenge, Quantrell, after recovering, joined this band of Kansas Jay Hawkers. He induced three of their number to come with him to Jackson county, Missouri, to the farm of a rich old man

325

named Morgan Walker. Their visit was for the purpose of stealing money from old man Walker, taking his mules and also taking his negroes to Kansas. This was about the beginning of the war. Quantrell betrayed these men, who were said to be the very men who murdered his brother. When the three went to the house of old man Walker, having been previously apprised of their coming, Walker and his neighbors fired upon them, killing one of them dead in the yard, two of them escaping, one being badly wounded. All search for them was unavailing for several days, when, as a negro drove down into the woods with an ox team, he saw one of the Jay Hawkers watching his wounded companion. He immediately raised the alarm. Quantrell, old man Walker and others went at once to the spot. Old man Walker was a splendid shot with a squirrel rifle and could knock a squirrel's head off every time, it was said. As the old man approached with his glasses on and his rifle in his hand, the well Jay Hawker ran through the woods, and looking back, the old man shot him in the forehead, killing him dead. George Quantrell went up and killed the wounded man. This occurrence actually took place.

Quantrell was born in Ohio and his father, before the war, was a union man. It was the killing of his brother by the Kansas men that brought the terrible revenge he and his band afterward visited upon them. He was, in contrast with most of the men who joined his band, an educated and rather refined man.

The war was now on and Quantrell remained in Jackson county, espousing the southern cause. He

raised a company of guerillas in Jackson, Clay, Lafayette and Cass counties, and became thereafter one of
the most famous guerillas in the world's history.

George Quantrell was killed, it is said, in Kentucky, toward the close of the war.

This band was recruited among young boys very
largely, many of whom were from good families. Some
went into it perhaps from their sympathies, or the
promptings of a vicious nature, but there is no doubt
that a majority were from families who had suffered
from the outrages that had been committed by the Kansas men and felt that they had a just cause for revenge.

Among these young men who joined this band
were the James boys and the Younger boys. We will
remember Cole Younger as he was in those days, a
broad-shouldered, splendid looking fellow, and while
he became an out-law and of course a bad man, he
was in our opinion the best of all the Jameses and
Youngers. Bob Younger was too young to be in the
war. Cole Younger was a man highly respected in
his neighborhood, and up to the time he joined the
band there was not a blot on his character. He was
one of the young men who felt that he had a wrong to
avenge in the death of his father, who was killed and
robbed by Kansas soldiers, not far from his home. He
was not killed for his sympathies, for he was a Union
man but for robbery only. The very fact that his
father, who was a most excellent man, and numbered
among the best citizens in the whole community,
should be so foully murdered by men who claimed to
be union soldiers, when his father had so gallantly

stuck to the union, and to his principles himself, although this side was in the insignificent minority in his neighborhood, and he was standing almost alone in his views. We do not believe that Cole Younger had any of the natural viciousness that characterized many of those men who, after the war, became out-laws. There is not a trace of it in his face. We believe that had George Quantrell never existed, he might to-day be holding most any office in his native county. The conduct of the Younger boys since being confined in the penitentiary at Stillwater, Minnesota, bears us out in the above statement, as they have at times been allowed to go as "trustys," going in and out as they pleased, and no men of a naturally desperate character or criminal instinct would have demeaned themselves as these men have done. This is not said in extenuation of what these men have done, for we have never recognized anything as heroic in their exploits, and their is nothing in the conduct of this or any other band of plunderers to be emulated by the youth of the country, or to excite the admiration of anybody. I believe the Younger boys would now say the same thing.

The Younger boys were finally captured at Northfield, Minnesota, on September 7, 1876.

The story of their terrible disaster at Northfield was a number of times related to by Dick Liddil, who said he obtained it from frequent conversations with Jesse James. It was as follows:

A fellow named Bill Chadwell, who had recently joined the band, claimed that he knew of a town named

Northfield, in Minnesota, where there was a bank in which a large amount of cash was always kept. With Chadwell as their guide the band went to Northfield on horseback, starting from Fort Osage township, in Jackson county, Missouri. There were eight members of this band—the three Youngers, Cole, Jim and Bob; the two James, Jesse and Frank, and Clell Miller, Bill Chadwell and Charlie Pitts, The true name of the latter was Sam Wells. We knew him well and were raised in the same neighborhood with him.

The tragedy at Northfield was a terrible one. The cashier of the bank refusing to give up his money was shot. The alarm was given, and the citizens of the town seizing their guns fired upon the robbers. Bill Chadwell and Clell Miller were shot dead upon the spot. Dick Liddil says that Jesse James claimed that one of their number shot Chadwell, believing that he had betrayed them, but the citizens seemed to think they killed him. Every one of the robbers, except possibly one of the Jameses was wounded, those being the least wounded taking their other comrades behind them on horseback and fleeing from the town. In their flight a Swede named Gustavason was killed. The people about Northfield for miles around congregated and joined in the chase. The James boys wanted to kill Bob Younger, who was too badly wounded to travel, but upon Cole's refusing to permit this the Jameses and Youngers parted. The wounded one of the James boys being hauled by his brother through the state of Iowa, western Nebraska, down to Missouri in a two-horse wagon. The

wounded man stopped at a house between Kansas
City, Missouri, and Independence.

The three Youngers and Charlie Pitts (Sam
Wells) were surrounded by citizens in Minnesota,
when a terrific fight ensued. All of the Youngers
being further wounded and Sam Wells being shot dead.
The Youngers were placed in the Minnesota penitentiary for life.

Frank and Jesse James were born near Kearney,
in Clay county, Msssouri. Frank was born in January,
1843, and was described by Dick Liddil, before
Frank's surrender as follows: "Generally dresses in
dark clothes—long coat, and when on a raid wears
black slouch hat. When settled down he wears a
derby hat or stovepipe. He wears a gold watch chain
with large and small links. It is a vest chain, with a
compass for a charm, which is suspended by a chain
about three inches. When he wears a black stock he
adorns it with a diamond pin, the stone of which is
about as large as a grain of corn and when he does
not use the stock he wears the pin in his shirt front.
He also wears a diamond ring on his left little finger,
with three stones in a row the central one being the
largest. Wears generally box-toed boots. He is very
thin through the temples. Eyebrows are medium
heavy; eyes are rather deep set and have a wrinkle over
them. Large mouth with scar on both sides of it,
where he was either shot or his gun kicked him; these
scars are in each corner. Chews a great deal of
tobacco. Doesn't smoke much. Drinks freely. Fre-
quents gambling halls and is a good poker-player.

Walks like a string-halted horse. Wears black overcoat generally. He wears a pair of nickel-plated Remington pistols, caliber 44, single action. He wears number seven boot and fourteen and one-half collar. Has a bullet hole through right leg above the knee.''

Jesse James was born in 1848 and is described by Dick as follows:—''Height five feet ten and one half inches, weight one hundred and eighty-five pounds, eyes blue, complexion light, snaps his eyes when talking, they are large. Wears seven and one-eighth hat and number eight boot. Nose short and turned up at the end. Round features, fleshy face. Hair is dyed black. Whiskers sandy and worn all over the face about two inches long, at least they were so on New Year's day, 1882. The first joint of third finger on left hand is gone. There are two bullet holes about three inches apart near the right nipple. Is bow-legged and steps very quickly. Is very graceful rider. Walks and rides erect, rides with long stirrup. He is a great horse thief. Has two suits of clothes, one a light colored coarse goods, sack coat, etc. Either wears a derby or stove pipe hat. When on a raid dresses very common, dark calico shirt and ducking overalls, pants in boots. Has white smooth hands, wears gloves.''

The band taken as a whole existed from the Liberty Bank robbery at Liberty, Missouri, 1866, to the surrender of Frank James October 5, 1882. There were in all during its whole career twenty one men in this band. As a man was killed another man was recruited, until its final downfall. Of this twenty-one men all are now dead except Frank James, living in St.

Louis; Dick Liddil, running a string of race horses in the northern states; Jim Cummings, farming in Arkansas; Tucker Basham, farming in Kansas and Cole and Jim Younger in penitentiary at Stillwater, Minnesota. It is not known what has become of Bill Ryan. Out of the fifteen members of the band not here accounted for, all but one met a violent death, and many of them were killed by members of the band. Clarence Hite died from consumption in three days after having been pardoned out of the Missouri Penitentiary.

The following are some of the robberies attributed to this band with the tragic results attendant upon their perpetration. The amounts of money obtained on each occasion are variously estimated and can not here be definitely stated It may be said, however, that in all the published accounts in the last ten or fifteen years the amounts of money obtained by them have been greatly exaggerated. The following is a list of their principal robberies:

Liberty, Missouri, bank robbery, February 14, 1866; Young Wymore, about sixteen years of age, killed.

Lexington, Missouri, bank robbery, October 30, 1886.

Savannah, Missouri, bank robbery, attempted, and Judge McLain, cashier, wounded, March 2, 1867.

Richmond, Missouri, bank robbery, May 23, 1867; Mayor Shaw, B. G. Griffin and son, citizens of Richmond, killed.

Russellville, Kentucky, bank robbery, March, 1868; Mr. Long, cashier, and Mr. Owens, a citizen, wounded.

Gallatin, Missouri, bank robbery, December 7, 1869; John W. Sheets, cashier, killed.

Corydon, Iowa, bank robbery, June 3, 1871.

Columbus, Kentucky, bank robbery, April 29, 1872 ; cashier killed.

Kansas City fair robbery, September 26, 1872.

St. Genevieve, Missouri, bank robbery, May, 1872

Robbery of Chicago, Rock Island and Pacific train in Adair county, Iowa, July 21, 1873; train derailed and engineer killed.

Gad's Hill, Missouri, train robbery, February, 1874 ; express car and passengers robbed.

Muncie, Kansas, train robbery, December 13, 1874.

Huntington, West Virginia, bank robbery, September 1, 1875.

Missouri Pacific train robbery at Otterville, Missouri, July 7, 1876.

Northfield, Minnesota, bank robbery, September 7, 1876.

The following are some of the principal robberies by the band as reorganized by Jesse James after the attempted Northfield robbery:

Glendale train robbery in Jackson county, Missouri, on Chicago & Alton railroad, October 7, 1879. Committed by Jesse James, Ed Miller, Wood Hite, Bill Ryan, Dick Liddil and Tucker Basham. Frank James was not in this robbery.

Winston train robbery, on Chicago, Rock Island & Pacific railroad, July, 5, 1881 ; Conductor Westfall and Frank McMillan, railroad laborer, killed.

Committed by Jesse and Frank James, Wood and Clarence Hite and Dick Liddil.

Blue Cut robbery in Jackson county, Missouri, on Chicago & Alton railroad, September, 7, 1881, committed by Frank and Jesse James, Wood and Clarence Hite, Dick Liddil and Charlie Ford.

Mussell Shoals, Alabama, robbery, March, 1881. U. S. Paymaster Smith robbed of $5,200. Committed by Jesse and Frank James, Dick Liddil and Bill Ryan.

Many of the friends of the James and Youngers have claimed that their depredations after the war, were committed in pursuance of a kind of just revenge, and that Union men and United States government property were the objects of this revenge. The records show this claim to be absolutely without any foundation.

The records show that with the exception of the attempted robbery of the bank of Northfield, Minnesota, about every bank ever robbed by them was in a southern state, the stock and deposits of which constituted the property of southern people. In their different raids they took a good horse from a southern man as readily as from a northern man. Probably five sixths of all the money they ever obtained was from banks. In several of the bank robberies above mentioned more money was obtained than in the Blue Cut, Glendale and Winston train robberies all combined. These train robberies can not be said to have been committed from any motive of just revenge as they can not be taken to be the property of any southern or northern man.

It will thus be seen that the charge that has been disseminated throughout the length and breadth of the United States to the effect that the James and Youngers confined their depredations to northern men is also totally without foundation. The truth is that their depredations sprung from no motive of revenge or outrages upon their families nor from any political or sectional cause whatever. So that both the charges of their enemies and their friends in this behalf are alike without foundation.

THE FINAL DOWNFALL OF THE GANG.

After the Liberty Bank robbery the James boys became outlaws and were hunted by the officers. Many good men and brave officers met their death trying to capture this daring band of desperadoes, who had taken a solemn oath never to be taken alive. But their cunning, the aid of their many friends, and their bold and audacious conduct, made their capture the most difficult task ever undertaken by officers or detectives. It is said that the Pinkerton Detective Agency lost five men trying to capture the James boys. Many posses were sent out in pursuit of them and raids were frequently made, but somehow they always managed to escape. As to how cautious they were is illustrated by the fact that they had an established rule that when in a country where there was any danger of a raid they slept in the woods at night. If any special danger they had one man on guard while the others slept. If traveling through a country where known they traveled at night. Another great difficulty in capturing these desperadoes was the want of an accurate description, which the officers could not obtain, as it will be borne in mind that they went into the war when boys, and were never known to any community after that and when grown to manhood and had lead such lives as they did, their appearance would naturally be greatly changed, to say nothing of their constant disguise. Their communication was conducted in such a way that no clue could be gained from this source. They never addressed a letter to each other but always sent them indirectly and they were generally written in a kind of code language adopted by them. The following will afford an interesting specimen of their correspondence and is copied from the original letter, which is one written by Jesse James to one of the other members of the gang. It is as follows:

"St. Joseph."

"Dear Bro., cum quick beeves fat 20000 cwt. must be slumped Platt City O. K.-49-83-61 Bob will meet you grounded mother at home Kan. no good.

Bro. —— ——"

Of course there were many people who knew them and saw them frequently, but these people were their friends and nothing ever escaped their lips. There were some people, doubtless, who knew them and knew something of their whereabouts and would have informed the officers if they had dared, but they well knew that it meant death for them if it should ever be known that they told. Several people were killed by the band for this very cause. They had terrorized their family neighbors and many officers, and that

officer is certainly a brave man who would dare to face
these desperate and blood-thirsty creatures, after reading of the horrible death of the Pinkerton Detective
who was tied on the back of a horse and tortured before
he was finally killed. But there were brave men and
they made earnest efforts to catch these outlaws.

The Glendale train robbery took place in Jackson
county, Missouri, during the political campaign in the
fall of 1879, and Mr. Wm. H. Wallace who was a can-
didate for the office of prosecuting attorney stumped
the county denouncing the "James gang" and
pledging himself to do all in his power to break up
the gang and was elected. He was perhaps the first
man to go among the friends of the James boys and
openly denounce them. Tucker Basham had been
caught, made a confession, pleaded guilty to participation in the Glendale robbery, and was sent to the
Penitentiary from Jackson county.

In March 1880, Bill Ryan was captured just east
of Nashville, Tennessee and brought back to Jackson
county.

The facts attending this arrest, stated in brief, are
as follows:

A man neatly dressed, riding a splendid horse, and
carring two revolvers, had become engaged in a controversy and assaulted a man near Nashville, Tennessee.
A man named Earthman came up behind this man,
threw his arms around him to prevent his shooting,
and he was thus taken in charge. He was somewhat
intoxicated and declared that he was a desperado and

22

an outlaw, and that his name was Tom Hill. Upon
being searched it was found that he had two revolvers
and wore a buckskin waistcoat next to his person, in
which was contained something like one thousand dollars in gold coins.

The following is a graphic description of the trial
of Bill Ryan as related by Mr. Wallace:

"The next thing was to convict the prisoner. No
train robber had ever been tried by a jury in Missouri
and it was generally believed that no jury in Missouri
would dare to convict one of the James boys. I informed the officials of the Chicago & Alton Railroad
company that Ryan was now in custody, charged with
robbing one of their trains at Glendale, October 7,
1879, and that I wished them to send all the train men
to the trial at Independence.

"One of their agents told me that after full consultation about the matter the railroad officials requested
that I should not insist upon the railroad or its train
men having anything to do with the trial; that one of
the James boys could not be convicted by a Missouri
jury, and that if they did anything in the matter it
would simply anger the James boys against their railroad and cause them to single their road out for other
robberies.

"I insisted upon their sending the train men, which
they did, but when they reached the trial at Independence and saw the complexion of the crowd formed in
the courthouse, they said they could swear nothing, and
importuned me to release them from testifying, which
I did.

"I proved the fact that there was a robbery, by Mr. Grimes, the express messenger, who was knocked senseless by one of the robbers, and of course, knew nothing except that about nine thousand dollars was taken from his safe.

"In anticipation of the fact that the state would lack evidence, I had suggested to Governor Crittenden that it would be wise to pardon a green fellow named Tucker Basham, then in the penitentiary, and let him testify against Ryan, who was a shrewd and bold member of the gang. This the govenor consented to do. Whig Keshlear and Captain Maurice Langhorne, then deputy marshals, had arrested Basham because of the sudden and lavish expenditure of money he was making and on account of certain admissions which had fallen from his lips.

"Mr. Peak, then prosecuting attorney, had had an indictment preferred against him, and Langhorne and Keshlear obtained a full confession from him, and he plead guilty. Hayes, brother of Up Hayes, a confederate colonel, brought Basham from the penitentiary in Jefferson City and kept him constantly under guard during the whole trial to prevent his assassination, I myself holding his pardon in my pocket until just in the act of placing him on the witness stand, when I handed it to him in full view of the jury, stating to the court that this made the full release of Basham, and that I had promised him the pardon, through the governor, in the event of his willingness to testify in the case.

"The friends of Bill Ryan were so incensed at the appearance of Basham at Independence that they set fire to his house, an old log cabin, in the Cracker Neck country, and when the oak floor refused to burn they took the family effects out into the yard, placed them in a pile and burned them up. Basham fled a short time after the trial, imploring me to go with him, stating that there was no question that both he and I were to be killed. I took the precaution of taking him to a photographer and having his photograph taken, telling him that I intended to bring him back as a witness in case another of the James boys was ever on trial. I never saw him afterwards.

"I shall never forget the Bill Ryan trial. It was by all odds the most exciting trial I have ever witness and, I believe, the most exciting ever had in the west.

"The excitement attending it was ten-fold greater than the excitement at the Frank James trial at Gallatin, Missouri. The Frank James trial was a set and thoroughly arranged proceeding for which both sides had been preparing for more than a year. James had the most eminent lawyers in the west present with thoroughly prepared and magnificent speeches to deliver in his behalf.

"The Bill Ryan trial was a pell mell encounter between the poorly organized forces of the law and thoroughly organized and defined forces of outlawry. Magnificient counsel represented Ryan—Captain Franklin, for many years a congressman from this district; Hon. R. L. Yeager and Major B. L. Woodson. It was a test case. The banner of the law was pitted

for the first time against the mask and the black flag of
the bandit. The friends of the outlaw band, backed by
two or three daily newspapers, were certain that these
men were being mistreated and had a right to do whatever they had done and that one of them ought not to
be, and could not be convicted by a Missouri jury.

"I had been to Nashville, Tennessee, and brought a
large number of witnesses from there, but, of course,
they knew nothing of Ryan's connection with the robbery, and aside from the testimony of a young man
named Miller, who testified that on the night of the
robbery several men passed by his house on horseback
and that he recognized the voice of one of them as the
voice of Ryan. I practically had no testimony except
that of Tucker Basham, who was about as good material as an expert cross-examiner could wish to get
hold of. The court room was packed from sunrise to
sundown with the friends of the outlaw band, armed to
the teeth. Many of them staying all night in the court
house and the court house yard so that they could get
seats when the trial commenced.

"It is safe to say that the crowd in the court house
stood twenty-five for the defendant to one for the state.
The balance of the James gang were then in close
proximity to Independence, and I knew it. Dick Liddil afterwards told me that the rescue of the prisoner
by the assassination of the officers was seriously con-
templated.

"During the Frank James trial at Gallatin, one or
more of his friends who had a wide reputation as
fighters, openly stated on the streets in the presence of

many of the most reputable citizens of the town, that they intended to kill me before the trial was over, but I regarded this as simply bluff and it gave me no uneasiness whatever. But when during the Ryan trial my assistant, Colonel Southern, a courageous man, and myself received a letter which I knew through a detective then in the cell with Ryan, was sent with his approval and threatening that if we did not desist our lives were in danger, I confess I was uneasy. It is the secret threat that counts. When other threats than this came to our ears, and officers of the court who had been in the confederate army said to me frankly that they thought the probabilities were that I would be shot, I confess that I was anxious. But I was into it, and as I regarded it, to show the white feather meant disgrace for life, and I resolved that both the path of duty and safety was to be found by making the very boldest fight I could.

"Bill Ryan was convicted and his punish men assessed at twenty-five years in the penitentiary. No jury ever sat who were more justly entitled to the thanks of the commonwealth than the jury in that case. Many of them were thoroughly acquainted in eastern Jackson county and they sat facing the friends of the accused, who thronged into the court house until the more prominent among them occupied nearly every seat inside of the bar and were actually in touching distance of me when I spoke.

"Many of these jurors had to go to their homes in the very midst of the friends of the defendant. One of them, I remember, a brother of ex-Sheriff Hickman, lived in the edge of the woods within a few miles of the farm upon which Bill Ryan was raised. Nor can too much praise be given to Cornelius Murphy, the marshal who summoned this jury in person.

"In their motion for a new trial the counsel for the defendant laid much stress upon the fact that the governor of the state, hearing of the great excitement existing at the trial, had sent a box of guns to Independence, and that the jury was thus overawed by the state. I believe the guns came but the box was never opened. In fact, I never saw one of the guns in the hands of anyone, and I am satisfied no one else did, I obtained an affidavit from each of the jury to the effect that during the whole trial they were kept together in charge of the marshal and that they never heard about the guns being shipped to Independence until their verdict had been returned, and that they were governed only by the law and the evidence in the case."

The jury which convicted Bill Ryan broke the backbone of outlawry in the state of Missouri. Thousands of mouths in Jackson and adjoining counties which had been locked by fear were opened, and the denunciation of train robbery was open and unstinted. The desire to rid Missouri of the stain of outlawry reached fever heat, and the officers of the law were greatly encouraged and posses of men began to search in every direction for the bandits.

The depredations of this band had become intolerable to the good people. The Glendale robbery had taken place October 5, 1879; the Winston robbery July, 15, 1881, and the blue Cut, on September 7, 1881, while the trial of Bill Ryan was in progress as if in utter defiance of the law. Just after the Winston robbery, the governor of Missouri, issued the following procla-- mation:

"PROCLAMATION OF THE GOVERNOR OF MISSOURI !

REWARDS FOR THE ARREST OF EXPRESS AND TRAIN ROBBERS.

STATE OF MISSOURI, ⎫
Executive Department. ⎰

WHEREAS, It has been made known to me, as the Governor of the State of Missouri, that certain parties, whose names are to me unknown have confederated and banded themselves together for the purpose of committing robberies and other depredations within this State; and

WHEREAS, Said parties did, on or about the Eighth day of October, 1879, stop a train near Glendale, in the county of Jackson, in said state, and, with force and violence, take, steal and carry away the money and other express matter being carried thereon; and

WHEREAS, On the fifteenth day of July, 1881, said parties and their confederates did stop a train upon the line of the Chicago, Rock Island and Pacific Railroad, near Winston, in the County of Daviess, in said State, and, with force and violence, take, steal, and carry away the money and other express matter being carried thereon; and, in perpetration of the robbery last aforesaid, the parties engaged therein did kill and murder one WILLIAM WESTFALL, the conductor of the train, together with one JOHN McMILLAn, who was at the time in the employ of said company, then on said train; and

WHEREAS, FRANK JAMES and JESSE W. JAMES stand indicted in the Circuit Court of said Daviess County, for the murder of JOHN W. SHEETS, and the parties engaged in the

robberies and murders aforesaid have fled from justice and
have absconded and secreted themselves:

Now, THEREFORE, in consideration of the premises, and
in lieu of all other rewards heretofore offered for the arrest or
conviction of the parties aforesaid, or either of them, by any
person or corporation, I, THOMAS T. CRITTENDEN, Governor of
the State of Missouri, do hereby offer a reward of five thousand
dollars ($5,000.00) for the arrest and conviction of each person
participating in either of the robberies or murders aforesaid,
excepting the said FRANK JAMES and JESSE W. JAMES; and
for the arrest and delivery of said

FRANK JAMES AND JESSE W. JAMES,

and each or either of them, to the sheriff of said Daviess
County, I hereby offer a reward of five thousand dollars,
($5,000.00), and for the conviction of either of the parties last
aforesaid of participation in either of the murders or robberies above mentioned, I hereby offer a further reward of five
thousand dollars, ($5,000.00).

IN TESTIMONY WHEREOF, I have hereunto set my hand
and caused to be affixed the Great Seal of the
[SEAL]   State of Missouri. Done at the City of Jefferson
on this 28th day of July, A. D., 1881.
THOS. T. CRITTENDEN."
By the Governor:
MICH'L K. McGRATH, Sec'y of State."

This reward was really offered by the railroad companies through the governor; the companies placing sufficient cash in the hands of the governor, together with that already authorized by the legislature, to pay the rewards offered.

It was but a few weeks after the conviction of Bill
Ryan until Mattie Collins, the common law wife of
Dick Liddil came to Whig Keslear, a deputy marshal,
and told him she desired an interview with Mr. Wallace

with reference to the surrender of Dick Liddil. She said the James boys were greatly discouraged; that they were very suspicious of each other; that Jesse James and Dick Liddil had parted company, Jesse threatening to kill the latter on sight, and that the officers were pursuing Dick in the Six-mile country, and on several occasions had barely missed capturing him.

With Jesse James on one side and the officers on the other, Dick Liddil was between the devil and the deep sea, and he wanted to give up and tell everything that he knew if promised protection.

Friends of Dick's went to see the governor, who promised him immunity if he would come in, and directed him to surrender to Sheriff Timberlake, of Clay county, Missouri.

While these negotiations were in progress, Dick Liddil and Bob Ford killed Wood Hite, as told in another part of this volume. Bob Ford was largely instrumental in bringing about Dick Liddil's surrender. Shortly after Dick's surrender, through the aid of Bob Ford, Clarence Hite was located at his father's home at Adairsville, Kentucky, and H. H. Craig of Kansas City, Sheriff Timberlake of Clay county, Bob Ford and Dick Liddil went after him; Bob and Dick going out to the house, as did also Ben Jeter, the marshal of Adairsville. This party also expected to capture one of the James boys there. Clarence was there and was taken without incident. Bob and Dick were kept in the back ground on the return trip and Hite never knew that they were there until after he had pleaded guilty to the Winston train robbery and sent to the penitentiary for twenty-five years. Jeter was compelled to leave Adairsville as his life was in danger from the sympathizers of the James boys. He went to Kansas City at the invitation of Police Commissioner Craig and was given a position on the police force in that city.

Shortly after the trip to Kentucky Bob Ford informed Sheriff Timberlake and Mr. Craig, that Jesse James and Charlie Ford were in that part of the country and that in all probability Charlie would visit his uncle's at some time during their stay. Mr. Craig sent to Mr. Ford's house two of the bravest officers on the Kansas City police force, with Dick Liddil; and Sheriff Timberlake sent two of his best deputies. Bob Ford was already there. These men stayed at the Ford house for several days, when the Governor wanted to see Liddil, who was sent to Jefferson City. Court convened at Liberty and Sheriff Timberlake found need for his deputies, and the party was withdrawn, leaving Bob Ford alone. In a day or two after these men left Jesse James and Charlie Ford came up and called Bob out. They wanted him to go with them to do a job. After a hurried conversation Bob went in the house and told his uncle to tell Timberlake he had gone with Jesse James and as soon as he got a chance he would let him know where they were located, and if they did not hear from him in ten days they would know he had been killed. It was the plan of this twenty year old boy, concocted on the spur of the moment. He went to St. Joseph, Missouri, with Jesse, but did not get a chance to notify Timberlake. There was no thought on the part of Ford or anyone interested in the plan, of killing Jesse, when Ford left with him. As Ford tells it the shooting came about in this way. Jesse had asked Bob if Liddil had surrendered and Bob told him no. On the morning of the shooting Jesse had gotten a paper containing the account of Liddil's surrender. Ford says he expected Jesse to shoot him right there, but thinks he didn't want to do it before his wife and children. That they had planned to go to Platte City, Missouri, that night to rob the bank and that Jesse intended to wait until they got on the road. Ford says he embraced the first opportunity to save his own life.

Frank James surrendered October 5, 1882. Thus ended the existence of the most notorious band of outlaws that ever existed in this country.

THE END.